# Adaptive Education Strategies

# Adaptive Education Strategies
## Building on Diversity

by

*Margaret C. Wang, Ph.D.*
Professor and Director
Center for Research in Human Development and Education
Temple University
Philadelphia, Pennsylvania

with contributions by

*Patricia A. Gennari, Ed.D.*
Mon Valley Education Consortium
McKeesport, Pennsylvania

*JoAnn Manning, Ed.D.*
William Penn School District
Delaware County, Pennsylvania
and

*Eva D. Vaughan, Ph.D.*
Department of Psychology
University of Pittsburgh
Pittsburgh, Pennsylvania

·P·A·U·L·H·
BROOKES
PUBLISHING CO.

Baltimore • London • Toronto • Sydney

**Paul H. Brookes Publishing Co.**
P.O. Box 10624
Baltimore, Maryland 21285-0624


Copyright © 1992 by Paul H. Brookes Publishing Co., Inc.
All rights reserved.


Typeset by Brushwood Graphics, Inc., Baltimore, Maryland.
Manufactured in the United States of America by
The Maple Press Company, York, Pennsylvania.

**Library of Congress Cataloging-in-Publication Data**
Wang, Margaret C.
Adaptive education strategies : building on diversity / by Margaret C. Wang,
 with contributions by Patricia A. Gennari, JoAnn Manning, and Eva D.
 Vaughan.
   p.    cm.
Includes bibliographical references and index.
ISBN 1-55766-084-0
 1. Individualized instruction—Handbooks, manuals, etc.   2. Individualized instruction—Planning—Handbooks, manuals, etc.   3. Classroom
management—Handbooks, manuals, etc.   I. Title.
LB1031.W35   1992
371.3′94—dc20                                                   91-28669
                                                                    CIP

# Contents

# Preface

Individual differences in learning and the implications for providing effective education has long been a topic of concern in research on learning and innovative program
efforts to improve schooling outcomes. Students differ in interests, learning styles,
knowledge, and the amount of time needed for learning, and these student differences
require different approaches and varying amounts of instructional support. Although the
recent development of educational practices that are adaptive to student differences can
be traced as far back as the early 1900s, advances in theories and research on adaptive
education, particularly during the 1980s and 1990s, have become associated with school
improvement efforts aimed at ensuring equity in educational outcomes for the increasingly diverse student populations schools today are challenged to serve.

There appears to be growing receptivity to the implementation of adaptive education
approaches as an alternative strategy to provide for student diversity. Educators seem
more open to trying educational approaches that are tied to the direct assessment of each
student's capabilities and learning needs and that build on each student's motivation and
competence for achieving schooling success. Widespread implementation of adaptive educational practices, however, has not been forthcoming. The lack of practical expertise
and a well-developed delivery system is considered a primary reason for the less than
optimal level of implementation of adaptive education in schools.

*Adaptive Education Strategies: Building on Diversity* has been developed to provide
school personnel with the theoretical and practical information required to design, implement, and evaluate adaptive education programs. This information is based on more
than two decades of systematic research associated with the development and school implementation of an adaptive education program known as the Adaptive Learning Environments Model. Although much of the content of this book is based on the experience of
this program, it is intended to be a generic practical guide for school personnel and
teacher educators interested in designing and implementing innovative programs using
the adaptive education approach as an alternative for providing for student diversity.

The book is intended for use by schools and as a reference for preservice education
courses that cover implementation of the adaptive education approach. It consists of eight
chapters. The first chapter, "The Theory and Practice of Adaptive Education," is primarily informational and presents the theoretical and research bases of adaptive education. Brief discussion of the essential features of adaptive education and descriptions of
several adaptive education programs are included.

In Chapter 2, "Needs Assessment and Implementation Planning," methods are discussed for gathering information about school and district resources preparatory to designing a site-specific program delivery system, and these are followed by a description of
the steps and processes in implementation planning, including scheduling, staffing, and
conducting pre-implementation activities. Chapter 3, "Building Program Support," provides a practical guide for informing interested parties—teachers, administrators, par-

ents, and others—about the adaptive education program at an early stage of program implementation. Discussions include the content and presentation of awareness information for various audiences and how to mobilize families and the community as partners in efforts to improve student outcomes. In Chapter 4, "Curricular Resources for Implementing Adaptive Education," methods are described for analyzing the school curriculum in various subject areas (including district-designed curricula, basal texts, and supplementary materials) and for organizing and adapting curricular resources to meet the learning needs of individual students.

Chapter 5, "Instructional Management," provides a description of a management system that uses interactive teaching, exploratory learning centers, and student self-schedules to facilitate classroom management and development of student abilities to take increasing responsibility for their own learning and behaviors. Chapter 6, "Pre-implementation Staff Training," is concerned with the content and delivery of pre-implementation training for school staff, as well as the development of classroom implementation plans for individual teachers. In Chapter 7, "Implementation Assessment and Staff Development," the development and use of formal and informal measures of program implementation are discussed, and guidelines are presented for using the results to diagnose implementation needs and to design and deliver ongoing, individualized training support to school staff based on these needs. Chapter 8, "Evaluation of Program Effects," discusses issues and strategies for identification and measurement of cognitive, affective, and behavioral program outcomes and the use of the data for program evaluation and improvement.

The chapters have been designed so that they may be used as separate training modules or in any combination. School administrators planning to design and implement an adaptive education program "from scratch" will find that the eight chapters, used in sequence, provide a step-by-step guide to all stages of their work, from initial conceptualization through installation and evaluation in classrooms. A school seeking to strengthen the staff development component of an ongoing program, however, may choose, for example, to use only Chapter 7, "Implementation Assessment and Staff Development." This work, or selected chapters, may also serve as an educational resource in workshops, courses, or other training offered by colleges of education or by state, intermediate, or local educational agencies.

This book could not have been possible without the help and support of many individuals who have worked closely with me at the University of Pittsburgh, Temple University, and many of our collaborating schools across the United States and abroad during the past 20 years. In particular, I wish to acknowledge the three individuals who have contributed much to the writing of this book: Patricia Gennari, who worked closely with me in the field testing and refinement of the Adaptive Learning Environments Model and developed much of the fine training material used as examples throughout this volume; JoAnn Manning, who spearheaded the training and technical assistance program enabling school leaders and teachers to use adaptive strategies, as well as provided practical wisdom and invaluable feedback in validating the work discussed in this book; and Eva Vaughan, my co-author of the *Handbook for the Implementation of Adaptive Instruction Programs*. Much of the theory and practice presented in *Adaptive Education Strategies: Building on Diversity* was articulated in an earlier form in that handbook.

My special thanks goes to Joan Nikelsky for her editorial assistance and for overseeing the final stages of revision. Her organizational skills and responsiveness to last-minute suggestions at the final stages of the editorial process were central to successful completion of this manuscript.

I wish to also express my deep gratitude to the individuals whose contributions in the various stages of the writing, field testing, school-based implementation, and evaluation helped make *Adaptive Education Strategies: Building on Diversity* possible. They include: Maynard Reynolds from the University of Minnesota; Deborah Bott from the University of Kentucky; Dorothy Winter and Betty Cline from the Waterloo Community

School District, Iowa; Rosie Dehli from the Montevideo School District, Minnesota; Jackie Bright and Barbara Korn from the Randolph County Schools, West Virginia; Jeanmarie Belonga and Rosina Carbo from the New Orleans Parish Schools, Louisiana; and Felicia Renard and MaryAnn Provenza from the Riverview School District, Pennsylvania.

To Constance Clayton, Superintendent of the School District of Philadelphia, I owe a special personal thanks. Finally, and most importantly, I would like to particularly acknowledge the contribution of the many teachers and principals from the School District of Philadelphia and other schools across the country and abroad, which are too numerous to list. Their commitment to use research-based innovative practices to ensure schooling success of all of the diverse children with whom they work is most inspirational and central to my professional development and the publication of this book.

Much of the work discussed in this book was supported by funding for research and innovative program development projects from the Office of Educational Research and Improvement, the Office of Special Education and Rehabilitative Services, and the Office of Compensatory Education of the U.S. Department of Education. However, the opinions expressed are mine. They do not necessarily reflect the positions of the U.S. Department of Education and no official endorsement should be inferred.

*Margaret C. Wang*
*Philadelphia*

# Adaptive Education Strategies

*Chapter 1*

# The Theory and Practice of Adaptive Education

Successful design and implementation of adaptive education programs require knowledge of theories of individual differences in learning and requirements for effective instruction, as well as the practical know-how for implementing the best and most promising practices in regular school settings. This introductory chapter provides an overview of the theoretical underpinnings and practical knowledge for implementing the adaptive education approach as an alternative instructional delivery system to ensure schooling success for increasingly diverse student populations.

This chapter is organized in five sections, and it begins with a discussion of basic assumptions underlying adaptive education and presents a conceptual model for the design, implementation, and evaluation of adaptive education programs. The second section focuses on critical program dimensions for designing adaptive education programs. In the third section, the school implementation and effects of critical dimensions of adaptive education are discussed. The fourth section provides a brief summary of the research on school-based implementation and outcome of adaptive education. The final section includes descriptions of widely adopted alternative programs that include critical features of adaptive education.

## THEORY OF ADAPTIVE EDUCATION

Creating effective, practical school learning environments that are responsive to the diverse learning needs of students has been a continuing challenge in school reform efforts. Adaptive education has been noted by researchers, school staff, and policymakers as a promising alternative approach for accommodating the individual learning needs of students, including those with exceptional talents or special needs, in regular school settings (e.g., Corno & Snow, 1986; Council of Chief State School Officers, 1987, 1989; Gartner & Lipsky, 1987; Heller, Holtzman, & Messick, 1982; National Coalition of Advocates for Students, 1985; Task Force on General Education/Special Education, 1989). The development of educational innovations that effectively provide the educational and related service needs of an increasingly diverse student population has become a central issue in school improvement.

A basic premise of adaptive education is that success in learning is maximized when students are provided with experiences that build on their initial competence and that are responsive to their learning needs. Furthermore, effective school-based implementation of adaptive education is achieved through an instructional system that incorporates a variety of strategies for delivering inclusive and coordinated services. The instructional system must be flexible to support implementation of alternative learning options and to permit varying amounts of learning time for individual students.

Instructional programs that effectively respond to student diversity assume that variation in the learning progress of each student is expected by teachers, parents, and the students. No special labeling is needed to provide different instruction for different students, and momentary problems in learning are not viewed as failures, but as occasions for further teaching. Specialist teachers (i.e., special education or Chapter 1 teachers) and other related service professionals (e.g., speech pathologists or school psychologists) work with regular classroom teachers in a coordinated system. It is expected that most, if not all, students can be provided with instruction suited to their needs in regular classroom environments without having to resort to a segregated "second system" approach that provides "special" or compensatory services that, for the most part, have not been shown to be effective (Anderson & Pellicer, 1990; Braddock & McPartland, 1990; Gartner & Lipsky, 1987; Wang, Reynolds, & Walberg, 1988; Williams, Richmond, & Mason, 1986).

Discussions of adaptive education as an alternative educational approach can be traced back to the early 1900s (cf. Whipple, 1925). Advances in theory and practical knowledge of effective instruction created a significant conceptual shift in how individual differences are viewed and in the information that describes and analyzes learner differences (cf. Ackerman, Sternberg, & Glaser, 1989; Snow & Farr, 1987; Wang & Lindvall, 1984). Changes in the conceptualization of individual differences occurred simultaneously with developments in cognitive psychology and classroom process research. Instead of characterizing a student's learning by measures of outcome or input differences, the focus has shifted toward analysis of the learning processes intrinsic to competent performance.

Growing evidence suggests a great variability in the ways that students acquire, organize, retain, and generate knowledge and skills. Furthermore, these variations may be attributable to students' adoption of particular learning processes that they perceive to be pertinent to the task at hand (Brown & Campione, 1986; Wang & Palincsar, 1989). Such findings have resulted in attention to individual differences in learning processes. Student differences are less likely to be identified through traditional tests only. Instead, differences are identified and described in terms of how information is processed, the problem-solving strategies and mechanisms for short- and long-term memory, rules that students bring to the instructional environment, and the competence of individual students, rather than general abilities and aptitudes, which have been the predominant practice (Gardner, 1983; Sternberg, 1990; Wang & Lindvall, 1984).

Individual differences in students were traditionally assumed to be static bases for classifying groups of students and predicting future achievement.

Glaser (1977) referred to this as the "selective" education mode. Individual differences in learning are no longer considered static, but capable of modification either before the instructional process begins or as part of the process (Bloom, 1981). Findings that suggest the malleability of learning characteristics of individual students and studies on interventions to enhance student learning have led to increased recognition of the wisdom of school implementation of adaptive education as an alternative approach to provide for student diversity in regular classroom settings (Brophy, 1986; Council of Chief State School Officers, 1987; Heller et al., 1982; Wang, 1990b; Wang, Reynolds, & Walberg, 1988).

Thus, for programs using adaptive education approaches, student learning success is seen as a consequence of the responsiveness of the learning environment, rather than the result of differences in student learning characteristics and basic abilities. Furthermore, the task of the school is to provide learning environments that enable all students to experience success, regardless of initial ability. In addition to changes in psychological concepts and educational principles, adaptive education in regular school settings has been aided by efforts to provide quality educational opportunities for every student. The passage of the Education for All Handicapped Children Act (PL 94-142) by Congress in 1975, for example, mandated support systems to accommodate the needs of individual students in regular classrooms. For these reasons, school administrators and teachers are supportive of individualized instruction that combines direct assessment of student capabilities with direct instruction that builds each student's competence in basic skills.

We can be optimistic about the usefulness of adaptive education programs. Along with technical advances, adaptive instruction is establishing a strong theoretical base. Research and experience in school implementation of adaptive education programs have resulted in substantial knowledge and technical skills, both for providing adaptive instruction and for motivating school personnel to implement programs.

## What Adaptive Education Is and Is Not

In light of inadequate and often inaccurate characterizations of adaptive education, several distinctions should be noted. First, although adaptive education involves individualized planning for each student, it is not in opposition to the group instruction format. The adaptive education approaches utilize group-based instruction, as well as individual tutoring, problem solving, and exploratory learning processes. In classrooms using the adaptive education approach, instruction takes place in a variety of settings and grouping arrangements (individual, small-group, and whole-class) depending on the material to be learned and the learning characteristics and needs of the students. Group lessons are included among a variety of instructional delivery and management strategies to develop academic and social skills among students who differ in multiple dimensions (Wang, 1980). For example, even in highly individualized adaptive education programs, objectives related to communication and social cooperation are taught in interactive group settings, and new skills and procedures are often introduced to students in groups or in the entire class.

Adaptive education is an educational approach aimed at providing learning experiences that help each student achieve desired educational goals. The term "adaptive" refers to the modification of school learning environments to respond

effectively to student differences and to enhance the individual's ability to succeed in learning in such environments. In fact, by definition, effective implementation of the adaptive education approach mandates the incorporation of a
variety of instructional methods that provide learning experiences matched to
individual characteristics, talents, interests, and knowledge. Figure 1.1. provides
a sample list of features and outcomes of adaptive education.

Adaptive education does not mean that students work entirely alone, nor
that teaching is unstructured or inactive. Furthermore, adaptive education is not
synonymous with open education (Peterson, 1979) or other student-centered instructional approaches. Among the key features of adaptive education is development of higher order thinking and problem solving skills and student responsibility for learning and achievement motivation. Decisions of curriculum
content and sequence of instruction, however, are largely made by the teacher,
based on curriculum structure and the teacher's judgment about the needs and
characteristics of the students.

Thus, incorporation of alternative instructional strategies and curricular options to facilitate student learning are important in the design of adaptive education programs. These strategies include teacher-directed lessons in groups or
with individual students, student-initiated exploratory activities, and individual and cooperative learning. Most characteristically, such programs provide opportunities that adaptively meet diverse learning needs, interests, and styles of
students. Adaptive education programs involve direct intervention and coaching that increase each student's competence as a self-directed learner and confidence in his or her ability to learn and achieve schooling success.

## A Conceptual Model of Adaptive Education

Figure 1.2. is a schematic representation of a conceptual model of adaptive education. The model is based on the premise that the development of innovative
educational programs that effectively respond to students' diverse learning
needs requires an evolving process of program design, implementation, evaluation, and refinement. The model consists of three major components. The first
component is the design of adaptive education programs, which identifies
student characteristics and program goals that provide the basis for designing
school environments for implementing adaptive education. The second component relates to program implementation in schools. The third component is evaluation of the process and product outcomes of the program.

The program design features included in the model are not new ideas but
are practices that have been implemented in the classroom by effective teachers
in a variety of schools. What is unique about this model is the comprehensive
and holistic approach that recognizes the interdependent effects of the critical
program dimensions of adaptive education and the requirement of systematic
implementation of the critical program dimensions to create and maintain
school learning environments that are effective in responding to student diversity. A particular feature of the model is the inclusion of both product and process variables in program evaluation as indicators of outcomes. Process outcomes include the abilities students acquire and display while learning and
interacting. While process outcomes, such as the ability to plan and manage
learning activities and the willingness to assist other students, are viewed as
mediating variables that lead to intended product outcomes, they are also con-

sidered major schooling outcomes in their own right. As these desirable class-room processes are developed by students and integrated into their behavior repertoire, the students' capabilities to profit from their learning experiences are enhanced.

Product outcomes, as conceived in the model, include abilities and attitudes acquired by students, teachers, and parents. These expected program outcomes are indicators of implementation success and of needed improvement. Examples of product outcomes include achievement of basic skills, student perception of competence and personal control over learning, and teacher expectations of student ability to achieve learning success. As suggested by the arrows in Figure 1.2., program outcomes are evaluated in relation to:

1.  The presence or absence of critical program dimensions (the large circle in the figure)
2.  The extent to which implementation of program dimensions leads to specific classroom processes characteristic of adaptive education (e.g., teacher and student behaviors)
3.  The extent to which the classroom processes lead to student social and academic competence

The resulting information provides the basis to determine if program implementation can be achieved in a variety of schools, if the program produces the intended product and process outcomes, and how the school can improve its ability to achieve these outcomes.

## CRITICAL DESIGN DIMENSIONS OF ADAPTIVE EDUCATION PROGRAMS

Three categories of program dimensions are included in the design of adaptive education programs. These categories, as shown in Figure 1.2., are dimensions related to supporting the delivery of adaptive education, dimensions related to classroom support for program implementation, and dimensions related to school- and district-level support.

## Program Dimensions Related to Provision of Adaptive Education

Nine program dimensions are critical for effective provision of adaptive education in regular classroom settings:

> Creating and maintaining instructional materials
> Developing student self-responsibility
> Diagnosing student learning needs
> Instructing
> Interactive teaching
> Monitoring student progress
> Motivating
> Prescribing
> Record keeping

The objectives and characteristics of each dimension are discussed in this section.

*Creating and Maintaining Instructional Materials* Instructional materials, both commercial and teacher-constructed, are available for each learning objective in various curricula. In addition to the basic materials for each subject in the curric-

| Expected student outcomes | Development of positive attitudes toward learning | | | |
|---|---|---|---|---|
| Features of effective classroom learning environments | Enjoyment in taking part in learning activities | Viewing help-giving and help-receiving as positive experiences | Special interest in certain learning areas | Motivation for continuing to learn |
| Instructional content that is: | | | | |
| Essential to further learning | | | X | |
| Useful for effective functioning in school and society | | | X | X |
| Clearly specified | | | | |
| Organized to facilitate efficient learning | | | | X |
| Assessment and diagnosis that: | | | | |
| Provide appropriate placement in the curricula | | | | X |
| Provide frequent and systematic evaluation of progress and feedback | | | | X |
| Learning experiences in which: | | | | |
| Ample time and instructional support are provided for each student to acquire essential content | X | | X | X |
| Disruptiveness is minimized | X | | | X |
| Students use effective learning strategies/study skills | | | | X |
| Each student is expected to succeed, and actually succeeds, in achieving mastery of curriculum content, and accomplishments are reinforced | X | | X | X |
| Alternative instructional strategies, student assignments, and activities are used | X | | | X |
| Management of instruction that: | | | | |
| Permits students to master many lessons through independent study | | | | X |
| Permits students to plan their own learning activities | X | | | X |
| Provides for students' self-monitoring of their progress with most lessons | X | | X | X |
| Permits students to play a part in selecting some learning goals and activities | X | | X | X |
| Collaboration among students that: | | | | |
| Enables students to obtain necessary help from peers | X | X | | |
| Encourages students to provide help | X | X | X | |
| Provides for collaboration in group activities | X | X | X | |

**Figure 1.1.**    Selected features of classroom learning environments and expected student outcomes. The X indicates that findings from studies on effective teaching and learning suggest relationships between the implementation of specific features and the achievement of particular student outcomes. (From Wang, M.C., Reynolds, M.C., & Walberg, H.J. [1986]. Rethinking special education. *Educational Leadership, 44,* 28–29; reprinted with permission of the Association for Supervision and Curriculum Development. Copyright 1986 by ASCD. All rights reserved.)

| Acquisition of a variety of learning skills | | | Mastery of subject matter content | | Development of positive self-perceptions | | | |
|---|---|---|---|---|---|---|---|---|
| Ability to study and learn independently | Ability to plan and monitor learning activities | Ability to obtain assistance from others | Mastery of content and skills for effective functioning | Mastery of content and skills for further learning | Confidence in one's ability as a learner | Confidence in oneself as a contributing member of the school/community | Confidence in one's ability to take self-responsibility for learning and behavior | Perceptions of internal locus of control |
| | | | X | X | X | | | |
| | | | X | X | | | | |
| X | X | | X | X | X | | X | |
| X | X | | X | X | X | | X | |
| | | | | | | | | |
| X | | | X | X | X | | | |
| X | X | X | X | X | X | | | |
| | | | | | | | | |
| | | | X | X | X | | | X |
| X | X | | X | X | | | X | |
| X | X | X | X | X | X | | X | |
| | | | | | | | | |
| | | | X | X | X | X | X | |
| X | X | | X | X | X | | | |
| | | | | | | | | |
| X | X | | X | X | X | | | X |
| X | X | | X | X | X | | | X |
| X | X | | X | X | X | | X | X |
| X | X | | X | X | X | | X | X |
| | | | | | | | | |
| | X | X | X | X | X | | X | X |
| | | X | X | X | | X | | X |
| | X | X | X | X | X | X | X | X |

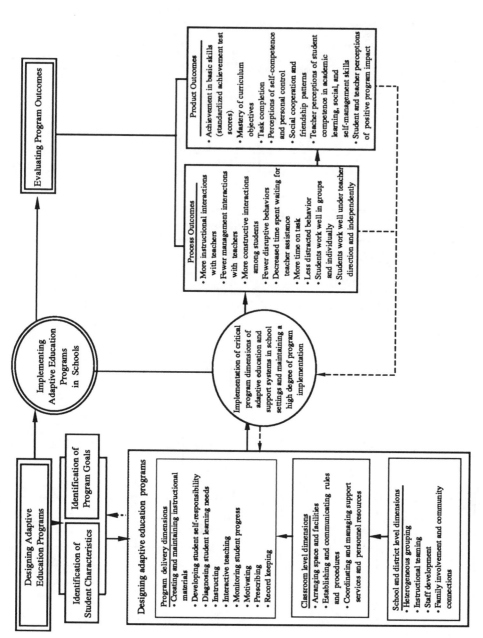

**Figure 1.2.**   A conceptual model for the design and school implementation of adaptive education. (Solid line = program development and implementation process, dotted line = program refinement process.)

ulum such as textbooks and workbooks, materials are created by teachers and instructional staff as needed, and all materials are maintained and updated. A variety of instructional materials (including those used individually by students or in small groups) allow students a choice and accommodate individual student learning needs and styles. Teacher-constructed learning materials are accompanied by directions understandable to students, a list of materials for each task, the task objective, and questions teachers can use to evaluate task performance.

***Developing Student Self-Responsibility*** This dimension concerns fostering student ability to be self-instructive and engage in self-directed learning, a critical outcome for sustaining lifelong learning. Indicators of student responsibility in learning include:

> Planning and managing one's own learning
> Engaging in higher order thinking and problem solving
> Managing work space
> Locating and returning all materials and equipment
> Carrying out assigned tasks with minimal supervision and assistance
> Focusing on curricular learning or constructive peer interaction while waiting for assistance
> Choosing activities and schedules
> Evaluating one's own work progress
> Asking for assistance when needed
> Providing assistance to others when asked
> Engaging in cooperative learning activities

***Diagnosing Student Learning Needs*** A key element to design of adaptive education programs is identification of student learning needs. In this approach, criterion-referenced and curriculum-based diagnostic techniques determine the level of the student beginning a unit of instruction in the curriculum. Frequent diagnostic checks monitor student progress toward curriculum objectives and determine mastery of a curricular unit. Each student is provided the appropriate level of instructional support and time required to achieve mastery. All students are expected to achieve the criterion for one unit before proceeding to the next unit.

***Instructing*** Regularly scheduled instruction in new tasks and review lessons is provided in small groups, individually, and for the whole class. A variety of effective techniques (e.g., questioning, explaining, cuing or prompting, structuring, restructuring, giving feedback, demonstrating, modeling) are used to provide instructional support to foster student learning.

***Interactive Teaching*** Interactive teaching provides for individual differences among students. To monitor student completion of assigned or self-selected tasks, teachers continually move in all areas of the classroom, responding to student requests or initiating contact with students for instruction and management. Examples of interactive teaching activities include providing on-the-spot instruction, adjusting prescriptions (assignments) based on reassessment of student performance and learning needs, and giving feedback and reinforcement to enhance motivation and efficiency. Each student contact is relatively short. When extended assistance or tutoring is required, sessions for individuals or small groups are scheduled for a later time.

***Monitoring Student Progress*** Teachers evaluate student learning on an ongoing basis to identify learning difficulties before they become established problems. Teachers use their knowledge of the curriculum, the student, and information from school staff and parents. Teachers check work in the students' presence and provide feedback. They determine the source of student difficulty and modify instruction or learning plans accordingly.

*Motivating*    A variety of motivation techniques help students assume increased responsibility for their learning and behavior. Teachers communicate their expectations for student success verbally and nonverbally and encourage self-discipline, independence, and cooperation. Teachers show personal regard for each student and give praise and corrective feedback when appropriate.

*Prescribing*    Teachers use the information from diagnostic tests and other curricular assessments as well as informal observations to develop instructional plans and prescribe individualized learning plans (assignments) to ensure student mastery of curriculum objectives. Explicit curriculum objectives, learning options, and specific tasks (e.g., a list of learning tasks or workbook pages to be completed, titles of chapters or books to be read, activities to be completed) are included in the learning plan.

*Record Keeping*    Progress records for each student are updated regularly and include documentation of individual student progress in mastering the objectives of each curricular area. Student progress records can be kept by computer or longhand. Students are taught to keep their own progress records when they are able to assume this responsibility.

## Program Dimensions Related to Classroom Support for Program Implementation

As shown in Figure 1.2., three program dimensions are critical for supporting program implementation at the classroom level:

> Arranging space and facilities
> Establishing and communicating rules and procedures
> Coordinating and managing support services and personnel resources

*Arranging Space and Facilities*    The classroom is designed to foster student independence and responsibility for learning behaviors. Furniture and equipment are arranged to allow easy movement between areas, storage and display areas are accessible to students, learning materials are organized to permit independent selection and replacement by students, and systems monitor the number and movement of students in activity areas.

*Establishing and Communicating Rules and Procedures*    Rules and procedures are clearly defined to support student self-management of the learning environment and activities and to provide consistent communication about classroom management. For example, procedures govern the use and maintenance of equipment and materials, the scheduling of activities, work completion, and independent movement about the room.

*Coordinating and Managing Support Services and Personnel Resources*    Classroom teachers meet with specialists (e.g., special education teachers, Chapter 1 reading teachers, and school psychologists) and support staff (e.g., paraprofessionals and classroom volunteers) regularly to plan and specify roles and tasks that provide for student needs. While classroom teachers assume primary responsibility for their classes, implementation of adaptive education calls for a team approach that requires classroom teachers, specialists, and support staff to collaborate to meet the diverse needs of the students. Regular discussion of individual student performance, including concerns about behavior, achievement, and plans for intervention, are integral to the teaching process.

## Program Dimensions Related to School- and District-Level Support

Four dimensions are critical to school- and district-level support for implementation of adaptive education programs:

> Heterogeneous grouping
> Instructional teaming
> Staff development
> Family involvement and community connections

The first two are strongly recommended but not absolutely essential for effective provision of adaptive education. Staff development and family involvement are vital to the success of any education program, but especially for an innovative program that requires major restructuring, such as adaptive education.

*Heterogeneous Grouping* Heterogeneous grouping in the context of adaptive education is broadly defined to include multi-age or ungraded classrooms that accommodate students with slow, average, and fast learning rates. In heterogeneous classes, individual differences are viewed by teachers, peers, and parents as the norm rather than the exception. Students are not labeled or tracked in adaptive classrooms, because student diversity is assumed to be the beginning point of instructional planning and intervention. The classroom and curriculum are organized to support flexibility in teachers' instructional time, to foster peer modeling, and to encourage peer tutoring. Students are described in terms of their instructional needs rather than their chronologic age.

Although teachers are the primary instructional resource for students, heterogeneous classes provide a natural setting for spontaneous and planned peer modeling and tutoring, which contribute to the academic and social development of tutor and tutee alike. Students have the opportunity to serve as social and academic resources for each other. Heterogeneous grouping is a classroom organizational structure particularly suited for schools with diverse populations. Adaptive education focuses on individual differences rather than differences between groups.

*Instructional Teaming* Instructional teaming refers to formal or informal arrangements of two or more teachers sharing resources as well as students. Teaming provides flexible and effective utilization of teacher time and talents, instructional styles, and scheduling. Students in programs that feature instructional teaming have been found to spend more of their school time receiving instruction than students in traditional one-teacher, self-contained classrooms. Consequently, greater student achievement and improved self-worth and attitudes toward school are fostered. Other effects include closer collaboration among school staff and more learning alternatives for students.

Instructional teaming has been found to be particularly effective in settings where students with special needs (i.e., students in special or compensatory education and gifted and talented students) are integrated in regular classes. In such programs, the regular teacher and specialists coordinate their work to provide for the diverse needs of all of the students. Professionals work together in and out of the classroom to plan and deliver instructional services designed to meet the individual needs of all students.

*Staff Development*    Adequate staff development is the key to successful implementation of innovative school programs that require fundamental changes in classroom practice, such as adaptive education. Systematic staff development programs provide the technical support for staff to become self-sufficient in monitoring and diagnosing their implementation needs and to maintain a high degree of implementation of adaptive education.

Staff development can take place in weekly planning meetings, topical seminars, or workshops conducted by school staff or outside experts. The specific content and the amount of staff development are determined by implementation and training needs of the individual staff. It is essential that staff development opportunities are scheduled on a regular basis, even after a high degree of program implementation is achieved. Continual staff development is necessary for program maintenance.

*Family Involvement and Community Connections*    Society educates children and youth for various purposes and through various channels, and the ultimate goal of education is to provide individuals with skills and abilities to function as competent and productive adults. Although the task of educating children and youth continues to depend primarily on the activities carried out in schools, schools can be enhanced by an appreciation of the role of the family and community in preparing children for adulthood.

The family and the community are critical sources, often overlooked, of support for effective implementation of adaptive education in schools. Given the limited school day, students in even the most effective education programs can benefit from instructional reinforcement and additional learning approaches at home and in the community. In addition to increasing learning time and educational resources, it is expected that student motivation increases when families and adults in the community express interest in school activities and achievement (Walberg, 1984). The community includes government and local human and health services, businesses, religious institutions, social service and youth agencies, and the media. Finding ways to mobilize the energies and resources (often latent) of families and communities is an important task in implementing adaptive education programs.

Family involvement provides critical support for student learning and the work of the school. The wisdom of involving families to enhance student schooling success has been advocated by educators and substantiated by research evidence (Ascher, 1990; Bempechat, 1991; Epstein, 1986; Walberg, 1987; Wang, Haertel, & Walberg, 1990). Family involvement with school has been shown to facilitate increased communication between school and home, and to promote active participation of family members in student learning. Research evidence shows that educational intervention programs designed to involve family members are significantly more effective than programs aimed exclusively at students (Bronfenbrenner, 1986; Epstein, 1986; Walberg, 1984).

In the broadest sense, family involvement in school includes not only active participation on the level as an audience for school events, as volunteers, and as planners of school activities and operations, but also, perhaps more importantly, as mediators of learning (Williams & Chaukin, 1989). Family involvement may take a variety of forms such as information sharing, volunteering in the classroom, or home tutoring. Opportunities should be provided for parents to learn about the school program and to participate in program decisions for their children such as the development of Individualized Education Programs, or IEPs. Such activities ensure that families are knowledgeable about their children's learning plans, the school curriculum, and their children's progress in the curriculum. Furthermore, as the first teachers of children, families play a significant role in the socialization and schooling process. The involvement of families in supporting student learning is especially important in the implementation of school programs aimed at adapting to student differences, particularly students with special needs who require exceptional educational and service support.

Students and schools need connections to the community. Exciting new modes of cooperation between schools and communities are being explored across the country (Davis, 1991; Scannapieco & Wang, 1992). For example, the School of the Future project in four Texas cities (Austin, Dallas, Houston, and San Antonio) coordinates preventive and treatment services for families and delivers these in a central neighborhood location (Holtzman, 1991). A similar project is being implemented in San Diego, California (San Diego City Schools, 1990). Another initiative is the Minneapolis Youth Trust, a community collaboration led by executive administrators, corporations, and elected officials from the school district, the city, unions, and community organizations (Kyle, 1991). The Youth Trust recruits and trains mentors for students of all ages and emphasizes work readiness and the development of work-related skills. As noted by Fantini and Sinclair (1985), children and youth spend a large proportion of their awake hours (estimated to be 70%) out of school. The more this time can be made constructive for academic, social, and occupational development, the better the chance for schooling and later success. Student learning efficiency and school achievement can be greatly increased through community efforts to enlarge the learning and work experience and to increase academic motivation (Benne & Tozer, 1987; Mitchell & Cunningham, 1990).

School staff need to seek out good ideas and practices that help promote promising connections. Fantini and Sinclair (1985) urge

> Now is the time for us to reassess our system of education, regroup our educational resources in the school and the community outside the school and systematically link the school and non-school environments to support learning for all people. (p. 65)

There is a growing interest to stimulate more links among families, schools, and communities. Educators are enlisting families and communities to engage children in academic activities outside of school to enhance schooling success, particularly for those students requiring exceptional support. Some schools are experimenting with child care, recreational, and extracurricular activities that were once the exclusive tasks of parents. Similarly, business leaders are assisting educators by lending their expertise in management, inventory, transportation, and other tasks, as well as in traditional work–study and vocational extension programs for young people. There is a growing realization that families and community agencies can serve as places of education and multiply the efforts of schools to increase student learning.

## SCHOOL IMPLEMENTATION OF ADAPTIVE EDUCATION PROGRAMS

The program dimensions described above are design features and classroom practices that have been shown to be effective based on research and practical experience (cf. Anderson & Pellicer, 1990; Wang, Haertel, & Walberg, 1990; Wang, Reynolds, & Walberg, 1990; Wang & Walberg, 1985; Williams et al., 1986; Wittrock, 1986). The presence of only a single dimension is, however, unlikely to lead to effective adaptive education. Rather, the implementation of clusters of dimensions as part of a comprehensive system is essential. Interactions among the dimension clusters lead to desired classroom processes and outcomes (see Figure 1.3.). In this section, some of the hypothesized interactive effects of clusters of program dimensions are discussed to illustrate their specific functions in program implementation.

### Integrated Diagnostic–Prescriptive Process

An integrated diagnostic–prescriptive process is central to adaptive education (Glaser, 1988; Wang, 1988). Dimensions that link diagnosis to instructional planning and intervention include:

Diagnostic testing
Monitoring and diagnosing
Prescribing
Record keeping

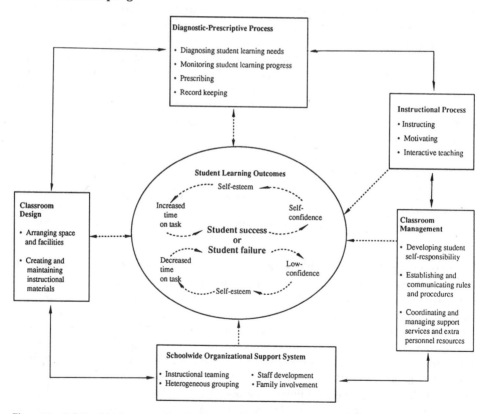

**Figure 1.3.** Relationships between selected adaptive education program dimensions and outcomes.

Diagnostic–prescriptive processes allow for assessment of each student's learning behaviors and performance at entry (diagnosing student learning needs), development of individualized learning plans (prescribing), and continual monitoring and assessment of each student's learning progress (monitoring student progress, record keeping). These dimensions are intervention strategies to provide successful learning experiences that lead to competent performance, even for students who are ill-prepared in their experience, knowledge, and skills.

Critical elements in the diagnostic–prescriptive process are clear short- and long-term curriculum objectives that are organized in psychologically and pedagogically meaningful learning units. The categorization and ordering of learning tasks enable teachers to structure learning experiences so that mastery of initial curriculum objectives provides knowledge and skills required for mastery of later objectives. Meaningful clustering and sequencing of curriculum objectives form the basis for curriculum-based assessments for monitoring student progress. Curriculum-based assessment provides information to determine the presence or absence of specific knowledge and skills required for competent performance.

Programs that incorporate such a diagnostic–prescriptive process enable placement of each student at an appropriate point in the curriculum. Through the use of the diagnostic–prescriptive process, students do not repeat tasks that they have mastered, or work on objectives for which they lack critical prerequisite skills. Checkpoints in the curriculum permit students who have acquired skills to move ahead to more complex tasks. Systematic implementation of an ongoing diagnostic–prescriptive process not only ensures student mastery of academic skills, but more important, ensures development of a sense of competence that, in turn, increases self-confidence. Such heightened self-esteem has been found to result in more time spent on learning, as well as greater achievement, motivation, self-direction, and responsibility for learning (Peterson, Heistad, Peterson, & Reynolds, 1985; Shepard, 1989; Snow & Farr, 1987; Wang & Peverly, 1987; Zimmerman, 1986).

## Systematic Provision of Instructional Learning Options

A variety of learning options and alternative instructional strategies is a requirement of implementing adaptive education. Five program dimensions directly relate to providing a wide range of instructional choices:

Creating and maintaining instructional materials
Arranging space and facilities
Interactive teaching
Coordinating and managing support services and personnel resources
Instructional teaming

For example, when commercial and teacher-constructed materials (creating and maintaining instructional materials) are combined with adequate space and facilities (arranging space and facilities), effective interaction with students (interactive teaching), and utilization of professionals and other support staff (coordinating and managing support services and personnel resources, instructional teaming), opportunities are increased for accommodating the learning needs of each student and the skills to be mastered. An anticipated outcome is consistent success in learning by every student.

## Instructional Learning Management System

Scheduling learning activities and instructional time and the availability of resources and facilities have posed major problems for implementing adaptive education programs. Establishing and communicating rules and procedures and developing student self-responsibility are two dimensions that have been shown to facilitate effective management of classroom instruction in general, and adaptive education in particular. Under traditional systems of education, choices in scheduling are limited to group instruction versus individual instruction, free choice versus teacher-prescribed activities, and teacher instruction versus independent student work. Effective management of the adaptive education approach, however, enables the inclusion and orchestration of all these alternatives.

Support must be provided for efficient use of time, space, and material resources by teachers and students. Thus, the establishment and explicit communication of rules and procedures (establishing and communicating rules and procedures) and delegation of increased responsibility to students for planning and completing their own learning tasks (developing student self-responsibility) are crucial dimensions for effective classroom management. Incorporation of these dimensions into classroom management frees teachers from routine management tasks, such as monitoring access to materials and equipment, and allows them to concentrate on teaching and establishing an orderly learning environment that is intellectually and socially stimulating (Evertson, 1989). This learning environment builds on the strengths of teachers and students and allows for the flexibility to effectively respond to student diversity.

A major expected outcome of an effective management support system is a decrease in the information overload that teachers are bound to experience in implementing adaptive education. In this complex process, teachers are required to process information about each student's learning progress on an ongoing basis. Teachers need to evaluate and design plans to facilitate mastery of learning objectives. Instructional decisions are based not only on student cues, but also on the availability of alternative strategies and materials. Implementation of strategies is complicated by each teacher's beliefs about education and the particular instructional practices, as well as his or her perceptions of individual student needs and characteristics. Limitations inherent in human information processing make it difficult for teachers to accomplish all of these tasks simultaneously. Therefore, designing program implementation support for adaptive education has been focusing on ways to reduce the information processing required of teachers. Effective instructional learning management systems ensure such support by teaching students to take more responsibility for their own learning. Teaching students to become effective managers of their classroom learning and behavior has been found to allow teachers more time for teaching and related instructional matters and less time for managing students (Wang, 1979; Wang & Walberg, 1983).

Fostering student self-responsibility has a positive impact on students and teachers. Research suggests a close relationship between self-management and efficient learning (e.g., Sternberg, 1988; Sternberg, Okagaki, & Jackson, 1990;

Thomas, 1980; Wang & Peverly, 1986). Students who are competent self-managers tend to show more initiative and make more use of learned principles of problem solving than do other students. In addition, the development of self-management skills increases student motivation and reduces the amount of system-imposed distraction in the learning environment. Strengthening basic academic and self-management skills is a way of increasing a sense of self-efficacy or personal control over learning. At the same time, students are more willing to spend the time needed for learning. Student acquisition of self-management skills is also seen as a way of maximizing the time actually dedicated to learning and instruction. In turn, it is anticipated that more instructional time, if wisely used, is likely to improve the quality of instruction and reduce the time needed for learning.

## School-Wide Organizational Support System

One of the most frequently cited causes of unsuccessful school implementation of innovative practices is the lack of well-defined organizational supports (Conley, 1991; Fullan, 1985; Goodlad, 1983; Reynolds & Wang, 1983; Skrtic, 1990). Adaptive education requires effective use and management of all available resources in ways that lead to increased learning and instructional alternatives. This requirement demands a major rethinking of the role of teachers, administrators, specialized professionals, parents, and policymakers and also a restructuring of the school organization and staffing, program delivery systems, and resource utilization to support the implementation of adaptive education.

An important step to prepare for implementation of adaptive education is the development of a process of school-based planning. Planning should involve the school staff, community, and businesses to form partnerships to improve the school's ability to coordinate resources to respond to the diverse learning characteristics and needs of the students. Among the design dimensions directly related to the development of a well-defined, organizational support system are:

> Heterogeneous grouping
> Instructional teaming
> Staff development
> Family involvement and community connections

## Staff Roles in Adaptive Education:
## A Transdisciplinary Team Approach to Delivery of Educational Services

A basic condition for providing educational services that are responsive to the individual student is collaboration among all educational professionals who affect student learning outcomes, particularly in classes with ethnically and socioeconomically diverse students, and students with special needs who are integrated in regular classes. The ultimate goal of such collaboration among school staff is to strengthen the school's capacity to address student differences through substantive understanding and help, while holding the school staff responsible for the progress and schooling outcome of every student. Implementation of such educational vision requires major rethinking and restructuring of current school organizational structures and practices (Conley, 1991; Lewis, 1989; Lieberman & Miller, 1990; Smith & Scott, 1990).

Restructuring for implementation of adaptive education requires creating professional environments that empower administrators, teachers, and support staff to plan how best to use their resources to provide for the needs of each student. This task requires renegotiation and definition of the roles of regular and special education personnel, changes in the roles of specialists, and changes in the roles of administrators and other professionals who provide instructional leadership and support that facilitates implementation (e.g., negotiating waivers in policy or funding for educational accountability of student outcomes, see Wang, Reynolds, & Walberg, 1988).

An effective environment for school implementation of adaptive education is a transdisciplinary structure that fosters school staff teaming for shared responsibility. The term "transdisciplinary" to describe a collaborative approach to program implementation denotes the significance of integrating information about all aspects of student learning and development with the expertise of professionals from a variety of fields. The following sections describe the roles of school staff members within a transdisciplinary team approach.

***Role of the Regular Classroom Teacher***   The regular classroom teacher assumes the central responsibility for coordinating adaptive education. The role of the regular classroom teacher in adaptive education programs remains largely the same as that of teachers in more traditional programs. For example, the teacher in an adaptive education program provides instruction for students in large groups, small groups, or individually with the appropriate curriculum. The instructional resources used by the regular teachers using the adaptive education approach—basal texts and various supplementary curricular materials— are also similar.

Adaptive education programs primarily differ from traditional programs in the premise that *all* students should be provided with opportunities and instructional support to achieve expected outcomes. In operation, the major difference between classes implementing adaptive education and those implementing a traditional program is a focus on the learning needs of individual students and the achievement of schooling outcomes of each student. The emphasis is on providing greater than usual support for the students requiring it in regular classroom settings through a coordinated delivery system that includes the expertise and resources of specialists on the instructional team. Adaptive education programs emphasize diagnosing the learning needs of each student and prescribing a variety of learning tasks based on those needs. Support for a structured approach to diagnosis and prescription is provided, for example, by careful sequencing of curricula, coordinated scheduling of resources and expertise of specialized professionals, and a learning management system that encourages student self-management and the use of peers as learning resources.

It is important to note that when adaptive education is effectively implemented through a transdisciplinary team of regular and specialist teachers, students with special needs can be integrated in regular classes on a full-time basis because the responsibility for instruction is divided among the team. Special interventions for individual students can usually be provided in the regular classroom rather than in pull-out settings where students are labeled and segregated from their peers and miss out on the variety of experiences in regular classes. Research conducted on students with special needs integrated full time in regular classrooms with special interventions shows that such students demonstrate substantial achievement gains, positive attitudinal changes, and a number of desirable process outcomes (Sobehart, 1991; Wang & Walberg, 1985; Wang & Zollers, 1990; Waxman, Wang, Anderson, & Walberg, 1985).

Typically in the implementation of adaptive education, two or more regular teachers and specialist colleagues form a team to provide coordinated services to students. They combine classes and share their resources and expertise among all students in these classes. Instructional teaming is a key to facilitating management and successfully accommodating a range of student learning needs and teaching styles. A major advantage of instructional teaming is the flexibility in allocating teacher resources to effectively meet the needs of individual students and in providing mutual support for problem solving and staff development. A variety of instructional groupings and optimal use of teacher interests, talents, and time are possible with instructional teaming.

**Role of the Specialist**  Traditionally, specialists in the school such as special education teachers, school psychologists, or Chapter 1 reading teachers function both physically and instructionally separately from regular classroom teachers. Specialists generally either have their own full-time classes or teach or practice in resource rooms where students come to them for part of the school day. Under these circumstances, there is minimal interaction between regular classroom teachers and specialists. When students with special needs are integrated in regular classrooms, specialist educators are required to work more closely with regular classroom teachers. Although they may not have their own special classes or rooms, they are responsible for collaborating with regular teachers to plan and deliver instruction and related services directly or in consultation with regular classroom teachers.

Because of their extensive training and experience with the diagnostic–prescriptive process and with individualization of instruction, special education teachers and other specialist professionals are in an excellent position to provide unique support to regular teachers, particularly in adaptive education classes. For example, special education teachers can offer consultative services to regular classroom teachers or provide pre-referral interventions for students. In addition, special education teachers who work in the classroom with students who require extraordinary attention can serve as role models for regular teachers. When a student experiences learning difficulties, special education teachers can intervene before the problem becomes a real handicap to the student.

Thus, in the context of a transdisciplinary team providing effective responses to diverse student characteristics and needs, the specialist educator plays an expanded role as both clinical staff providing direct services to students and as an expert consultant to support the work of regular teachers (Reynolds, 1989; Reynolds, Wang, & Walberg, 1987). These roles, while not entirely new to special educators, represent a change from the usual separation between special and regular teachers. By virtue of their training, special educators are ideally suited to perform these crucial support roles in successful implementation of an adaptive education program that responds to the special needs of individual students in regular classes.

**Role of the Principal as Instructional Leader**  In addition to the administrative, policy making, and public relations functions of the principal, research on effective schools has clearly shown that the school principal is particularly important for promoting and maintaining innovative school improvements. Research on innovative school programs shows that principals determine whether a change, once adopted, will be maintained (cf. Kyle, 1985). These studies referred to school principals as the gatekeepers of change, and their support for educational innovations through project training and the creation of a supportive organizational climate is crucial to program continuation. Research findings also show that effective schools tend to have principals who function primarily as instructional rather than administrative leaders (Fullan, 1985; Montgomery & Leithwood, 1983; Sergiovanni, 1990; Walberg & Keefe, 1988). As instructional leaders, principals work with teachers to:

1. Implement a diversity of alternative instructional strategies
2. Actively develop solutions to classroom problems
3. Participate in and provide inservice activities
4. Lead formal and informal staff development programs
5. Observe and provide feedback to teachers
6. Work with teachers to identify instructional goals and means for ensuring student achievement

To promote the flexibility of adaptive education programs, restructuring the relationships among school personnel and providing ongoing training support are important instructional leadership functions.

## THE RESEARCH BASE ON PROGRAM OUTCOMES

As Figure 1.2. shows, the model of adaptive education hypothesizes two kinds of program outcomes: process outcomes and product outcomes. Process outcomes include a variety of desirable classroom behaviors and interactions (such as increased time on task and fewer disruptive behaviors). Product outcomes include gains in student learning (cognitive outcomes), positive student interactions and friendship patterns (social outcomes), and improved student and teacher attitudes (affective outcomes).

Evaluation of the efficacy of adaptive education requires assessing the effects of adaptive education on both types of outcomes. Readers interested in data supporting the success of particular programs can refer to reports by program developers in the list at the end of this chapter. Until the 1980s, research comparing outcomes of adaptive education programs was characterized by inconsistent and inconclusive results. This was primarily due to two factors: a dearth of relevant studies and the lack of a consistent conceptual framework to describe features and outcomes of adaptive education. Since the 1980s, however, the number of studies has multiplied. With this greater pool, a meta-analysis by Waxman et al. (1985) was able to select studies based on a definition of adaptive education consistent with the conceptual model shown in Figure 1.2. Findings from selected studies of the effects of adaptive education are summarized below.

Waxman et al. (1985) conducted a meta-analysis of the results of 38 studies, which included a total of 309 comparisons between adaptive and nonadaptive (control) instruction programs. The studies involved a variety of programs, social settings, grade levels, subject matter, and research methodologies. Thirty-two of the studies examined cognitive outcomes (usually performance on standardized achievement tests), twelve examined affective outcomes, and three examined behavioral (or process) outcomes other than cognitive ones.

Using the meta-analysis procedures (Glass, McGaw, & Smith, 1981), effect size was computed for each comparison and the weighted effect size was computed for each study. The overall mean weighted effect size was .45, about one half of a standard deviation. This result suggests that the average student in an adaptive education program scored at the 67th percentile of the distribution scores for the control group students (those in nonadaptive programs). The mean weighted effect sizes for cognitive, affective, and behavioral outcomes were .39, .60, and .69, respectively. These effects did not vary significantly as a function of specific program characteristics, methodological rigor, social context of the study, subject area, grade level, or other student characteristics. Overall, the findings from the meta-analysis study support the hypothesized positive relationship between adaptive education and both process and product outcomes.

An observational study of features of adaptive education was conducted by Wang and Walberg (1986). The study examined how different combinations of features and implementation conditions are integrated into existing programs to produce classroom processes and student outcomes commonly associated with effective instruction and learning. Seven widely implemented programs were selected for investigation from instructional programs or models that include the goal of providing for individual differences. The seven programs were the Adaptive Learning Environments Model (Wang, 1980; Wang, Gennari, & Waxman, 1985), the Bank Street Model (Gilkeson, Smithberg, Bowman, & Rhine, 1981), the Behavior Analysis Model (Beckwith & Stivers, 1982; Ramp & Rhine, 1981), Individually Guided Education (Klausmeier, 1975), the Mastery Learning Approach (Bloom, 1968), Team-Assisted Individualization (Slavin, 1985), and the Utah System Approach to Individualized Learning ( Jeter, 1980).

Classrooms representing exemplary implementation of these programs were identified by the program developers and served as the sample for the study. Data on seven categories of variables—program features, classroom processes, classroom climate, student perception of responsibility, student achievement, teacher attitudes, and student socioeconomic status—were collected and analyzed for a total of 65 second, third, and fourth grade classrooms. Findings from the study suggest that programs that feature student choice, task flexibility, systematic teacher monitoring, peer tutoring, student-initiated requests for assistance from teachers, a wide variety of curriculum materials, and task-specific instructions tended to produce student outcomes that included high levels of self-management, substantive rather than management-related interactions with teachers, and frequent work in small groups. Overall, programs and classrooms that were observed to feature the greatest use of strategies for individualizing instruction, as well as clear task-specific directions, were associated with high levels of student responsibility.

On average, the programs that predominantly utilized adaptive education practices and strategies produced student achievement levels as great as, and often greater than, achievement levels under more teacher-directed and group-paced programs. Moreover, several sample programs that included features of adaptive education had positive results in additional outcomes considered by educators, parents, and students to be of value. Among these outcomes were constructive student interactions with peers, independent work, individual diagnosis and prescription, cooperative learning, and exploration. The data also indicate that no single feature seemed to distinguish effective programs from less effective programs. Instead, the combination and coordination of several features in carefully implemented programs appeared to produce a wide range of positive student outcomes.

## THEORY INTO PRACTICE: DESCRIPTIONS
## OF SELECTED ADAPTIVE EDUCATION PROGRAMS

Many research-based innovative programs aimed to respond to student diversity have been widely implemented (Wang & Walberg, 1985). Several programs are described below to provide illustrations of school implementation of adaptive education. They do not represent an exhaustive survey, but illustrate the types of adaptive education programs being implemented in school settings. These programs, which owe much to earlier efforts such as the Winnetka Plan and similar programs developed in the 1920s (Whipple, 1925), have provided a substantial database for demonstrating the feasibility of providing adaptive education in regular school settings. Table 1.1. provides a summary of selected models featuring implemented adaptive education practices. The table is based on a research synthesis study of variables considered important to learning by education professionals (Wang, Haertel, & Walberg, 1990). The study was conducted to develop a database that would provide a common language for researchers to describe program features, implementation, and effects of different innovative school programs. The table lists two major categories of variables: marker variables important to learning and important program emphases. A marker variable in the context of this study is a variable identified from research and by the consensus of experts in the field as sufficiently important to learning that it is useful for synthesizing and analyzing findings across studies. In Table 1.1., the marker variables considered important to learning are grouped under six categories, and six model programs are included as examples of widely implemented alternative programs that provide for student diversity in regular classroom environments.

## Adaptive Learning Environments Model

The Adaptive Learning Environments Model (ALEM) is an educational program with the overall goal of ensuring the learning success of each student through an adaptive educational and service delivery system that effectively responds to the diverse social and academic needs of individual students in regular learning environments. An underlying premise of the ALEM design is that students learn in different ways and require different amounts and rates of instruction. Furthermore, it is assumed that effective school programs accommodate and build on these differences through a variety of instructional methods, alternative learning sequences, and options suited to the learning needs of individual students. Specific interventions are designed to enhance each student's ability to acquire basic academic skills and develop social competence and self-esteem. Under the ALEM, students are taught to take responsibility for their own learning by participating in the planning and management of their educational tasks. Regular students and students with special needs, including students in special or compensatory education programs as well as those considered to be academically gifted, receive appropriate instruction in ALEM classes without experiencing the negative effects of special labeling or segregation.

The ALEM was initially developed as a comprehensive school-based program for preschool and early elementary grades as one of the model programs of

**Table 1.1.** Summary of selected adaptive education models and programmatic emphases

| Variables | Model program | | | | | |
|---|---|---|---|---|---|---|
| | Adaptive Learning Environments Model | Curriculum-Based Assessment | Johns Hopkins Cooperative Learning Model | Johnson and Johnson Cooperative Learning Model | Johnson City Mastery Learning Model | Project Link |
| I. Marker Variables Considered Important to Learning | | | | | | |
| A. State and district variables | | | | | | |
|   1. District-level demographic variables | X | | X | | | |
|   2. State-level policy variables | X | X | X | | X | X |
| B. Out-of-school contextual variables | | | | | | |
|   1. Community variables | X | X | | | | |
|   2. Peer group variables | X | | | | X | |
|   3. Home environment and parental support variables | X | | | | | |
|   4. Student use of out-of-school time variables | X | | | | | |
| C. School-level variables | | | | | | |
|   1. Demographic variables | X | | X | | | |
|   2. Teacher/administrator decision making variables | X | | | | | |
|   3. School culture variables (ethos conducive to teaching and learning) | X | | | | | |
|   4. School-wide policy and organizational variables | X | X | | X | X | X |
|   5. Accessibility variables | X | | | | X | |
|   6. Parental involvement policy variables | X | | | | X | X |
| D. Student variables | | | | | | |
|   1. Demographic variables | X | | | | | |
|   2. History of educational placements | X | X | | | | |
|   3. Social and behavioral variables | X | | X | X | X | X |
|   4. Motivational and affective variables | X | X | X | X | X | X |
|   5. Cognitive variables | X | X | X | | X | X |
|   6. Metacognitive variables | X | | | | | |
|   7. Psychomotor variables | X | | | | | |

(continued)

**Table 1.1.**  (continued)

| Variables | Model program | | | | | |
|---|---|---|---|---|---|---|
| | Adaptive Learning Environments Model | Curriculum-Based Assessment | Johns Hopkins Cooperative Learning Model | Johnson and Johnson Cooperative Learning Model | Johnson City Mastery Learning Model | Project Link |
| **E. Program design variables** | | | | | | |
| 1. Demographic variables | X | | X | X | | X |
| 2. Curriculum and instructional variables | X | X | X | X | X | X |
| 3. Curriculum design variables | X | | | | | |
| **F. Implementation, classroom instruction, and climate variables** | | | | | | |
| 1. Classroom implementation support variables | X | X | X | X | X | X |
| 2. Classroom instructional variables | X | X | X | X | X | X |
| 3. Quantity of instructional variables | X | X | X | X | X | X |
| 4. Classroom assessment variables | X | X | X | X | X | X |
| 5. Classroom management variables | X | X | X | X | X | X |
| 6. Student and teacher interactions: Social variables | X | X | X | X | X | X |
| 7. Student and teacher interactions: Academic variables | X | X | X | X | X | |
| 8. Classroom climate variables | X | | X | X | | X |
| **II. Important Program Outcomes** | | | | | | |
| A. Student learning outcomes | X | X | X | X | X | X |
| B. Teacher expertise and attitudes | X | X | X | X | X | X |
| C. Administrator/instructional leader expertise and attitudes | X | X | X | | X | |
| D. Family expectation attitudes | X | | X | | | |
| E. Program cost effectiveness | X | X | | | | X |

(From Wang, M.C., Reynolds, M.C., & Rosenfeld, S. (1989). *Variables important to learning: A consensus from the field.* Philadelphia, PA: Temple University Center for Research in Human Development and Education; reprinted by permission.)

the National Follow Through Program (Wang, 1980; Wang, Leinhardt, & Boston, 1980). Program development and implementation in a variety of school settings have extended the application of the ALEM as a mainstreaming program for students with special needs in elementary and selected middle and senior high schools (Manning & Quandt, 1990; Peterson et al., 1986; Sobehart, 1991; Wang & Birch, 1984; Wang, Reynolds, & Schwartz, 1988; Wang & Zollers, 1990).

The ALEM design offers an educational philosophy and specific strategies for technical assistance to strengthen the teacher's ability to adapt instruction to student differences as well as a systematic structure for supporting program implementation. The delivery of adaptive instruction is facilitated by individualized progress plans, a diagnostic–prescriptive monitoring system, and the Self-Schedule System, which is a classroom instructional learning management system that helps students take responsibility for their own behaviors and learning progress. Features that support the implementation of adaptive instruction include a program delivery system, a systematic staff development sequence known as the Data-Based Staff Development Program, school and classroom organizational supports, and family involvement.

The ALEM adaptive program delivery system supports school personnel in making systematic adjustments to use school resources and staff expertise to achieve school improvement goals. A site-specific plan for implementing the ALEM is developed based on assessments of school characteristics such as student needs, staffing patterns, curricula options, operating practices, record-keeping procedures, and physical resources. Support for introducing and maintaining the ALEM is provided through the Data-Based Staff Development Program. This training sequence for school personnel includes three levels. The first, basic training, provides an overview of the ALEM and a working knowledge of the requirements for program implementation. The second, individualized training, is keyed to the particular functions of each staff role. The third, inservice training, consists of an ongoing process of program assessment, feedback, planning, and staff development.

At the school level, the ALEM calls for staffing patterns that promote coordination and collaboration among the school staff. Specialized professional staff work closely with regular education teachers to plan and serve in a variety of implementation support functions. The specialized staff provide technical and instructional support by assisting in the diagnostic–prescriptive process, with direct instruction, and by serving as consultants. At the classroom level, the ALEM design utilizes heterogeneous or multi-age grouping, flexible scheduling, and continuous progress plans. The ALEM also includes a systematic plan to implement a family involvement program to increase the communication and cooperation between home and school, and it includes family and community support for the school and its programming goals.

Data are collected from schools using ALEM components on implementation, classroom processes, and student learning outcome measures such as student achievement, student attitudes, and the attitudes of teachers and parents. Findings from over a decade of research provide consistent evidence that high degrees of ALEM implementation have been obtained in regular classes in a variety of school settings, and that effective implementation leads to positive changes in classroom processes, such as increases in student–teacher interactions for instructional purposes, decreases in student–teacher interactions for management purposes, and increases in the time students spend in cooperative learning and peer tutoring. Among the most noteworthy findings are that ALEM students tend to exhibit unusually high rates of on-task behavior, a high frequency of student-initiated interactions with teachers for instructional purposes, a high frequency of student-selected exploratory activities and constructive interactions among peers, and high levels of student self-responsibility in managing their behaviors and the classroom learning environment (e.g., Peterson et al., 1986; Sobehart, 1991; Wang & Zollers, 1990).

## Johnson and Johnson Cooperative Learning Model

The Johnson and Johnson Cooperative Learning Model emphasizes the effectiveness of peer cooperation and a cooperative versus competitive learning environment in the classroom. This approach is appropriate for most instructional situations. Competition, individual action, and cooperation do have their place in the classroom, and the cooperative learning model stipulates that these goal structures should be used, but emphasizes avoiding inappropriate classroom competition and teaching students when competition is appropriate. The model concentrates on peer collaboration in the learning environment, and a goal is that students freely participate in the learning process without comparing their abilities to those of their peers. Cooperative learning groups are typically heterogeneous, composed of students with varying abilities and personal characteristics. Heterogeneous groupings have been shown to increase the achievement of successful as well as less successful students and to teach social skills and democratic values ( Johnson & Johnson, 1975; Johnson, Maruyama, Johnson, Nelson, & Skon, 1981; Johnson, Skon, & Johnson, 1980; Kagan, 1989–90). Further, the cooperative environment encourages students who are less knowledgeable to exert themselves in order to share in the satisfaction of group efforts.

All members share responsibility for leadership functions as well as for other group tasks. Good interpersonal relationships between members are important. Students provide help and encouragement to each other to ensure that all group members complete assignments. Teachers do not automatically assume that students possess small group skills, and the skills are taught directly so that students are able to work collaboratively. These skills include communication, trust, leadership, and conflict management. Students are also taught to assess how well the group is working. Teachers observe groups, analyze problems, and intervene as necessary. Feedback is given to groups regarding individual student performance, group performance on assignments, and group process management ( Johnson, Johnson, & Holubec, 1986).

Classroom materials are arranged so that students have access to other students, the teacher, and instructional materials. The classroom arrangement clusters students in small groups with easy access to materials and other students. Members of each cluster are seated with a clear view of the members of their group so that they are able to speak to each other without disturbing the rest of the class. Groups may share a table, push desks together, or sit in a small circle, and the groups should be as far apart as possible. The teacher must have access to all groups in order to observe and assist.

The cooperative learning model emphasizes ways that teachers can structure goals to promote valued behaviors among students and cooperative behaviors by clearly describing their expectations. Quality of instruction not only involves the value and appropriateness of informational assistance by the teacher, but also includes how clearly "social" learning goals are communicated. Students are encouraged to interact and to perceive each other as major resources for learning. Therefore, students use the teacher less for ideas and solutions as they learn to use each other more, and the teacher directs students to each other. Students know where materials are, how to use them, and how to use other students as sources of information. The cooperative learning model seeks to improve student achievement, the social acceptance of students with academic handicaps, student self-esteem and attitudes toward school, student behavior, and teacher attitudes, particularly attitudes toward mainstreaming.

Teachers can assist in achieving program implementation by consciously providing the groundwork necessary for students to work collaboratively. One such step is to discuss with students the idea of working together, and to help them identify skills that they need to begin collaborative efforts. The teacher can then facilitate development of these skills by helping students clearly understand, both conceptually and behaviorally, the nature of the skill; providing practice situations; giving each student feedback on skill performance; encouraging students to persevere in practicing; providing situations for successful use of the skill; providing opportunities for the skill to be used so that it is integrated into the students' repertoire; and establishing classroom norms that support the use of the skill. There are several types of skills that are important to successful collaborative efforts. The classroom teacher can facilitate implementation of the program by understanding and instructing students in communication skills, building and maintaining a climate of trust, managing controversial interactions, self-examination of personal behavior, and positive competition skills.

In this program design, teachers shape classroom activities by selecting the appropriate goal structure for classwork, which involves recognizing the qualities of the instructional goals and the materials. This process requires the following steps: deciding what material is to be mastered and the desired cognitive and affective outcomes; ascertaining the nature of the instructional task; selecting the instructional climate and the interaction to facilitate the learning objectives; determining the difficulty of the instructional task and if the material is new or to be reviewed; identifying the learning outcomes, interaction, and climate promoted by the goal structure; identifying the conditions for using the goal structure; and, finally, choosing the appropriate goal structure.

The goals or expected outcomes of the model include high interaction among peers, effective communication, utilization of other students as resources, sharing and helping, emotional involvement of all students, coordination of efforts and division of labor, original and risk-taking thinking, and little comparison of self with others. This model stresses affective as well as cognitive outcomes at every step of planning, implementation, and assessment.

Cognitive structures best addressed by the cooperative approach are retention, application, and transfer of factual information, concepts, and principles; mastery of concepts and principles; verbal abilities; problem-solving abilities; cooperative skills; creative abilities such as original or risk-taking thinking and productive controversy; awareness and use of one's own abilities; and role-taking abilities.

## Johns Hopkins Cooperative Learning Model

The Johns Hopkins Cooperative Learning Model focuses on instructional, motivational, and classroom management issues involved in teaching students with a wide range of abilities in a classroom setting (Slavin, 1985). In general, the five programs (STAD, TGT, Jigsaw II, TAI, and CIRC) combine powerful classroom organization elements. The socialization effects of cooperative learning, which has been found to have a positive effect on race relations and attitudes toward mainstreamed students with academic handicaps, allow more direct instructional time by the teacher in individualized instructional programs that meet student academic needs.

Students with learning disabilities, students with mental retardation, and students with emotional disabilities are integrated with students without disabilities in regular classes to the maximum extent possible. Students with the most severe learning and/or emotional problems only are maintained in special education classes, and every attempt is made to move these students into regular classrooms as soon as they are ready. Once mainstreamed, students are integrated into the heterogeneous learning teams along with other students.

Students receive most of their academic instruction through cooperative learning methods designed to accommodate a wide range of performance levels. Students work on instructional tasks in heterogeneous learning teams. Team members receive points based on individual performance on tests and compositions, and these points are used to compute a team score. This provides a basis for individual accountability for mastering new material and team incentives that reward performance and motivate students to help, tutor, test, and encourage each other to achieve. Mainstreamed students are integrated into the heterogeneous teams. Since team members have equal status, this helps develop better peer relations and more positive attitudes toward mainstreamed students with academic handicaps. Parent involvement in cooperative learning models is actively encouraged in many forms and specific activities. The use of home-based reinforcement methods is introduced for students experiencing behavioral difficulties in school. Brief descriptions of specific programs follow.

*STAD and TGT*   Student Teams Achievement Divisions (STAD) and Teams Games Tournaments (TGT) are generic cooperative learning processes that can be used in any subject area. In both programs, the teacher presents new material or skills, which students study cooperatively in learning teams. In STAD, students take a test or quiz on the new content, and individual scores are used to compute a team score by which teams are recognized. In TGT, following team study, students engage in tournaments with students of similar ability levels, and ask one another questions and check each other's answers. Teams are rewarded based on individual team member performance in the tournaments.

*Jigsaw II*   In Jigsaw II, students from each team are assigned by the teacher to "expert groups." Each expert group is given a portion of new content to investigate and to learn. After the expert groups have gathered the information for their area, students return to their teams and exchange this information with their team members, who were in other expert groups. Team members help each other master the new material in preparation for a quiz, and the scores are used to determine team scores and rewards.

*TAI*   The Team-Assisted Individualization math program focuses on math instruction for third through eighth grade. In TAI, students proceed through math units at their own rates, based on unit tests. The TAI program uses initial instruction in small groups by the teacher for new concepts or skills. Teammates check each other's work and give corrective feedback during student practice. Teams earn points for a team score and awards as team members pass unit tests.

*CIRC*  The Cooperative Integrated Reading and Composition program focuses on reading instruction for second through sixth grade. The CIRC program uses instruction in reading groups by the teacher followed by cooperative learning, guided practice, and independent practice activities. Students work on a specific sequence of activities involving silent and oral reading, vocabulary practice, grammar activities, reading comprehension and practice, and writing about the story. Students discuss their work, correct each other's activities, and provide corrective feedback. Quizzes at the end of the instructional cycle are used for individual accountability and to determine team scores.

Teachers receive training in general cooperative learning principles and in specific strategies for the program being implemented. CIRC and TAI are complex programs in specific subject areas and, therefore, require extensive training in instructional methods. Program coordinators at the district or school level address implementation concerns and provide training for program expansion. Since cooperative learning strategies are often used to accommodate the needs of students with special needs in mainstreamed classrooms, resource room teachers, reading specialists, and other special education staff are involved in implementation as much as possible. These personnel also receive extensive training and usually work with the regular education teacher to help special students in the mainstreamed classroom.

## Johnson City Mastery Learning Model

The Johnson City Mastery Learning Model, also known as the Outcomes-Driven Developmental Model, is based on the philosophy that all students can achieve subject mastery if given sufficient time and the proper learning conditions. The model provides a comprehensive, systematic process that is applied to all aspects of school operation, including instruction, curriculum design, climate, leadership and management, staff development, and flow of communication.

Although the program works best for average students, the model seeks high levels of achievement for all students in all areas of learning, K–12. Students with mild physical or learning impairments can be fully integrated into all academic classes, and students with more severe impairments can largely be integrated. Students are not excluded from enriched learning experiences according to IQ or other criteria but are encouraged to participate to their highest level of motivation and performance.

The Johnson City system involves extensive curriculum planning and ongoing revision. Curriculum development is provided for school staff and is based on research. Teams of teachers, coordinators, and principals develop objectives for disciplines and units. The curriculum is constantly revised and tailored to meet the needs of individual classes. Student groups are based on the performance of students within the curriculum, and staff are assigned according to student needs. The special education teacher is a consultant to other teachers. A strong emphasis is placed on communication at all levels with administrators, teachers, parents, and students.

Mastery is evaluated on an ongoing basis, and students performing below standards are provided with additional instructional time. Students performing at a standard level may choose enrichment and exceptional learning experiences, and students progress to the next phase of instruction when they demonstrate mastery of a phase.

There are 18 basic components of the Johnson City Mastery Learning Model, each designed according to district needs. Changes are made in stages, and trained administrators and teachers provide inservice training to other teachers. Providing time and funds for staff training are key resource requirements.

All components of the system must be in place for implementation. The model is based on research and requires that a school district base all decisions on the best research literature. A mission statement related to student outcomes is developed and understood by all members of the school and community. Philosophical beliefs concerning academic excellence are made clear, and psychological knowledge about learning and motivation guides instruction. A team of administrators and teachers is chosen and trained to provide leadership for transformation. Administrative support is required for staff development, communication, problem solving, change, and improvement of classroom climate. Instruction incorporates the essentials of good teaching, and the curriculum is organized to support the instructional process. Agreement by the team is reached on the evidence of student learning, time management, and student assignment to groups. Regulations for classroom practices must be determined and endorsed by all members of the school community. School board policy is set in accordance with the best research practices, and the board is informed about the model and is expected to support it. Public support of the entire community is cultivated.

The model has succeeded in improving student achievement scores through improvement in both math and reading above expected levels. Morale, climate, and staff effectiveness have improved, and parents also have shown great enthusiasm for the program (Johnson City Central School District, 1989).

## Curriculum-Based Assessment for Instructional Design

Curriculum-Based Assessment for Instructional Design (CBAID) is an intervention system that can be implemented by a variety of personnel (including student peers) with students who are experiencing academic difficulties (Deno, 1985; Idol-Maestas, 1983). CBAID is based on principles of effective instruction and on the premise that an inappropriate match of curriculum to student needs is the primary cause of schooling failure. CBAID postulates a cognitive theory of learning, an instructional model, an implementation process, and an assessment strategy by which personnel determine the learning problem and the method of instruction needed. Measures of implementation integrity and teacher acceptability are included as program and teacher outcomes.

CBAID assesses knowledge of subject matter and skills in the basic academic areas of reading, math, and spelling for elementary grades. CBAID has also been applied to secondary-level academic areas such as pre-algebra and civics. Student motivation is informally assessed and incorporated into an intervention sequence that emphasizes success and minimizes failure. Feedback is routinely provided to students regarding their performance and progress.

The CBAID intervention system is based on thorough and ongoing training of school staff in the CBAID model and procedures and the characteristics of successful implementation. CBAID is used within existing curricula when the teacher or others notice problems in student performance in a basic academic area. Assessment of student performance in the curricular area begins with a specific definition of the student's problem. An intervention is designed based on the assessment and the CBAID model of instruction. The intervention may be short term (10 sessions or fewer) or long term (more than 10 sessions). Precise methods of instructional presentation minimize student frustration and memory requirements for learning. Data on fluency, accuracy, and comprehension are collected during each intervention session and summarized across sessions for team decisions. Teachers (both regular and special service) are viewed as intervention managers who direct the resources to ensure that all students learn. Teachers are encouraged to set specific goals for each intervention sequence. In addition to the teacher, aides, parents, and other students may be involved in implementing the interventions. Support from the principal and from central office administrators, which is incorporated into measures of implementation integrity, is emphasized.

Preliminary assessment of existing staffing and curriculum leads to implementation planning of CBAID at each building site. A school site contact person coordinates implementation with the school principal. Staff development is required for implementation of CBAID by teachers or staff. In some instances, the school structure may be altered to better address the needs of an identified group of students. Allocation of resources may be modified to meet the identified needs.

Follow-up by trained consultants with school personnel, teachers, and the staff implementing CBAID is an important component of program implementation. Follow-up consists of three processes: problem identification and exploration, observation and reinforcement of teacher skills, and assessment of degree of program implementation. Preliminary studies suggest that follow-up is indispensable to successful implementation of the model in schools. Measures in the CBAID system assess the degree of implementation of skills in the intervention as well as variables associated with successful program implementation.

The primary effect of the CBAID model is increasing local school capacity to address identified learning problems in a systematic manner. The use of an explicit instructional and cognitive model for learning helps teachers and staff to view decreased student performance as a professional problem solved by modifying the instruction. Teachers and others learn to approach the academic behavior of a student at risk of school failure as a solvable situational problem requiring careful intervention.

## Project Link

Project Link is a collaborative consultation process utilizing school-based teams. It provides a method of classroom problem solving that progresses in a series of steps and emphasizes interactive, nonhierarchical relationships among professionals. Any student in the school who is having academic or behavioral problems may be referred to a support team.

The Project Link model is characterized by the development of a permanent school-based teacher support team, which includes representatives from regular and special education staff, school support personnel, and school building administrators. Experts are available as consultants, and the educational agency of the region supports the model and provides crucial assistance. The team engages in a series of activities including needs assessment, developing a plan of goals and activities, scheduling meetings, team training, and developing a record-keeping system.

A teacher who refers a student to the team becomes part of the process by participating in team meetings about the student's problem. The case manager, assigned for each referral, initiates contact with the consultee, collects and organizes data, monitors consultation contacts, and reports to the team on progress.

For each case there are effective consultant and consultee communications regarding the problem to be resolved, and a mutual contract is developed. The discrepancy between actual and desired behavior is clearly defined. For academic problems, curriculum-based assessment analyzes skills. For behavioral problems, antecedents and consequences are analyzed, and data collected to identify problems. Goals are specified in behavioral terms, and intervention recommendations are implemented. Progress is evaluated and the decision to terminate, continue, or change the intervention is data-based.

Both the district and individual school administration support the school-based team. A regional administrator is responsible for the coordination of the team model. Communication is maintained between the team and faculty as well as other involved individuals. Training sources are developed and training is provided regularly.

Students progress in their own curriculum as academic and behavior problems are resolved. Teachers receive assistance in resolving classroom problems from the school support team and expert consultants.

## SUMMARY

Educators have shown increased interest in the development and implementation of education programs to accommodate a wider range of student differences than has been possible in conventional classrooms. By adapting instruction to meet the diverse needs of individual students and developing self-management skills, adaptive education programs enable regular classroom teachers to effectively instruct heterogeneous classes. A number of adaptive education programs have been developed and field tested with the goal of effective instruction for *all* students, and the evidence regarding their effectiveness is clearly positive. Implementation of these programs in schools has been hampered by the lack of systematic delivery systems for meeting teacher support needs and concerns about program implementation.

This chapter is intended as a source of background information that can help in designing delivery systems that support implementation of adaptive education. The ultimate goal, and indeed the expected outcome of a systematically designed school program using the adaptive education approach, is the development of a delivery system that empowers the school staff to work collaboratively in designing and implementing plans that ensure schooling success for all students in school.

## REFERENCES

Ackerman, P., Sternberg, R.J., & Glaser, R. (Eds.). (1989). *Individual difference*. New York: W.H. Freeman and Co.

Anderson, L.W., & Pellicer, L.O. (1990). Synthesis of research on compensatory and re-medial education. *Educational Leadership, 48*(1), 10–16.

Ascher, C. (1990). *Improving the school–home connection for poor and minority students.* New York: ERIC Clearinghouse on Urban Education, Teachers College, Columbia University.

Beckwith, G., & Stivers, M. (Eds.). (1982). *A guide to classroom training: A manual for classroom trainers.* Waukegan, IL: Waukegan Behavior Analysis Follow Through Project.

Bempechat, J. (1991). *The role of parent involvement in children's academic achievement: A review of the literature.* New York: ERIC Clearinghouse on Urban Education, Teachers College, Columbia University.

Benne, K.D., & Tozer, S. (1987). *Society as educator in an age of transition.* Chicago: National Society for the Study of Education.

Bloom, B.S. (1968). Learning for mastery. *Evaluation Comment, 1*(2), 74–86.

Bloom, B.S. (1981). *All our children learning: A primer for parents, teachers, and other educators.* New York: McGraw-Hill.

Braddock, J.H., & McPartland, J.M. (1990). Alternatives to tracking. *Educational Leadership, 47*(7), 76–79.

Bronfenbrenner, U. (1986). Ecology of the family as a context for human development: Research perspectives. *Developmental Psychology, 22,* 723–742.

Brophy, J.E. (1986). Research linking teacher behavior to student achievement: Potential implications for instruction of Chapter 1 students. In B.I. Williams, P.A. Richmond, & B.J. Mason (Eds.), *Designs for compensatory education: Conference proceedings and papers* (Vol. IV, pp. 121–179). Washington, DC: Research and Evaluation Associates.

Brown, A.L., & Campione, J.C. (1986). Psychological theory and the study of learning disabilities. *American Psychologist, 41,* 1059–1068.

Conley, D.T. (1991). Restructuring schools: Educators adapt to a changing world. *ERIC/CEM Trends and Issues Series, No. 6.* Eugene, OR: ERIC Clearinghouse on Educational Management, University of Oregon.

Corno, L., & Snow, R.E. (1986). Adapting teaching to individual differences among learners. In M.C. Wittrock (Ed.), *Handbook of research on teaching* (3rd ed., pp. 605–629). New York: Macmillan.

Council of Chief State School Officers. (1987). *Assuring school success for students at risk.* Washington, DC: Author.

Council of Chief State School Officers. (1989). *Family support and involvement: A guide for state action.* Washington, DC: Author.

Davis, D. (1991). School reaching out: Family, school, and community partnerships for student success. *Phi Delta Kappan, 72*(1), 376–382.

Deno, S.L. (1985). Curriculum-based measurement: The emerging alternative. *Exceptional Children, 52*(3), 219–232.

Epstein, J.L. (1986, November). *Toward an integrated theory of school and family connections* (Report No. 3). Baltimore: Johns Hopkins University Center for Research on Elementary and Middle Schools.

Evertson, C.M. (1989). Classroom organization and management. In M.C. Reynolds (Ed.), *Knowledge base for the beginning teacher* (pp. 59–70). Oxford: Pergamon.

Fantini, M.D., & Sinclair, R.L. (1985). *Education in school and nonschool settings.* Chicago: National Society for the Study of Education.

Fullan, M. (1985). Change processes and strategies at the local level. *Elementary School Journal, 85*(3), 391–422.

Gardner, H. (1983). *Frames of mind: The theory of multiple intelligences.* New York: Basic Books.

Gartner, A., & Lipsky, D.K. (1987). Beyond special education: Toward a quality system for all students. *Harvard Educational Review, 57*(4), 367–395.

Gilkeson, E.C., Smithberg, L.M., Bowman, G.W., & Rhine, W.R. (1981). Bank Street Model: A developmental-interaction approach. In W.R. Rhine (Ed.), *Making schools more effective: New directions from Follow Through* (pp. 249–288). New York: Academic Press.

Glaser, R. (1977). *Adaptive education: Individual diversity and learning.* New York: Holt, Rinehart & Winston.

Glaser, R. (1988). Cognitive and evaluative perspectives on assessing achievement. In E.F. Freeman (Ed.), *Assessment in the service of learning: Proceedings of the 1987 ETS invitational conference* (pp. 37–44). Princeton, NJ: Educational Testing Service.

Glass, G.V., McGaw, B., & Smith, M.L. (1981). *Meta-analysis in social research.* Newbury Park, CA: Sage Publications, Inc.

Goodlad, J.I. (1983). *A place called school: Prospects for the future.* New York: McGraw-Hill.

Heller, K., Holtzman, W., & Messick, S. (Eds.). (1982). *Placing children in special education: A strategy for equity.* Washington, DC: National Academy of Sciences Press.

Holtzman, W. (1991, August). *Psychology in the School of the Future: Community renewal, family preservation, and child development.* Paper presented at the annual convention of the American Psychological Association, San Francisco.

Idol-Maestas, L. (1983). *Special educator's consultation handbook.* Rockville, MD: Aspen Systems.

Jeter, J. (Ed.). (1980). *Approaches to individualized education.* Alexandria, VA: Association for Supervision and Curriculum Development.

Johnson City Central School District. (1989). *ODDM—The Outcomes-Driven Developmental Model: A program for comprehensive school improvement.* Johnson City, NY: Author.

Johnson, D.W., & Johnson, R.T. (1975). *Learning together and alone: Cooperation, competition, and individualization.* Englewood Cliffs, NJ: Prentice Hall.

Johnson, D.W., Johnson, R.T., & Holubec, E.J. (1986). *Circles of learning: Cooperation in the classroom.* Edina, MN: Interaction Book Co.

Johnson, D.W., Maruyama, G., Johnson, R., Nelson, D., & Skon, L. (1981). Effects of cooperative, competitive, and individualistic goal structures on achievement: A meta-analysis. *Psychological Bulletin, 89,* 47–62.

Johnson, D.W., Skon, L., & Johnson, R. (1980). The effects of cooperative, competitive, and individualistic goal structures on student achievement on different types of tasks. *American Educational Research Journal, 17,* 83–93.

Kagan, S. (1989–90). The structural approach to cooperative learning. *Educational Leadership, 47*(4), 12–15.

Klausmeier, H.J. (1975). IGE: An alternative form of schooling. In H. Talmage (Ed.), *Systems of individualized education* (pp. 48–83). Berkeley, CA: McCutchan.

Kyle, J.E. (1991). Minneapolis Youth Trust. In J.E. Kyle (Ed.), *Children, families and cities: Programs that work at the local level.* Washington, DC: National League of Cities.

Kyle, R.M. (Ed.). (1985). *Reaching for excellence.* Washington, DC: E.H. White and Co.

Lewis, A. (1989). *Restructuring America's schools.* Arlington, VA: American Association of School Administrators.

Lieberman, A., & Miller, L. (1990). Restructuring schools: What matters and what works. *Phi Delta Kappan, 71*(10), 759–764.

Manning, J., & Quandt, I. (1990, April). *School-based innovation: Implementation issues and outcomes.* Paper presented at a meeting of the American Educational Research Association, Boston.

Mitchell, B., & Cunningham, L.L. (1990). *Educational leadership and changing contexts of families, communities, and schools.* Chicago: National Society for the Study of Education.

Montgomery, D.J., & Leithwood, K.A. (1983, April). *Evaluating curriculum implementation: A critical task for the effective principal.* Paper presented at the annual meeting of the American Educational Research Association, Montreal.

National Coalition of Advocates for Students. (1985). *Barriers to excellence: Our children at risk.* Boston: Author.

Peterson, P.L. (1979). Direct instruction reconsidered. In P.L. Peterson & H.J. Walberg (Eds.), *Research on teaching: Concepts, findings, and implications* (pp. 57–69). Berkeley, CA: McCutchan.

Peterson, J., Heistad D., Peterson, D., & Reynolds, M. (1985). Montevideo Individualized Prescriptive Instructional Management System. *Exceptional Children, 52*(3), 239–243.

Peterson, J., Nielsen, J., Dahl, P., Johnson, J., Nystrom, E., & Vaughan, E.D. (1986). *Integrating students with special needs in regular classes: Teacher roles and student outcomes at the secondary level.* Pittsburgh, PA: University of Pittsburgh, Learning Research and Development Center.

Ramp, E.A., & Rhine, W.R. (1981). Behavior analysis model. In W.R. Rhine (Ed.), *Making schools more effective: New directions from Follow Through* (pp. 155–200). New York: Academic Press.

Reynolds, M.C. (1989). Children with special needs. In M.C. Reynolds (Ed.), *Knowledge base for the beginning teacher* (pp. 129–142). Oxford: Pergamon.

Reynolds, M.C., & Wang, M.C. (1983). Restructuring "special" school programs: A position paper. *Policy Studies Review, 2*(1), 189–212.

Reynolds, M.C., Wang, M.C., & Walberg, H.J. (1987). The necessary restructuring of special and regular education. *Exceptional Children, 53*(5), 391–398.

San Diego City Schools. (1990). *New beginnings: A feasibility study of integrated services for children and families.* San Diego, CA: Author.

Scannapieco, M., & Wang, M.C. (1992). *Synthesis of the literature on inner-city school–community connection programs.* Philadelphia, PA: Temple University Center for Research in Human Development and Education.

Sergiovanni, T. (1990). Adding value to leadership gets extraordinary results. *Educational Leadership, 47*(8), 23–27.

Shepard, L.A. (1989). Why we need better assessments. *Educational Leadership, 46*(7), 4–9.

Skrtic, T.M. (1990). *Behind special education: A critical analysis of professional culture and school organization.* Denver, CO: Love Publishing Co.

Slavin, R.E. (1985). Team-assisted individualization: A cooperative learning solution for adaptive instruction in mathematics. In M.C. Wang & H.J. Walberg (Eds.), *Adapting instruction to individual differences* (pp. 236–253). Berkeley, CA: McCutchan.

Smith, S., & Scott, J. (Eds.). (1990). *The collaborative school.* Eugene, OR: ERIC Clearinghouse on Educational Management, University of Oregon.

Snow, R.E., & Farr, M.J. (Eds.). (1987). *Aptitude, learning and instruction: Vol. 3. Conative and affective process analyses.* Hillsdale, NJ: Lawrence Erlbaum Associates.

Sobehart, H.C. (1991). Implementing ALEM: An encouraging first year. In J.C. Lindle (Ed.), *Pennsylvania educational leadership yearbook 1990–1991* (pp. 12–19). Lancaster: Pennsylvania Association for Supervision and Curriculum Development.

Sternberg, R.J. (1988). Mental self-government: A theory of intellectual styles and their development. *Human Development, 31*, 197–224.

Sternberg, R.J. (1990). Thinking styles: Key to understanding student performance. *Phi Delta Kappan, 71*, 366–371.

Sternberg, R.J., Okagaki, L., & Jackson, A.S. (1990). Practical intelligence for success in school. *Human Development, 48*(1), 35–39.

Task Force on General Education/Special Education. (1989). *The general education/special education interface task force report: An advisory report to Patrick Campbell, assistant superintendent.* Sacramento, CA: California Department of Education, Special Education Division.

Thomas, J. (1980). Agency and achievement: Self-management and self-regard. *Review of Education Research, 50*(2), 213–240.

Walberg, H.J. (1984). Families as partners in educational productivity. *Phi Delta Kappan, 65*, 397–400.

Walberg, H.J. (1987). What works in a nation still at risk. *Educational Leadership, 44*(1), 7–11.

Walberg, H.J., & Keefe, J.W. (Eds.). (1988). *Rethinking reform: The principal's dilemma.* Reston, VA: National Association of Secondary Principals.

Wang, M.C. (1979). Implications for effective use of instruction and learning time. *Educational Horizons, 57*, 169–174.

Wang, M.C. (1980). Adaptive instruction: Building on diversity. *Theory into Practice, 19*(2), 122–127.

Wang, M.C. (1988). The wedding of instruction and assessment in the classroom. In E.F. Freeman (Ed.), *Assessment in the service of learning: Proceedings of the 1987 ETS invitational conference* (pp. 63–79). Princeton, NJ: Educational Testing Service.

Wang, M.C. (1990a). *Designing and evaluating school learning environments for effective mainstreaming of special education students: Synthesis, validation, and dissemination of research methods* (report). Philadelphia, PA: Temple University Center for Research in Human Development and Education.

Wang, M.C. (1990b). Programs that promote educational equity. In H. Waxman, P. Bap-

tiste, J. Anderson, & J. Walker de Felix (Eds.), *Leadership, equity, and school effectiveness* (pp. 132–154). Newbury Park, CA: Sage Publications, Inc.

Wang, M.C., & Birch, J.W. (1984). Effective special education in regular classes. *Exceptional Children, 50*(5), 391–398.

Wang, M.C., Gennari, P., & Waxman, H.C. (1985). The Adaptive Learning Environments
Model: Design, implementation, and effects. In M.C. Wang & H.J. Walberg (Eds.), *Adapting instruction to individual differences* (pp. 191–235). Berkeley, CA: McCutchan.

Wang, M.C., Haertel, G.D., & Walberg, H.J. (1990). What influences learning? A content
analysis of review literature. *Journal of Educational Research, 84*(1), 30–43.

Wang, M.C., Leinhardt, G., & Boston, M.E. (1980). *Individualized Early Learning Program*
(LRDC Pub. Series 1980–2). Pittsburgh, PA: University of Pittsburgh, Learning Research and Development Center.

Wang, M.C., & Lindvall, C.M. (1984). Individual differences and school learning environments. In E.W. Gordon (Ed.), *Review of research in education* (Vol. 11, pp. 161–225).
Washington, DC: American Educational Research Association.

Wang, M.C., & Palincsar, A.S. (1989). Teaching students to assume an active role in their
learning. In M.C. Reynolds (Ed.), *Knowledge base for the beginning teacher* (pp. 71–
84). Oxford: Pergamon Press.

Wang, M.C., & Peverly, S.T. (1986). The self-instructive process in classroom learning contexts. *Contemporary Educational Psychology, 11*, 370–404.

Wang, M.C., & Peverly, S.T. (1987). The role of the learner: An individual difference variable in school learning and functioning. In M.C. Wang, M.C. Reynolds, & H.J. Walberg
(Eds.), *Handbook of special education: Research and practice: Vol. 1. Learner characteristics and adaptive education* (pp. 59–92). Oxford: Pergamon Press.

Wang, M.C., Reynolds, M.C., & Schwartz, L.L. (1988). Adaptive instruction: An alternative educational approach for students with special needs. In J.L. Graden, J.E. Zins, &
M.J. Curtis (Eds.), *Alternative educational delivery systems: Enhancing instructional
options for all students* (pp. 199–220). Washington, DC: National Association of School
Psychologists.

Wang, M.C., Reynolds, M.C., & Walberg, H.J. (1988). Integrating the children of the second
system. *Phi Delta Kappan, 70*(3), 248–251.

Wang, M.C., Reynolds, M.C., & Walberg, H.J. (Eds.). (1990). *Special education research
and practice: Synthesis of findings*. Oxford: Pergamon Press.

Wang, M.C., & Walberg, H.J. (1983). Adaptive instruction and classroom time. *American
Educational Research Journal, 20*, 601–626.

Wang, M.C., & Walberg, H.J. (Eds.). (1985). *Adapting instruction to individual differences*. Berkeley, CA: McCutchan.

Wang, M.C., & Walberg, H.J. (1986). Classroom climate as mediator of educational inputs
and outputs. In B.J. Fraser (Ed.), *The study of learning environments 1985* (pp. 47–58).
Salem, OR: Assessment Research.

Wang, M.C., & Zollers, N.J. (1990). Adaptive instruction: An alternative service delivery
approach. *Remedial and Special Education, 11*(1), 7–21.

Waxman, H.C., Wang, M.C., Anderson, K.A., & Walberg, H.J. (1985). Synthesis of research
on the effects of adaptive education. *Educational Leadership, 43*(1), 26–29.

Whipple, C.M. (Ed.). (1925). *The twenty-fourth yearbook of the National Society for the
Study of Education*. Chicago: University of Chicago Press.

Williams, B.I., Richmond, P.A., & Mason, B.J. (1986). *Designs for compensatory education: Conference proceedings and papers*. Washington, DC: Research and Evaluation
Associates.

Williams, D.L., & Chaukin, N.F. (1989). Essential elements of strong parent involvement
programs. *Educational Leadership, 47*(2), 18–20.

Wittrock, M.C. (Ed.). (1986). *Handbook of research on teaching* (3rd ed.). New York:
Macmillan.

Zimmerman, B.J. (Ed.). (1986). [Special Issue] *Contemporary Educational Psychology,
11*(4).

## SUGGESTED READINGS ON THE THEORY
## AND PRACTICE OF ADAPTIVE EDUCATION

Ackerman, P., Sternberg, R.J., & Glaser, R. (Eds.). (1989). *Individual difference.* New York: W.H. Freeman and Co.

Barber, L.W. (Ed.). (1986). *Adapting instruction to individual needs: An eclectic approach.* Bloomington, IN: Phi Delta Kappa.

Bloom, B.S. (1981). *All our children learning: A primer for parents, teachers, and other educators.* New York: McGraw-Hill.

Clark, C.R., & Bott, B.A. (1991). Issues in implementing the Adaptive Learning Model. *Teacher Education and Special Education, 14*(1), 57–65.

Corno, L., & Snow, R.E. (1986). Adapting teaching to individual differences among learners. In M.C. Wittrock (Ed.), *Handbook of research on teaching* (3rd ed., pp. 605–629). New York: Macmillan.

Glaser, R. (1977). *Adaptive education: Individual diversity and learning.* New York: Holt, Rinehart & Winston.

Reynolds, M.C., & Wang, M.C. (1983). Restructuring "special" school programs: A position paper. *Policy Studies Review, 2*(1), 189–212.

Snow, R.E., & Farr, M.J. (Eds.). (1987). *Aptitude, learning and instruction: Vol. 3. Conative and affective process analyses.* Hillsdale, NJ: Lawrence Erlbaum Associates.

Wang, M.C., Haertel, G.D., & Walberg, H.J. (1990). What influences learning? A content analysis of review literature. *Journal of Educational Research, 84*(1), 30–43.

Wang, M.C., & Lindvall, C.M. (1984). Individual differences and school learning environments. In E.W. Gordon (Ed.), *Review of research in education* (Vol. 11, pp. 161–225). Washington, DC: American Educational Research Association.

Wang, M.C., Reynolds, M.C., & Schwartz, L.L. (1988). Adaptive instruction: An alternative educational approach for students with special needs. In J.L. Graden, J.E. Zins, & M.L. Curtis (Eds.), *Alternative educational delivery systems: Enhancing instructional options for all students* (pp. 199–220). Washington, DC: National Association of School Psychologists.

Wang, M.C., Reynolds, M.C., & Walberg, H.J. (1986). Rethinking special education. *Educational Leadership, 44*(1), 26–31.

Wang, M.C., & Walberg, H.J. (Eds.). (1985). *Adapting instruction to individual differences.* Berkeley, CA: McCutchan.

Wang, M.C., & Zollers, N.J. (1990). Adaptive instruction: An alternative service delivery approach. *Remedial and Special Education, 11*(1), 7–21.

Whipple, C.M. (Ed.). (1925). *The twenty-fourth yearbook of the National Society for the Study of Education.* Chicago: University of Chicago Press.

# Chapter 2

# Needs Assessment and Implementation Planning

A key to successful implementation of innovative educational programs in schools is matching local resources and expertise to program implementation requirements. Assessment of resources and expertise available for program implementation at the school is a first step in development of a site-specific implementation plan.

This chapter provides a practical guide for developing a needs assessment and site-specific implementation planning process to be used by school staff. Included are a description of procedures and instruments for collecting needs assessment information, as well as the sequence of activities that constitutes the needs assessment process. Information on the practicalities of conducting needs assessment to establish adaptive education programs in schools and how to use the assessment for planning is also included.

## NEEDS ASSESSMENT

Research and practical experience suggest that implementation of a program that incorporates local needs, resources, and constraints tends to promote a perception of "ownership" of the program and greater commitment for program maintenance and institutionalization (Ellett & Wang, 1987; Fullan, 1985). This sense of ownership and commitment is particularly critical to implementation of adaptive education programs that usually necessitate programmatic changes, which require restructuring school objectives and reallocations of school personnel and resources (Reynolds & Wang, 1983). Available resources and expertise need to be identified, and the discrepancies between those resources and the requirements for effective implementation of adaptive education should be delineated as a part of the planning process for program implementation.

Needs assessment is likely to involve a variety of people, particularly the school staff and administrators who are responsible for developing and implementing site-specific programs. Depending on the type of program to be implemented, the needs assessment process may involve input from decision makers of local school districts and state departments of education. Implementation planning, in contrast, is typically carried out by the school-based personnel responsible for program implementation at the school level. For example, those involved in needs assessment may include district administrators who are exploring the potential of adaptive education as an alternative approach to particular needs of their district, university or college faculty who are collaborating with the school district to upgrade educational or training programs, state and district policymakers who determine the need for policy waivers to provide program support, and curriculum specialists or program developers of the particular adaptive education program. Implementation planning is directed toward development of a delivery system for a specific school. Planning activities are site-specific and primarily involve school administrators and staff.

It is recommended that one person be appointed as the planning coordinator, responsible for all needs assessment and planning activities. This person may be external to the school district (e.g., a faculty member from a college or university collaborating with the district), a developer of the adaptive education program to be implemented, or a staff member of the school district. The planning coordinator ensures integration of all activities and timely communication among all parties. The coordinator works closely with central administrators of the school district and the school staff and is involved in discussions and other aspects of implementation planning.

## The Process of Needs Assessment

A comprehensive assessment of implementation needs at a school site consists of several stages that usually extend over a period of several months. The stages are:

1.  Discussion among district and building administrators, the school staff, parents, and others involved on the merits and constraints of implementing an adaptive education program as an alternative approach to meet their school improvement needs
2.  Discussion of the program and the requirements for implementation with appropriate school staff
3.  Collection of site-specific information at the school for planning purposes

These activities inform local policymakers and the school staff about the design, implementation requirements, and expected outcomes of the planned adaptive education program as well as collect information about local resources and expertise for supporting the program implementation.

The first stage of the needs assessment process is initiated by school or district leaders, school staff (teachers, principals, or psychologists), parents, or community leaders who are interested in developing and implementing improvement programs using the adaptive education approach. A major task at this stage of the process is to provide information about the program to district and school administrators. Their early involvement is important because they need to be aware of program requirements and identify specific school constraints and needs. Discussions among administrators at this stage include evaluating evidence on the feasibility of school-based implementation of the adaptive education approach and determining conditions for program success. When the decision is made to implement the new program, the process of needs assessment moves into the second stage.

In the second stage of the needs assessment process, discussions focusing on the coordination of program implementation and reassignment of school resources to meet the site-specific needs are initiated. School personnel are more fully informed about the program and its implementation requirements. Relevant factors and issues in this stage of the needs assessment process include site-specific characteristics, such as the targeted student population and programming needs (e.g., will the adaptive education program be a regular education program or a full- or part-time mainstreaming program). Building administrators are generally responsible for providing information for site-specific needs assessment, but all personnel directly and indirectly involved in program implementation should take part in discussions (e.g., regular education teachers, reading and math specialists, special education teachers, school psychologists, counselors, and building and district office administrators).

The final stage in needs assessment is the collection of detailed site-specific information at the participating school. The following sections discuss the information required for the analysis of needs, readiness, and planning at each potential implementation site.

Information to be gathered through the needs assessment process includes these general areas, which are discussed below:

1. Student population to be served
2. Staffing resources and patterns
3. Current school goals, policies, and practices
4. Classroom teaching practices
5. District and school curricula
6. Physical facilities
7. School records and documents
8. Family involvement

***Student Population To Be Served*** To design a site-specific delivery system for implementation, information about the following is needed: the number of students enrolled in the school and in a typical class, the number of special needs students, and the criteria and procedures typically used to assign students to classes.

If not all students and teachers will participate in the adaptive education program, information is needed on which students and teachers will participate in the program and how they will be selected. If the program is being implemented to mainstream students with special needs, additional information is required. This includes:

1. Specific classification of the students with special needs to be mainstreamed and the criteria used to determine their classification or placement
2. A description of the settings and programs of present placements
3. Criteria and procedures typically used to assign special needs students to classes and programs in the school
4. Whether additional criteria need to be developed for identifying program students and assignment of teachers

***Staffing Resources and Patterns*** Information about school and district personnel is required to design a site-specific program implementation delivery system and to plan staff development programs matched to staff needs. Specific information includes:

1.  Training and experience of the teachers in implementing innovative programs and the adaptive education approach
2.  Roles and functions of each staff member
3.  Schedule of planned inservice training activities
4.  Identification of full- or part-time personnel who may be reassigned to coordinate and provide daily support for program implementation

Administrators and resource persons also play vital roles in program implementation and support. To identify such persons and to define their roles in the program, information needs to be collected concerning:

1.  Instructional leadership functions performed by the principal or school staff
2.  Names and current assignments of school or district staff with expertise in adaptive education who may serve as program support or resource persons
3.  Names and assignments of specialized professional staff in the school
4.  Funding for such personnel
5.  Formal and informal mechanisms for coordinating activities of resource personnel
6.  Availability of paid or volunteer classroom assistants or student interns from collaborating universities to assist in program implementation

**Current School Goals, Policies, and Practices**   Goals, policies, and practices related to instruction, curriculum, student evaluation, and other aspects of education vary from school to school. Site-specific implementation goals for the adaptive education program should be closely matched to the school's goals, policies, and practices. Policies or practices incompatible with the practice of adaptive education should be clearly identified so that they can be modified to support implementation.

Program planners need to know:

1.  Goals of the school's education program
2.  Methods for tracking or grouping students
3.  School or district curriculum policies
4.  School evaluation system and promotion policy
5.  Use of practices related to effective implementation of adaptive education programs
6.  School involvement in other projects that may affect implementation of an adaptive education program

If the program is being implemented in regular classes that also serve mainstreamed special education students, additional information must be gathered concerning special education policies and procedures. They include state, district, and school special education funding and placement policies that may affect delivery of adaptive education; methods to identify students for special education services; procedures for assigning special education students to mainstream classes; and information about students for construction of IEPs. Similar considerations also apply to schools with a Chapter 1 program in operation.

Information about allocating instructional and noninstructional school time is needed to arrange schedules for classroom teachers, specialized professionals, and students. This information includes, for example, student schedules for the school day and extracurricular activities; distribution of teacher time, including scheduled in-class preparation time; daily and weekly school-wide activities (e.g., committee work, lunch room supervision); and the typical schedules of professional and paraprofessional staff.

**Classroom Teaching Practices**   To match staff development to the implementation support and training needs of individual staff, the particular instructional approaches and techniques used by the individual teacher must be assessed. This information includes, for example:

1. Percentage of class time teachers allocate to whole-group instruction, small-group instruction, and individual work
2. Management techniques used by teachers, including classroom rules and enforcement
3. Extent of teacher control (e.g., teacher-directed or prescribed activities) as well as student choice or self-management
4. Extent of cooperative planning and teaching
5. Extent to which learning options (e.g., alternative activities such as exploratory projects and learning centers) are available to students

**District and School Curricula**   A critical design consideration for implementing adaptive education is the extent to which basic curricula can be modified to accommodate student diversity (e.g., flexibility in pacing student progress, alternative sequencing, variety of learning materials and activity options). It is important to note that schools using the adaptive education approach do not need to develop a different set of curriculum materials for implementation. Contrary to the common belief that implementation of adaptive programs requires specially constructed curricula, curricula of the district and school are usually used (with some adaptation) with adaptive education programs. Commercial curriculum materials used in schools can be adapted easily for implementation. These materials typically include explicit and carefully sequenced objectives, varied activities for each objective, and tests for diagnosis and assessment of mastery. While some commercial basal series are more suited to individualizing instruction and for implementing the adaptive education approach, schools implementing adaptive education generally can, with minimal modifications, use available curriculum materials and other resources of their districts to enable students to enter at different points and progress at their own rate.

To prepare the existing curriculum resources of the school or district for implementing adaptive education programs, these materials first should be inventoried, and the means for obtaining needed additional supplementary materials determined. To this end, information is gathered concerning:

1. Curriculum guides of district-designed curricula and texts in use
2. Availability of adjunct materials such as workbooks, placement tests, and skill sheets
3. Supplementary materials and activities (commercial and teacher-constructed) available in the school
4. School or district resource center for curriculum materials and resource supports
5. Procedures for purchasing additional curriculum materials

**Physical Facilities**   Attention to the design and availability of physical facilities is essential to create a supportive environment for effective implementation of adaptive education programs. Classroom furniture and equipment should be arranged so that teachers and students can easily move about the room, and so learning materials can be stored for easy access. An inventory is needed of:

1.  Amount and arrangement of furniture in each classroom
2.  Available material storage and display facilities and their locations
3.  Special instructional equipment available (e.g., manipulative materials for student use, computers, tape recorders)
4.  Location of electrical outlets

*School Records and Documents*   School records provide a valuable source of information about the school and students for program planning, monitoring, and evaluation. Records indicate what kinds of baseline performance data are available and how the school collects such data on a routine basis. Information to be gathered includes:

1.  Data available in student records
2.  Standardized tests administered in the district and school and dates of testing
3.  Data available in standardized achievement test printouts
4.  Documents describing the community, the school, and the education programs

*Family Involvement*   Family support of a student's education program is vital to program success. To develop programs that meet family interests and needs, to provide families with information about adaptive education, and to plan for active family involvement, it is necessary to obtain information such as:

1.  Family awareness of the school or district education program generally and adaptive education specifically (goals and expected outcomes, schedule for program installation, description of program impact on daily classroom operations, and role of parents)
2.  Input of families in the program
3.  Organizational structure for family involvement (e.g., parent-teacher associations, parent academies, or family volunteer programs), percentage of families who are members, and the frequency of meetings
4.  Regular communication with families, such as by newsletter
5.  Frequency and circumstances of conferences with families
6.  Development programs for school staff to effectively communicate and involve families

## Instruments for Collecting Needs Assessment Information

The variety of needs assessment information required for comprehensive implementation necessitates a number of methods for data collection. A systematic procedure and data collection form will ensure that the required information is obtained in a usable form. Much of the information can be gathered by interviewing a school official, usually the principal. Some information (e.g., arrangement of classroom furniture, teacher and student behaviors) requires observation of classrooms and school facilities. Other information (e.g., data of past student achievement) is obtained by examining school documents and records. For illustrative purposes, Needs Assessment Forms developed for systematic collection of site-specific information for planning implementation of adaptive education programs are presented in Appendix 2.A and described below. Although the Needs Assessment Forms have been designed and used by schools mainly in conjunction with implementation of adaptive education programs, they may be used with some modification by schools interested in implementing other innovative school-based education programs.

The Needs Assessment Forms consist of three data collection instruments: the Principal Interview Form, Observation Notes, and a Records Checklist. Each instrument includes two or more sections (A–H in Appendix 2.A). The instruments and sections are described below.

***Principal Interview Form*** The Principal Interview Form consists of the School profile (Section A), Curriculum (Section B), and Evaluation/documentation (Section C). Section A is designed to obtain information about the goals of the school, staff assignments and responsibilities, and student demographic characteristics. Section B elicits information about the school curriculum, and Section C includes questions about methods of student evaluation and documentation.

The Principal Interview Form generally requires 30–45 minutes to complete. The information to be obtained during the needs assessment interview is generally routine, and most items are self-explanatory. The goal is to obtain complete and detailed information. If answers are not clear, the interviewer should request clarification or elaboration. If the principal is unable to answer questions, he or she should be asked to identify alternate sources for that information.

***Observation Notes*** The Observation Notes Form to assess specific classroom implementation needs consists of the Classroom observation (Section D), Teacher interview (Section E), and Analysis of physical design of the classroom (Section F). Administration of Section D involves observation in classrooms while instruction is in progress, and it concerns description of classroom environment, student behavior, management techniques, and teacher styles. Teacher interviews (Section E) are designed to obtain information regarding classroom routines and activities that supplements and clarifies the information obtained from classroom observation. School facilities and furnishings are tallied in Section F, and the information is obtained from classroom observations and from a tour of the school.

Several factors should be considered in selecting classrooms for observation. First, it is usually not feasible to conduct observations in all classrooms participating in the adaptive education program. Experience in conducting needs assessments of this type suggests that a sample of two or three classes is usually sufficient to yield a picture of typical methods of classroom instruction, especially combined with information from other needs assessment instruments. If implementation is planned for different grade levels such as primary and intermediate, it is recommended that one classroom be selected from each level to obtain a general overview of the school's programs. The building administrator should help to select classrooms for information on general operational procedures of a typical classroom in the school.

A total of 2½ hours (two 30-minute classroom observations, two 30-minute periods to interview teachers and examine curriculum materials and classroom facilities, and one 30-minute tour of the school) should be allowed for administration of the Observation Notes Form. Section D is completed during the 30-minute classroom observation. The observer should sit or stand where it is possible to observe the entire classroom without interfering with activities. Question 1, a brief description of classroom activities, can be answered after a quick scan of the room. The next 20 minutes are spent observing teacher and student interactions. The final few minutes are used to complete Questions 2–5. A note should be made in the Comments section of the form to obtain clarification from the teacher during the teacher interview (Section E) if there was not enough opportunity to observe a behavior. A separate form with Sections D and E should be used for each classroom observation.

Section E and the first question in Section F are completed during a 30-minute period when students are out of the classroom. This activity should take place after the classroom observation, but does not necessarily have to follow immediately. First, the teacher is asked to clarify any points that were unclear during the observation. Next, curriculum materials are examined to answer Questions 7–10, and the teacher can assist in locating curriculum components that are not readily evident. In questions 11 and 12, the teacher reports the percentage of student and teacher time spent in various instructional groupings and settings. The first question of Section F (Question 13) requires an inventory of classroom furnishings and should be completed at this time. Question 14 consists of a checklist that is completed during a tour of the school, which may be scheduled at any convenient time.

*Records Checklist*   The Records Checklist contains the School profile (Section G) and Documents (Section H). Local documents are examined to obtain information to complete both sections. The data recorded in Section G is based on the school roster and individual student record cards. In general, most of the information in Sections G and H is readily available from the school and district offices through computerized information systems. The principal should be asked to make available the school roster, individual student record cards, and school documents. It is helpful to have access to copying facilities during this time.

*Scheduling Needs Assessment Interviews*   The needs assessment interviews are generally conducted by the person coordinating needs assessment and planning activities. A full day is generally required for gathering all needs assessment information. If someone collaborates in data collection, time may be reduced. The principal and teachers to be interviewed should be given ample notice in order to arrange their schedules, and should be advised of the purpose of each scheduled interview or activity.

A sample schedule for a needs assessment is included in Figure 2.1. The schedule should be arranged and confirmed well in advance of the date. The schedule should be verified on the appointed day prior to collection of information. In particular, the time for observation, interviewing teachers, and taking inventory of classroom materials and facilities should be verified with teachers in advance.

## IMPLEMENTATION PLANNING AND DEVELOPMENT OF A SCHOOL-SPECIFIC DELIVERY SYSTEM

Implementation planning involves using the information obtained from needs assessment to design a program delivery system tailored to the goals and resources of a particular site. Thus, in implementation planning, decisions are

| | |
|---|---|
| 9:30–10:30 | Interview principal |
| 10:30–11:00 | Observe in Classroom A |
| 11:00–11:30 | Examine relevant school documents |
| 11:30–12:00 | Inventory curriculum materials and furnishings, interview teacher in Classroom A |
| 12:00–12:30 | Lunch |
| 12:30– 1:00 | Observe in Classroom B |
| 1:00– 1:30 | Tour school |
| 1:30– 2:30 | Examine relevant school documents |
| 2:30– 3:30 | Inventory curriculum materials and furnishings, interview teacher in Classroom B |

**Figure 2.1.**   Sample schedule for conducting needs assessment.

made at the building level concerning how the resources identified during needs assessment will be used, modified, and reallocated for adaptive education. For example, the description of the student population that includes the number of students with particular special needs is used to make decisions about the assignment of students with special needs to program classes, as well as the method for assigning them. While needs assessment yields information about curriculum and available material resources, implementation planning involves decisions about adapting and reallocating those resources and identifying additional resources that must be obtained.

Implementation planning, like needs assessment, takes place at the building level, because schools within a single district are likely to differ considerably in their human and material resources and in their implementation needs. Program planners should schedule one or more sessions soon after completion of the needs assessment so that they and building officials outline the areas for planning and the decisions to be made. Program planners and building officials should also develop guidelines for making decisions based on the information obtained from the needs assessment.

The major responsibility for designing a site-specific delivery system generally rests with the principal. It is essential that other administrative and instructional staff are involved in the implementation planning process to ensure ownership of the new program. Since implementation planning is an evolving process integral to program implementation, the principal's leadership and the active participation of school staff are central to successful implementation.

## Checklist of Tasks in the
## Development of a School-Specific Delivery System

Designing a school-specific delivery system involves decisions in eight areas:

1. Identification of program classes
2. Staffing
3. Student placements
4. Scheduling
5. Space, facilities, and materials
6. Program monitoring and evaluation
7. Communication and dissemination of information
8. Documentation of implementation planning

Each of these includes a set of specific tasks. The Checklist of Tasks in the Development of a School-Specific Delivery System is included in Appendix 2.B. The checklist provides a guide for site-specific planning. The following sections describe each area and task in greater detail. A final section deals with the development of the formal document, or the Implementation Plan, that serves as a systematic guide for carrying out the activities required for a school-specific delivery system.

## Identification of Program Classes

The tasks related to identification of classes include determining the number of classes that will participate in the program and identifying grade levels and the grade-level composition of participating classes. Implementation of an adaptive education program may be school-wide or limited to selected grade levels and classes. If some, but not all, grades or classes are involved, certain factors are involved in deciding how many and which grades and classes will use the program.

It is theoretically possible to implement an innovative program in only one or two classes. Initial implementation in at least four classes, however, is recommended. A vital collegial support system is established for participating teachers if a new program is introduced in a greater number of classes. This support system is important to dispel the feeling of isolation among participating teachers, which is typical in the first year of a new program. Having the opportunity to share ideas and concerns is fundamental to building teacher morale. The work of intensive pre-implementation activities such as curriculum preparation can be greatly reduced for individual staff members when the work of several teachers is pooled.

Instructional teaming among regular and specialist teachers is an essential element of effective implementation of adaptive education programs. Instructional teaming, however, requires some structural and attitudinal changes. More flexibility for student groupings, scheduling of activities, and division of teacher responsibilities is possible when instructional teaming is implemented. Teaming can occur between classes at the same grade level or between classes at consecutive grade levels (e.g., second and third grades).

Another factor in determining the number of participating classes is the availability of implementation support services for teachers. Such services are essential to help teachers establish and maintain implementation of innovative programs. Although principals provide support in their role as instructional leaders, their responsibilities leave them too little time to completely fulfill this requirement. Experience with implementation of innovative programs has shown that assignment of another staff member to serve as a program coordinator is vital to program success. The coordinator can work either full time or part time to provide implementation support and coordination of schedules, expertise, and resources.

Theoretically, the role can be filled by a school staff member, either assigned by the principal or nominated by colleagues. Ideally, the coordinator is someone highly regarded by his or her colleagues, and could be a regular education teacher, a special education teacher, a Chapter 1 supervisor, or a curriculum specialist. Our experience suggests that one program coordinator is needed for every 8–12 program classes, and a half-time program coordinator may suffice for fewer classes. The number of participating classes should be limited during the first year of the program, especially if a full-time program coordinator is not available. The selection and role of the program coordinator are more fully discussed in the section on staffing.

Adaptive education programs have been implemented most frequently in elementary and middle schools, although implementation of adaptive education is feasible at any school level. If the initial implementation is planned for a few classes, with later expansion possible, it is advisable to begin with the lowest grades in the school and add other grades in subsequent years. Whatever grade levels are chosen should be sequential (e.g., first, second, and third, rather than first, second, and fourth). This allows greater continuity from one grade to another, as well as facilitation of program activities such as curriculum preparation and instructional teaming.

School officials must also decide if each class will include students from a single grade, or two or more sequential grades (a multigrade or ungraded system). Multi-age grouping is recommended particularly for early elementary grades to provide flexibility in responding to student diversity through instructional grouping and more opportunities for peer modeling, peer tutoring, and cooperative learning. However, multigrade classes are not always possible because of local policy, teacher preference, or other factors. The decision concerning grade-level composition of classes must consider the interest and expertise of individual teachers and organizational and physical constraints, as well as possible advantages and disadvantages of each alternative.

## Staffing

Systematic planning to meet staffing needs is an essential requirement for effective implementation of adaptive education. In addition to classroom and specialist teachers, the program coordinator works closely with classroom teachers, specialists, principal, and other school and district resource persons to provide a variety of implementation and staff development services to support the program.

Because successful implementation of adaptive education requires reassignment of the school staff for collaborative and coordinated programming, the roles of resource personnel, such as special education teachers and Chapter 1 coordinators, are redefined in the context of program implementation. These roles and relations with classroom teachers and other instructional staff are likely to shift from traditional patterns. For example, when students with special needs are integrated in regular classes on a full- or part-time basis, regular and special educators work together far more closely in planning and implementation than in traditional settings.

The focus of the instructional staff in schools using adaptive education is on providing for the diverse needs of individual students. Thus, accommodating instruction to each student is the routine practice of the teaching staff. Students with special needs rarely need to be singled out for instruction, and, instead, regular teachers and specialists work as teams, combining their expertise to design and provide instruction to meet the needs of the students in regular classes.

Because of such shifts in staff roles and relationships, careful implementation planning for staffing is crucial. The following sections discuss identification, specification, and requirements of program participants, classroom teachers who assume the primary responsibility for programming implementation, specialized professionals who provide additional resources and coordination, and teacher assistants such as paraprofessionals and classroom volunteers who work closely with the instructional staff in support activities.

Program teachers should be recruited or assigned and involved in implementation planning as early as possible. All potentially participating teachers should be informed about the planned program, and program participants should be recruited from volunteers. If not enough teachers in the school express interest, transferring teachers among schools can be considered. Involuntary assignment to the program should be avoided. Although adaptive education programs have been successfully implemented in classes with teachers who initially expressed skepticism or opposition, it is obviously preferable to have wholehearted cooperation of teachers from the start.

*Selection of a Program Coordinator*   The program coordinator is central to successful implementation and maintenance of innovative programs. Therefore, this person must be selected with care. Although this person may be an administrator, a curriculum supervisor, or a teacher, experience in effective teaching and respect by the school staff are important determiners to select a person who might be referred to as a master teacher. The assignment of a teacher rather than an administrator as program coordinator is suggested for several reasons. First, research has indicated that teachers prefer staff development programs based on teachers helping teachers (Little, 1981). In addition, teachers are likely to be more supportive when implementation and training needs are provided by another teaching colleague who shares their perspectives and is presumably sympathetic to their implementation concerns. Above all, the coordinator selected from teaching staff is likely to be viewed as a member of the implementation team and a colleague who understands the teacher perspective, supports implementation, and provides peer coaching, rather than serving in an administrative or supervisory role.

Selection of a program coordinator should be based on the candidate's ability to work with the principal, support personnel, and teachers and specialists in performing a variety of functions. These functions may include, for example, formal and informal monitoring of program implementation; planning and delivery of staff development activities to improve implementation; consultation with teachers to solve instructional problems; curriculum coordination, maintenance, and revision; maintenance of program records and documentation of activities and effects; and establishment and maintenance of communication networks within the school and with others involved in the program, such as parents.

The program coordinator may be certified in regular and/or special education. The latter could be especially helpful if the adaptive education program includes full-time integration of special services in regular classrooms. In fact, assignment of a special education teacher as program coordinator is often an excellent way to utilize the special training and skills of a resource room or special class teacher. More important than the type of teaching experience and certification, however, is the rapport with, and the respect of, the staff, as well as skills for organizing and coordinating the activities described above.

In addition to selecting a program coordinator, a major planning task is to decide the specific functions of the coordinator and how program support is to be provided. For example, it is important to clarify responsibility for coordinating staff development activities: Is this a function of the principal or program coordinator? How will the work of planning and conducting staff development be allocated? Who will be responsible for carrying out staff development activities? These kinds of decisions must be made well before classroom implementation begins.

***Resource and Specialist Personnel and Their Program Roles*** Most schools are served by a variety of special resource personnel, school-based and itinerant, including special education teachers, curriculum specialists, school psychologists, social workers, Chapter 1 teachers, and others. Not all are directly involved in program implementation on a daily basis. Nevertheless, at the very least, all should be fully informed of the program, because it is likely to affect, and to be affected by, their activities. For example, the special interventions designed by a school psychologist for a student in an adaptive education program may differ from those designed for a student in a more traditional educational setting.

In many ways, the work of specialists is integrated into the ongoing regular education program more fully in adaptive education environments than in traditional programs. For example, in adaptive education, special education teachers usually collaborate with regular classroom teachers to serve students in their classrooms rather than at a special site. Furthermore, since instruction is individualized for all students, special interventions designed for particular students, usually an "add-on" in traditional instruction programs, in most cases can be incorporated into individual instruction programs.

Program teachers and other staff should plan to draw on the expertise of school and district resource personnel not directly involved in daily implementation. For example, a curriculum specialist may be helpful in resolving problems in the preparation or implementation of individualized reading or math curricula. As much as possible, the best utilization of human resources should be anticipated and planned well in advance of program implementation.

In adaptive education programs, classroom support staff such as instructional assistants, parent volunteers, and student teachers perform important functions, with teacher supervision. These functions include routine checking and recording of student work, helping individual students while the teacher is engaged in instruction, and constructing or copying learning materials. Although full-time classroom assistants may not be needed, half-time support personnel is recommended for each classroom or each team of two classrooms.

Classroom assistants may be paid paraprofessionals or unpaid volunteers. The school principal should make arrangements for hiring and assigning classroom assistants well in advance of program implementation. If classroom assistants are not available, program planners need to develop volunteer support well before classroom implementation. If volunteers are used as classroom assistants, it is important that they understand the duties, are willing to participate in required training, and commit their time on a regular basis.

## Student Placements

Assignment of students to classes should be carefully made if the school is including both program and nonprogram classes at the same grade levels. While site-specific constraints and policies must be taken into consideration, random assignment should be considered. Random assignment ensures initial comparability between program and nonprogram classes, so that comparisons are free of sampling bias. In addition, random assignment precludes charges of unfairness in student assignment to program or nonprogram classes by the school staff and, perhaps more importantly, conveys the message that *all* students can be accommodated effectively in adaptive education. Student diversity is therefore viewed as the norm and can be a strength in classroom organization. Student diversity can contribute to the resources of the class in meeting individual needs of students and for building on their talents and enhancing student development.

Random assignment is sometimes precluded by staff or parent preferences, however. For example, teachers may evaluate the program as particularly appropriate (or inappropriate) for particular students. Parental preference must be considered as well. It is important that parents have the opportunity to *decline* if the program is antithetical to their education philosophy or their children's needs. Parents should be given sufficient information about the new program well in advance so that they can exercise this option.

Class placement should ensure heterogeneous grouping regardless of assignment method. In addition to the research and practical bases that question the wisdom of homogeneous grouping (Oakes, 1985; Reynolds, Wang, & Walberg, 1987), a number of reasons point to heterogeneous grouping as an effective response to student diversity. First, in heterogeneously grouped classes, individual differences are assumed, and student differences are perceived as the norm rather than the exception. Second, students helping students or peer tutoring, an important component of the learning management system of adaptive education, usually leads to students at a higher level in a given subject helping students at a lower level in that subject. Third, teachers may find that the presence of students with a variety of backgrounds and abilities is not only stimulating and challenging but also enhances their effectiveness. For example, including highly capable students in class can provide students with added resources for tutoring and modeling and enable teachers to devote more of their time to those students who pose the greatest challenges to their teaching skills.

Assignment of students with special needs to adaptive education classes should be limited to a number that can be adequately served by the regular teacher with consultative services from specialists. It would be unwise to place more than three to five students with a behavior disorder in the same classroom.

The age of students with special needs in relation to other students should also be considered. A 12-year-old student with severe learning problems would undoubtedly be uncomfortable in a second grade class, even if his or her academic skills were at this level. This is another reason why multigrade classes are recommended in the implementation of adaptive education. Students with special needs in multigrade classes may be the same age as the older students while functioning academically at the level of younger students. A careful curriculum sequence and student progress monitoring system are crucial elements in multiage classes and in classes where students with special needs are integrated. Criteria for mastery must be explicit and followed by the entire instruction team of the regular classroom teacher and the specialist teachers.

Certain nonprogram factors should also be considered in deciding placement of students requiring special or remedial education services. The placement of special needs students is likely to be affected by state and district guidelines and mandates for special education. In addition, the IEPs of individual students may have particular educational requirements. These factors should be identified as early as possible and incorporated in planning so that all arrangements for placement of students with special needs are completed prior to program implementation.

A question often asked by school staff concerns the appropriate class size for effective implementation of adaptive education programs. Implementation of adaptive education, as with traditional programs, can be greatly facilitated with a small class size, especially in early elementary classes. Implementation of adaptive education programs can occur with the normal class size without additional personnel if the specialist staff can be redeployed to work as part of the implementation team. Fifteen-to-one is a reasonable teacher-to-student ratio for basic skills instruction in elementary and middle school classes using adaptive education. In classes integrating or mainstreaming students with special needs, it is critical that not more than 10%–15% of a class of 30 students be students with special needs.

## Scheduling

Scheduling of pre-implementation and implementation activities is one of the most important, and often one of the most difficult, aspects in designing a delivery system. The school principal must ensure that adequate time and resources are allocated for two pre-implementation activities: preparation of basic skills curricula for individualized instruction, and training school staff. In addition, the principal needs to construct a master schedule for the school so that all program features are effectively implemented.

*Curriculum Preparation* Some preparation of curriculum is generally required for implementing adaptive education. The amount of time required for preparing curriculum materials depends on available curriculum materials. Preparing curriculum materials involves an inventory and organization of curriculum materials into manageable instruction units that provide flexibility in accommodating student diversity. Identification and construction of supplementary materials, as well as development of a task assignment and a records system (e.g., prescription sheets to communicate assignments to individual students, and charts for recording student progress) are major curriculum preparation tasks. When the existing curriculum materials and implementation requirements are closely matched, major curricular revisions are not needed. Detailed discussions of curriculum adaptation are included in Chapter 4.

Curriculum preparation should take place well in advance of classroom program implementation. The amount of time needed depends on factors such as the number of grade levels in the program and the available curriculum materials. The number of grade levels determines the levels of the curriculum materials that must be analyzed and adapted. For example, curriculum development for four to six grade levels is likely to require 5 days, and less time is needed if two or three grade levels need to be prepared.

A second factor influencing the time required for curriculum development is if available curriculum materials include components such as diagnostic tests and individualized assignment sheets. The presence of such components reduces the time required to analyze the curriculum and develop prescription sheets. Another factor is if the school uses a single basal series in each subject or materials from several sources. Preparation of a curriculum based on a single basal series generally takes less time. Curriculum development may be facilitated if two or more sites implementing the adaptive education program use the same curriculum materials. In such cases, adaptations made in one site can be imported by the others with little change.

Curriculum preparation should be completed prior to staff training. The curriculum preparation process can be facilitated by clerical help for typing, copying, and organizing completed curriculum materials. Work space and materials should be reserved well in advance to ensure that curriculum preparation activities proceed smoothly.

***Staff Development***     Staff development is central to effective implementation of innovative programs that require considerable changes in classroom organization and teacher roles. This staff development consists of two major phases: pre-implementation training that occurs prior to program implementation and implementation training support that continues throughout the school year. During pre-implementation training, school staff acquire skills needed for effective implementation of program components in the classroom. Each teacher develops a classroom implementation plan that specifies activities and dates of phasing in the new program over the first few weeks of school.

Pre-implementation training ideally should be scheduled just before program implementation, and 3–5 days allowed for this training. The schedule depends on factors such as availability of staff and funds for training, the complexity of the adaptive education program to be implemented, and the readiness of the staff for implementation. Less time is needed if many program teachers have experience with the diagnostic–prescriptive process or other elements of adaptive education. Since school district funds are usually allocated before the start of a school year, discussions with district administrators concerning scheduling and funding of pre-implementation training should be initiated as early as possible.

Staff who need to be involved in pre-implementation training include classroom teachers, the program coordinator, paraprofessionals or other classroom assistants, school administrators, and specialist resource personnel whose work directly or indirectly affects program implementation. Classroom teachers and the program coordinator should attend the entire series of training sessions. Although it is beneficial to include everyone involved in program implementation in all the training sessions, financial and other considerations often preclude this step. In practice, other than overview sessions, classroom assistants, school and district administrators, and other specialist resource personnel usually only attend sessions that are directly relevant to their program roles.

Delivery of staff development training is primarily the responsibility of school and district administrators and the person responsible for the coordination of implementation planning. Other professionals may be called on to conduct training sessions. For example, experts on the specific program, local experts on adaptive education, or trained school staff can provide assistance. The program coordinator or other staff who participated in curriculum preparation should be responsible for conducting training sessions on preparing of classroom materials and developing classroom procedures and instructions.

Pre-implementation training is best conducted in the school where the program will be implemented. Teachers should have access to their classrooms during pre-implementation training for at least 2 days, if not for the entire training. Teachers need to prepare the classroom environment for program implementation by rearranging furniture, constructing learning centers, and developing, organizing, and labeling materials.

The principal or the program coordinator is responsible for planning and implementing the training program. He or she needs to contact all the people involved and arrange for necessary facilities and materials on the scheduled dates.

*A Master Schedule for the School* Constructing a master schedule generally falls to the school principal whose task is to find ways to reconcile entrenched school scheduling policies and practices with the scheduling requirements of program implementation. There are two basic requirements. The first is to allot one planning period each week for the entire program staff (or subgroups of the staff, such as all primary grade teachers) to meet and discuss common implementation problems, share ideas, and plan staff development activities. These common planning activities are vital to maintain program implementation.

The second requirement relates to allocation of class time. For elementary and middle school grades, it is recommended that large blocks of uninterrupted class time (2½–3 hours) be scheduled to be utilized flexibly for various basic skills subjects. (The ways in which the teacher can use this time are discussed in Chapter 5.) This block of time for basic skills subjects may be scheduled in the morning or afternoon, and the schedule may vary from class to class if teachers on the team can work at the same time. Classroom assistants should be assigned to the classrooms during this time block for basic skills instruction if possible. If there are fewer classroom assistants than classrooms, a possible solution is to schedule half the classes (or teams) for basic skills instruction in the morning, and the other half in the afternoon.

Developing a master schedule that meets pre-implementation and implementation requirements may require considerable juggling. The benefits are many, and enable ease of program management, facilitation of implementation, teaming, and program coordination.

## Space, Facilities, and Materials

Adaptive education programs use basically the same kinds of materials, facilities, and equipment as traditional programs. Therefore, planning in this area primarily involves rearrangement and reallocation of what the school already possesses rather than acquisition of new equipment and materials. Nevertheless, it is unwise to assume that everything needed already is in place. Implementation planning should include a detailed assessment of available resources so that deficiencies can be addressed before the program begins. Specific planning for space, facilities, and materials includes:

1. Confirming that sufficient curriculum materials are available
2. Identifying and acquiring supplemental instructional materials
3. Acquiring noninstructional materials
4. Allocating an office for the program coordinator
5. Locating needed storage facilities or furniture

*Curriculum Materials* After necessary curriculum components have been identified (part of curriculum preparation), an inventory should determine if shortages exist so that additional books and materials can be acquired before program implementation. It is important to remember that adaptive education classes are likely to include students working at different levels within the same curriculum. For example, although most students in a fourth grade class are probably working at a fourth grade math level, the class may include some students working at a third grade level and some at a fifth grade level. Single-grade classrooms should be allotted a few sets of curriculum materials that are both below and above the grade level of the class. Multi-age classrooms are likely to require materials for an even broader range of grade levels.

Additional curriculum materials are needed to tailor learning experiences to individual student needs. These materials may include placement tests, diagnostic tests, unit pre- and post-tests, skill sheets, and teacher-constructed learning tasks. (The materials needed are discussed in chap. 4, this volume.) Often, such materials are available in the school or district and should be constructed or purchased if not. Curriculum-embedded tests, as well as ditto masters, skill sheets, and adjunct learning aids associated with basal curricula, are usually available from the publishers of the series.

***Necessary Noninstructional Materials***  Noninstructional materials consist of the same kinds of supplies such as tablets and other paper, pencils, crayons, paints, and erasers as used in traditional instruction. These should be inventoried and any additional materials purchased to ensure an adequate supply for student needs. Implementation of adaptive education may require special materials. Such materials should be constructed or purchased in time for use on the first day of class.

An item that implementors of adaptive education programs have found to be indispensable is the pocket folder, a commercially available folder with a pocket on each side. Students use the folders to hold their prescription sheets, current assignments, and other materials. Each student should have several pocket folders—one for each basic skills subject and one for other activities that holds the self-scheduling sheet and materials related to self-selected activities. Color coding is recommended, such as red folders for reading, blue for math, and green for other activities.

***Space and Facilities***  The program coordinator needs a room to store learning materials and to confer with individual teachers and students. In addition, the program coordinator's room often becomes a resource center for materials such as extra skill sheets and workbooks, supplementary learning materials, materials and equipment for instruction of students with special needs, and equipment and supplies that may be useful to classroom teachers. Therefore, the room should be large enough to comfortably accommodate at least two people, plus assorted books, learning materials, and equipment such as a computer, bookbinder, or laminator. The room should have a desk, at least two chairs, and bookcases, cabinets, and shelves.

Implementation of adaptive education programs does not require particular classroom furniture, and most classrooms are adequately equipped and only rearrangement of existing furniture is necessary. Nevertheless, it is a good idea to check each classroom to determine if additional equipment is needed. In addition to seating and working space for teachers and students, the following are necessary:

> Tables or other work space for learning centers, small-group activities, and individual work with students
> A table to accommodate the teacher and 5–10 students for small-group instruction—an alternative is to place smaller tables or desks together
> Adequate shelves, cabinets, or storage space for curriculum and learning materials such as books, workbooks, work sheets, kits, and games

Adequate storage facilities for all the materials required for adaptive education programs is sometimes a problem. If furniture cannot be located or purchased, it is often possible to construct storage facilities relatively easily and inexpensively. For example, boards on piles of blocks or bricks make adequate shelves, and boxes, cartons, and other containers can be used to store many things. Teachers, parents, and students can be asked to help. For the imaginative principal or teacher, there are many inexpensive ways to build a physical environment to support effective implementation of adaptive education.

## Program Monitoring and Evaluation

Maintaining a high degree of program implementation throughout the school year requires continual monitoring of the program delivery and staff development support. In addition, desired effects of the program must be identified and measured and the results used to improve program delivery (formative evaluation) and to assess program success in meeting goals (summative evaluation). Planning implementation monitoring and evaluation include:

1. Establishing a system for monitoring implementation and using the results for staff development
2. Identifying appropriate measures of program effects or outcomes
3. Developing a schedule for collecting outcome data

Regular monitoring of implementation by the program coordinator and classroom teachers is vital for maintaining successful implementation of the adaptive education program. The program coordinator's schedule should be planned to include frequent visits to program classes while instruction is taking place. During these informal observations, implementation problems can be noted and plans made to address the problems. The program coordinator's schedule should provide for regular observation of all classrooms and be flexible to permit extra visits to classes needing special attention.

A shortcoming of informal observations is the potential to overlook important aspects of implementation. Therefore, informal observations should be supplemented with more formal, systematic, and comprehensive measurements of classroom implementation. An instrument, the Implementation Assessment Battery for Adaptive Instruction, has been designed for this purpose (Wang, Catalano, & Gromoll, 1986). The assessment battery is used to collect data on the 12 critical design dimensions of adaptive instruction elaborated in Chapter 1.

For maximum program benefit, the Implementation Assessment Battery (or a comparable assessment instrument) should be administered at least three times a year: in fall (mid- to late October), winter (January or February), and spring (April or May). The results of fall and winter testing can be used to identify, for the school as a whole and for individual teachers, aspects of implementation that require strengthening. The results of spring testing are useful for planning for the following school year. Comparison of the year's assessment results provides data on changes in implementation over the year.

Both formal and informal assessments of implementation provide data that form the basis for staff development. At weekly staff conferences, common implementation problems can be handled, either through discussion or formal or informal training. In addition to staff conferences, the schedules of the program coordinator and teachers should include time for a specialist to work with individual teachers on specific classroom problems.

It is important for teachers to know that frequent formal and informal classroom observations are an integral component of the delivery of adaptive education. To ensure teacher cooperation and to maximize successful implementation, teachers must be convinced that the purpose of the observations is to help them solve implementation problems or to improve their implementation effectiveness rather than to evaluate their ability to teach. This requires that the principal and program coordinator work to create and maintain open communication, good rapport, and feelings of trust among all members of the program staff.

**Appropriate Measures of Program Outcomes**   Two goals of adaptive education programs are to effectively meet the individual learning needs of diverse students and to foster students' ability to take responsibility for their own learning. Additional goals mentioned by developers and implementors of adaptive education programs include positive attitudes of teachers and students, improved classroom interactions, increased time on task, decreased inappropriate student behaviors, improved student self-concepts, and greater integration of special needs students into the world of the classroom. The particular goals or their priorities are likely to vary from school to school. Early in program planning, school administrators must decide and precisely define the outcomes they wish to produce in students, teachers, school administrators, and parents.

Important categories of program outcomes include:

1.  Classroom processes (behavioral outcomes)
2.  Student cognitive, social, motivational, and attitudinal outcomes
3.  Positive attitude and support of program goals by teachers, parents, and administrators
4.  Costs

Desirable classroom process outcomes include positive changes in student behavior, in teacher–student interactions, and in student–student interactions. Expected student cognitive outcomes include achievement gains in basic skills and other subjects and steady progress through the curriculum. Desired student motivational and attitudinal outcomes include improved attitudes toward school and self and greater willingness to take responsibility for one's own learning. Program outcomes for teachers, parents, and administrators include positive assessment of the program's effects on themselves and students, as well as receptive attitudes toward adaptive education programs and integration of special needs students in regular classes. Finally, cost outcomes include district costs for instruction, plus additional expenses or savings specific to the adaptive education program.

The above list is by no means exhaustive. Suggesting important types of outcomes with examples, however, may serve to determine the specific outcomes in each category that are important for a school.

When desired program outcomes have been identified and defined, methods and instruments to measure program progress and outcomes should be identified. For some types of outcomes, standardized published measures are available. If such measures do not exist or are inappropriate, and if the outcome is judged to be sufficiently important, then school officials and program planners must design and develop appropriate methods of assessment. Given the considerable time and effort to construct reliable and valid measuring instruments, it is obvious that planning for the measurement of program outcomes should begin well before data are needed. (Methods for identifying and measuring program effects for program improvement and evaluation are provided in chap. 8, this volume.)

**Schedule for Collection of Outcome Data** Collection of outcome data should be scheduled to best serve formative and summative evaluation purposes. For decisions concerning program effectiveness and continuation (summative evaluation), the year-end or spring data are usually appropriate. Outcome data collected at other times are more useful for program planning (formative evaluation). For example, measures of implementation and of classroom processes that are obtained in fall and winter may be valuable for suggesting revisions to improve program delivery.

Another factor to consider in scheduling data collection is the information desired. If, for example, school administrators wish to assess the extent to which certain outcomes changed from pre-program levels, baseline measurements are needed of these outcomes prior to program implementation. If trends over time are of interest, multiple periodic measurements must be made. Another factor to consider in scheduling data collection is the particular population to be sampled. Obviously, program students, teachers, parents, and administrators are likely sources of outcome data. It is useful also to collect data from nonprogram classes comparable to program classes in the school or district for comparisons.

When a schedule for data collection has been formulated, the principal must ensure that all necessary testing materials and supplies are available when needed and that all the involved teachers, test administrators, and others are informed well in advance of the dates and times for data collection.

## Communication and Dissemination of Information

Program participants and others involved should be regularly informed about the new education program, beginning with the decision to adopt the program and continuing throughout the program. Clear and open communication builds support and enables those involved to deal with their concerns and to identify possible problems and solutions. Specific planning includes:

1. Developing an awareness plan to inform people about the program
2. Establishing an internal network for communicating among program staff
3. Establishing a network for disseminating information to parents, community members, and district administrators

**An Awareness Plan** The first step to build support for and commitment to a new program involves developing awareness of the program and its expected effects. Awareness presentations for various audiences need to be planned and delivered. Obviously, teachers, school and district administrators, and school board members must be informed at or before the time of formal adoption. However, many other parties also have an interest in the program. The earlier and the more completely such involved individuals are informed about the program, the greater the likelihood that they will support the program and the easier the implementation process is likely to be. Therefore, school administrators should plan as early as possible for dissemination of information.

Information can be written (e.g., a newsletter to parents), presented directly, or communicated by video. Direct presentation has the advantage of the exchange of concerns, questions, and ideas. An effective method is to begin with a brief printed communication followed by a meeting with the presentation of more detailed information. For example, a note might be sent to parents that contains a paragraph description of the new program and includes an invitation to a meeting at which the program will be more fully discussed.

Different parties require different information. For example, parents are most interested in how the program will affect their children, while policymakers are likely to be concerned about costs. The information needed by different groups and suggestions for planning and conducting awareness presentations are discussed in detail in Chapter 3.

**Establishing an Internal Network for Communication Among Program Staff** Openness and trust constitute the foundation for a successful education program. A communication network that facilitates frequent interchange of information, problems, and ideas among program staff serves to strengthen that foundation. Regular weekly staff meetings provide a formal communication channel, and informal channels should also be available. Both the principal and the program coordinator should arrange their schedules to include time convenient for individual teachers who have suggestions or who need to talk about a problem. It is important for the principal to foster an atmosphere in which teachers and staff members feel free to express their feelings and concerns without fear of criticism or other adverse effects.

**Establishing an External Network for Disseminating Information** Parents, members of the community, district and state administrators, and policymakers need to be regularly informed about the program's progress. This can be done in a variety of ways. For example, parents can receive regular updates through a newsletter and parent–teacher organization meetings. The community can be informed of developments by articles in a local newspaper and television or radio broadcasts. Letters can be sent periodically to district and state policymakers concerning the program, and policymakers can be invited to visit the school and see the program in operation. These and other possibilities should be considered by the school principal in planning for establishing and maintaining communication with all involved parties.

## Documentation of Implementation Planning

The many components of implementation planning, the large number of people affected, and human fallibility make accurate and thorough documentation of all planning processes and decisions imperative. Proceedings of implementation planning meetings should be recorded as written or taped minutes. If this is not possible, summaries should be prepared as soon as possible after meetings. All planning by individuals, such as scheduling decisions by a school principal, should be similarly recorded.

To provide an accessible guide to implementation in the school, records of planning processes and results should be incorporated into an Implementation Plan. The Implementation Plan should be prepared and filed prior to preimplementation activities such as curriculum preparation and staff training. Some plans may be incomplete at that time, but records of subsequent planning decisions can be appended.

The Implementation Plan can be written in narrative form, but to ensure complete information and facilitate access to particular planning components, a format such as that shown in Appendix 2.C is recommended. The form is organized according to the planning components discussed in this chapter, and school administrators, staff, and planners need merely to record planning decisions in the appropriate places. Additional sections or pages can be added as needed.

After the Implementation Plan has been prepared, copies should be distributed to all who have a role in planning and coordinating program implementation. These include school and district administrators, program support personnel, and other collaborators in program and training development.

## SUMMARY

Implementation of an adaptive education program begins well before the first day the program goes into effect. A comprehensive needs assessment is the first, and perhaps the most essential, task for program success. Planners for program implementation need clear knowledge about the resources and limitations of the particular site. Implementation planning involves decisions concerning the classes that will participate in the program, program staff members and their roles, and student placements. Planning also involves scheduling pre-implementation activities and planning the operation of the program throughout the year. Space, materials, and facilities are inventoried and reallocated, constructed, or purchased. Plans are developed for program monitoring and evaluation and for internal and external communication and dissemination of information.

Results from systematic needs assessment serve as the basis for implementation planning that ensures effective site-specific delivery. A well-designed and carefully documented site-specific delivery system eases the transition from the current practice to the new program; builds enthusiasm, commitment, and support among program participants and others; and increases the likelihood of program success.

## REFERENCES

Ellett, C.D., & Wang, M.C. (1987). Assessing administrative leadership components of program implementation in an innovative ECE program. *Journal of Research in Childhood Education*, 2(1), 30–47.

Fullan, M. (1985). Change processes and strategies at the local level. *Elementary School Journal*, 85(3), 391–422.

Little, J.W. (1981). *School success and staff development: The role of staff development in urban desegregated schools*. Boulder, CO: Center for Action Research.

Oakes, J. (1985). *Keeping track: How schools structure inequality*. New Haven: Yale University Press.

Reynolds, M.C., & Wang, M.C. (1983). Restructuring "special" school programs: A position paper. *Policy Studies Review*, 2(1), 189–212.

Reynolds, M.C., Wang, M.C., & Walberg, H.J. (1987). The necessary restructuring of special and regular education. *Exceptional Children*, 53(5), 391–398.

Wang, M.C., Catalano, R., & Gromoll, E. (1986). *Training manual for the Implementation Assessssment Battery for Adaptive Instruction* (Vols. 1 & 2). Philadelphia, PA: Temple University Center for Research in Human Development and Education.

# Needs Assessment Forms

NEEDS ASSESSMENT FORMS

School _____

District _____

Location _____

Date Filed _____

Person Completing Form _____

*Adaptive Education Strategies*

## I. PRINCIPAL INTERVIEW FORM

Directions:   Schedule a 90 minute meeting with the principal and complete all questions in sections A, B, and C.

### I.A. School Profile

1. What is the composition of the student population (ethnic background, English as second language)?

   \_\_\_\_\_ % Black/Afro-American

   \_\_\_\_\_ % White/Caucasian

   \_\_\_\_\_ % American-Indian/Native American

   \_\_\_\_\_ % Mexican American/ Chicano

   \_\_\_\_\_ % Oriental/Asian American

   \_\_\_\_\_ % Puerto Rican (Mainland/Borinquen)

   \_\_\_\_\_ % Other_____

   \_\_\_\_\_ % English as second language

2. How are students assigned to classes?

3. Is there a school-wide system for grouping students according to ability (e.g., homeroom assignments, specific academic grouping)?\_\_\_\_\_If so, describe.

4. Are any classes grouped together?_____If so, which ones?

5. What criteria have been used for assigning teachers to these classes?

6. Check individualization practices used by classroom teachers.

   _____ Teach small groups

   _____ Use the diagnostic-prescriptive process

   _____ Provide supplemental assignment as needed

   _____ Other _____

7. How often do inservice and/or clerical days occur?

8. What types of inservice activities are currently planned?

9. Who hires and supervises paraprofessionals?

10. Describe a typical schedule of a student in a general education class.

   a) Starting Time _____

   b) Length of Lunch Period _____

   c) Length of Recess _____

   d) Number and Type of Special Classes per Week _____

   e) Length of a Special Class _____

   f) Dismissal Time _____

   g) Comments:

I. A.  School Profile (cont.)

11.  Describe a typical schedule of a general education classroom teacher.

  a) Starting Time _____

  b) Length of Lunch Period _____

  c) Number of Preparation Periods per Week _____

  d) Length of a Preparation Period _____

  e) Type of Non-instructional Duties _____
  _____

  f) Frequency of Non-instructional Duties _____

  g) Quitting Time _____

  h) Comments:


12.  Describe a typical shedule of a paraprofessional.

  a) Starting Time _____

  b) Length of Lunch Period _____

  c) Number and Length of Breaks _____

  d) Type and Frequency of Non-instructional Duties _____
  _____

  e) Special Guidelines for Duties _____

  f) Quitting Time _____


13.  Identify district/school personnel with expertise in adaptive instruction (individualization).

| Name | Position |
|------|----------|
|      |          |
|      |          |
|      |          |
|      |          |


14.  Check the functions of instructional leader currently performed by the principal.

  _____ Observes classroom teachers

  _____ Discusses results of observations with staff

  _____ Holds regularly scheduled staff meetings

  _____ Plans inservice training

  _____ Maintains a master schedule

  _____ Follows a systematic procedure for appropriate placement of students with special needs

  _____ Makes decisions regarding school policies

  _____ Holds regularly scheduled meetings with parents

  _____ Other _____

15. Describe the present philosophy and goals of the school.

16. List any resource personnel available.

| Position | Name | Responsibilities |
|---|---|---|
| Speech Pathologist | | |
| Adaptive PE Teacher | | |
| Special Ed Teacher | | |
| Chapter I Teacher | | |
| Psychologist | | |
| Counselor | | |
| Social Worker | | |
| Nurse | | |
| Home-School Visitor | | |
| Others _____ | | |

17. Who is responsible for coordinating activities and assignments of resource personnel?

18. How are parents informed about new projects?

19. Is there a PTA or PTO?

20. If there is a parent organization, how often does the group hold meetings?

21. What percentage of parents participate in this organization?

I. A. School Profile (cont.)

    22. In what areas do parents have input?

    23. Does the parent group circulate a newsletter?

    24. How often are parent conferences scheduled?

    25. Is there a parent volunteer group?

    26. Is there any other type of volunteer program? _____ If so, describe.

    27. Are practicum students assigned to this school? _____ If so, from which college?

    28. Are there any other pilot or special projects currently operating within the school? _____ If so, describe the program and the students served.

I.B.  Curriculum

    29. Describe any specific district policies regarding curriculum (e.g., number of hours for reading and math). To what degree can these be modified?

30. By what date are curriculum materials ordered? Who orders the materials?

31. Can additional curriculum materials be purchased during the school year? How much money is usually budgeted per class?

32. What basal math series is used at each grade level?

33. What other math series are available in the district?

34. List any other available math materials.

35. Which basal reading series is used at each grade level?

36. What other reading series are available in the district?

37. List any other available reading materials.

38. Is there a materials resource center where learning materials can be borrowed or made?

39. List other kinds of equipment available for use in the classroom.

I. B.  Curriculum (cont.)

    40.  Which curriculum guides are available?

I. C.  Evaluation/Documentation

    41.  What type of grading system is used?

    42.  How often are report cards given out?

    43.  What is the district's promotional policy?

    44.  What standardized tests are given?

    45.  When are students tested? (Which grade levels are tested?)

    46.  Who tests the students?

    47.  Where are student records filed?

    48.  How are students identified as needing special education services?

    49.  Who is responsible for overseeing the placement process?

    50.  How is the parent informed that a special education placement is being considered?

    51.  Who writes the Individualized Education Program (IEP)?

    52.  Where are IEP s filed?

    53.  How often are special education placements for individual students reviewed?

    54.  How much time do students from a resource room typically spend in general education classes?

## II. OBSERVATION NOTES

Directions: Two classrooms should be observed while the students are present for 30 minutes each. An additional 30 minutes should be scheduled to interview the teacher and examine materials in each classroom while the students are absent. Use two copies of this form, one for each of two classrooms. Record the classroom, grade level, and teacher name in the place provided.

Section D: Answer question 1 upon entering the classroom. Observe the teacher and student interactions for 20 minutes. Then complete questions 2 - 5. Circle Y for yes or N for no, or 1 - 4 (1 - never; 2 - some of the time; 3 - most of the time; 4 - always). Write short comments for any of the areas where sufficient information was not included in the question.

Section E: While students are out of the classroom, examine curricular materials and discuss classroom activities with the teacher (questions 6 - 10).

Section F: Tally the amount of available furniture and equipment while examining classroom materials and check school facilities during the tour of the building.

D.    Classroom Observation (with students present)

Classroom _____

Grade Level _____

Teacher _____

1. Describe the classroom activity upon entering the room. (What are most of the students doing? Is there a paraprofessional in the room? What is that person doing?)

2. Physical Environment

    a) Are classroom rules posted?          Y   N

    b) Are desks arranged in rows?          Y   N

    c) Do students choose where they will sit?          Y   N

    d) Are learning centers set up in the room?          Y   N

    e) Comments:

3. Style of Instruction          *Never*        *Always*

    a) Does the teacher instruct the class as a whole?    1   2   3   4

    b) Does the teacher work with small groups?    1   2   3   4

    c) Do students work alone while completing seatwork?    1   2   3   4

    d) Does the teacher move around the room giving feedback to individuals or small groups?    1   2   3   4

    e) Comments:

4. Management Techniques

    a) Does the teacher verbally praise students?    1   2   3   4

    b) Does the teacher give reminders regarding rules?    1   2   3   4

II. D. Classroom Observation (cont.)

    c)  Does the teacher raise his/her voice when reprimanding students?    1  2  3  4

    d)  Does the teacher isolate or exclude students who are misbehaving?    1  2  3  4

    e)  Comments:

5.  Student Behavior

    a)  Do students raise their hands for teacher assistance?    1  2  3  4

    b)  Do students ask permission to move around the room?    1  2  3  4

    c)  Do students ask permission to leave the room?    1  2  3  4

    d)  Do students talk to one another whenever they wish?    1  2  3  4

    e)  Comments:

II. E. Examination of Classroom and Teacher Interview (with students absent)

6.  If during the classroom observation, you had questions about any activity, clarify these points with the teacher.

7.  Which of the following components are available for the reading and math series?

| Component | Reading | | Math | |
|---|---|---|---|---|
| a)  Textbook | Y | N | Y | N |
| b)  Placement Tests | Y | N | Y | N |
| c)  Pre/Post Tests | Y | N | Y | N |
| d)  Record Keeping System | Y | N | Y | N |
| e)  Work Book | Y | N | Y | N |
| f)  Ditto Masters | Y | N | Y | N |
| g)  Related Kits | Y | N | Y | N |
| h)  Related Games | Y | N | Y | N |

8.  If learning centers are present in the classroom, which of the following components are included?

| Components | | |
|---|---|---|
| a)  List of Materials | Y | N |
| b)  Script of directions for each activity | Y | N |
| c)  Activities that accommodate various levels of difficulty | Y | N |

9. List the teacher-made parallel activities available in the classroom.

| Subject Area | Description |
|---|---|
|  |  |
|  |  |
|  |  |
|  |  |
|  |  |

10. List the names of any commercially made activities available in the classroom.

| Type of Material | Name of Materials |
|---|---|
| Instructional Kits |  |
| Games |  |
| Basal Series |  |
| Others |  |

11. Ask the teacher approximately what percentages of reading and math time are spent on the following activities.

_____ % students work independently on paper-pencil tasks

_____ % students work in small groups with teacher assistance

_____ % students work with other students without teacher help

12. What percentages of the day does the teacher engage in the following?

_____ % instructing the class as a total group

_____ % working with small groups of students

_____ % moving around giving feedback to individual students

II. F. Physical Plant

    **13.** List the amount of available furniture and equipment in the classroom

| Item | Number Available |
|---|---|
| Student desks | |
| Group tables | |
| Bulletin board | |
| Clock | |
| Storage cupboards | |
| Lockers | |
| Outlets | |
| Sinks | |
| Carrels | |
| Computer | |

    Comments:  (Describe any features of the classroom design that would facilitate or hinder program implementation.)

    **14.** While touring the school check which of the following facilities can be found.

        _____ Art room                _____ Auditorium

        _____ Music room            _____ Gym

        _____ Science room        _____ Media center

        _____ Library                 _____ Computer center

        _____ Cafeteria             _____ Other _____

        _____ Chapter I rooms
                  (reading and/or math)

## III. RECORDS CHECKLIST

Directions:  1) Examine the school roster and student record cards and complete Section G.

2) Obtain copies of documents listed in Section H.

G. School Profile

|  | Grade | Number |
|---|---|---|
| 1. How many general education classes are there at each level? | K | |
| | 1 | |
| | 2 | |
| | 3 | |
| | 4 | |
| | 5 | |
| | 6 | |

2. How many children are enrolled in the school?       Total: _____

3. How many special education classes are in the school? (List locally used label and number of each type of class provided in the school.)

| Classification | Locally Used Label (if different) | Number of Classes |
|---|---|---|
| Learning Disabled | | |
| Emotionally Disturbed | | |
| Physically Handicapped | | |
| Mentally Retarded | | |
| Other _____ | | |
| _____ | | |

4. Check any information typically included on student record cards.

_____ Student ID number

_____ Birth date

_____ Previous class placements

_____ Achievement test scores

_____ Report card grades

_____ Other _____

5. Check information that is available from achievement test reports.

_____ Individual scores

_____ Class summary

III. G. School Profile (cont.)

_____ Grade-level summary

_____ School summary

_____ Summary for special education students

III. H. Documents

6. Check items that are available in the school. If possible, obtain one copy of each.

_____ 1. School calendar

_____ 2. Staff handbook

_____ 3. Parent handbook

_____ 4. Student handbook

_____ 5. Curriculum guides

_____ 6. District curriculum development directives

_____ 7. Sample IEP

_____ 8. School organizational chart

_____ 9. District organizational chart

_____ 10. Summary report of achievement scores for previous year

# Checklist of Tasks in the Development of a School-Specific Delivery System

## CHECKLIST OF TASKS IN THE DEVELOPMENT
## OF A SCHOOL-SPECIFIC DELIVERY SYSTEM

A.  Identification of Program Classes

_____     Determine the number of classes that will participate in the program.

_____     Select grade levels and grade-level composition of classes.


B.  Staffing

_____     Assign teachers to program classes.

_____     Select a program coordinator.

_____     Identify resource and special personnel, and define their roles in the program.

_____     Identify/hire paraprofessionals and/or arrange for other classroom support staff.


C.  Student Placements

_____     Assign regular education students to program classes.

_____     Make arrangements for placement of special needs students in the classes.


D.  Scheduling

_____     Designate time, place, and personnel for curriculum preparation.

_____     Designate time, place, and personnel for pre-implementation training of staff.

_____     Construct a master schedule for the school compatible with program requirements.


E.  Space, Facilities, and Materials

_____     Confirm that sufficient materials (i.e., textbooks, workbooks) are available.

_____     Identify/acquire supplemental instructional materials, if needed.

_____     Acquire necessary noninstructional materials.

_____     Allocate a room for the program coordinator.

_____     Locate storage cabinets and other furniture for program classrooms.


F.  Program Monitoring and Evaluation

_____     Establish a system for monitoring program implementation and using the results for staff development.

_____     Identify appropriate measures of program outcomes.

_____     Develop a schedule for collection of outcome data.


G.  Communication and Dissemination of Information

_____     Develop a plan to inform stakeholders (e.g., parents, school board members) about the program.

_____     Establish an internal network for communication among program staff.

_____     Establish an external network for disseminating information to parents, community members, district administrators, and others about the program.

H. Documentation of Implementation Planning

_____ Record and/or summarize proceedings of implementation planning meetings.

_____ Prepare Implementation Plan.

_____ Distribute Implementation Plan.

*Appendix 2.C*

# Implementation Plan Forms

## IMPLEMENTATION PLAN

School        _____

Principal     _____

School Year   _____

Date Filed    _____


### PART 1: STAFFING AND STUDENT ASSIGNMENTS

I. A. Participating Classroom Teachers and Classes

Anticipated Number of Students

| | | | General | Special | |
|---|---|---|---|---|---|
| 1. | Teacher | Grade Level | Education | Education | Chapter 1 |

_____

_____

_____

_____

_____

_____


2.   List the names of aides/paraprofessionals available to be assigned to the program.  Indicate the number of hours they will work, and their classroom assignment.

| Name | Number of Hours | Classroom Assignment |
|---|---|---|
| _____ | _____ | _____ |
| _____ | _____ | _____ |
| _____ | _____ | _____ |
| _____ | _____ | _____ |


I. B. Additional Program Staff

1. Name of Program Coordinator (or Candidate)     _____

2. Current Position     _____

3. Percentage of Time Commitment to Program     _____

4. Room Assignment     _____

I. B.  Additional Program Staff (cont.)

5. List any available resource personnel.

| Position | Name | Role in Adaptive Education Program |
|---|---|---|
| Special Ed Teacher | _____ | _____ |
| Chapter 1 Teacher | _____ | _____ |
| Speech Pathologist | _____ | _____ |
| Adaptive Physical Education Teacher | _____ | _____ |
| Psychologist | _____ | _____ |
| Counselor | _____ | _____ |
| Social Worker | _____ | _____ |
| Nurse | _____ | _____ |
| Home-School Visitor | _____ | _____ |
| Other | _____ | _____ |

I. C.  Tasks and Personnel Responsible for Supporting School
    Implementation of the Adaptive Education Program

| TASKS TO BE CARRIED OUT IN CONJUNCTION WITH IMPLEMENTATION OF ADAPTIVE EDUCATION | PERSON(S) RESPONSIBLE FOR CARRYING OUT THE TASKS |
|---|---|
| Administer Implementation Assessment Battery a minimum of three times during the school year. | |
| Monitor program implementation through weekly informal classroom observations. | |
| Monitor pupil progress toward learning objectives on a monthly basis. | |
| Review the use of curricula in the classroom on a monthly basis in order to determine the need for modifications. | |
| Coordinate the individualization of curricular materials as modifications are needed or when additional levels will be added. | |
| Identify supplemental materials and learning activities to facilitate individualization of the curricula. | |
| Establish/coordinate a system and central location for the supply and distribution of materials. | |

| TASKS TO BE CARRIED OUT IN CONJUNCTION WITH IMPLEMENTATION OF ADAPTIVE EDUCATION | PERSON(S) RESPONSIBLE FOR CARRYING OUT THE TASKS |
|---|---|

Diagnose learning needs of individual students who regularly show mastery of curricular objectives within a reasonable period of time.

Work with teachers to develop instructional plans for students who have been diagnosed as needing revised learning plans.

Plan pre-implementation training for program staff and volunteers.

Design staff development plan for individual teachers.

Confer biweekly with individual teachers in order to discuss targeted areas of training.

Plan/conduct weekly group meetings in order to address training areas relevant to all teachers.

Coordinate data collection on program effects a minimum of three times during the school year.

Maintain student rosters for each class.

Document individual and group staff development activities.

Maintain a master schedule for instructional staff that reflects requirements of implementing the adaptive education program.

Implement process for the identification and placement of special needs children.

Establish a network or structure for communicating about the adaptive education program's implementation with parents, community, and others.

Establish a network or structure for communicating among teachers implementing the adaptive education program.

Conduct awareness sessions for various stakeholders.

Designate and clearly communicate responsibilities to program staff.

Meet with other persons responsible for support functions to discuss program implementation.

Participate in family and community activities.

Organize ongoing activities to involve parents in the program.

## PART II. PRE-IMPLEMENTATION ACTIVITIES

II. A. <u>Awareness Presentations</u>

| <u>Audience</u> | <u>Topic(s) and Medium of Presentation</u> | <u>Date</u> |
|---|---|---|
| 1. School Administrators | _____ | _____ |
| | _____ | _____ |
| | _____ | _____ |
| | _____ | _____ |
| | _____ | _____ |
| 2. Teachers | _____ | _____ |
| | _____ | _____ |
| | _____ | _____ |
| | _____ | _____ |
| | _____ | _____ |
| 3. Parents | _____ | _____ |
| | _____ | _____ |
| | _____ | _____ |
| | _____ | _____ |
| | _____ | _____ |
| 4. Other | _____ | _____ |
| | _____ | _____ |
| | _____ | _____ |
| | _____ | _____ |
| | _____ | _____ |

II. B. <u>Curriculum Preparation</u>

1. Dates     _____

2. Place     _____

3. Participants

_____

_____

_____

_____

4. Subjects Areas to Be Individualized

_____

_____

5. Curriculum Preparation Profile  (Prepare one copy of the following curriculum preparation profile for each subject to be individualized.)

Subject                        _____

Title of Basal Series          _____

Copyright Date                 _____

Levels to be Prepared          _____

II. C. Pre-implementation Training

1. Dates        _____

2. Place        _____

3. List the person(s) responsible for preparation and delivery of training.

_____

_____

_____

_____

4. List of Trainees and Days of Training Required

| Names of Trainees | Number of Days of Training Required |
|---|---|
| School Administrators | |
| _____ | _____ |
| _____ | _____ |
| Teachers | |
| _____ | _____ |
| _____ | _____ |

II. C.   Pre-implementation Training (cont.)

Education Specialist(s)

_____          _____

_____          _____

Administrators

_____          _____

_____          _____

Paraprofessionals or Aides

_____          _____

_____          _____

Other

_____          _____

_____          _____

What arrangements have been or will be made for paying staff or providing other incentives to attend training?

## PART III. SCHOOL AND CLASS SCHEDULES

1. Weekly Conference Time for Program Staff:

    Day    _____

    Time    _____

2. Schedule of Program Coordinator (Complete in as much detail as possible.)

3. For elementary grades, each class needs an uninterrupted block of time each day during which instruction in the individualized components of the curriculum take place.  Attach a copy of the master schedule showing the 2 1/2 to 3 hour block or list the information below.

    Teacher                  Time of Instructional Block

## PART IV. NEEDED CLASSROOM FURNITURE AND EQUIPMENT

Item Needed                          Plan for Obtaining

_____          _____

_____          _____

_____          _____

_____          _____


## PART V. PROGRAM MONITORING AND DATA COLLECTION

|                                |            | Person      | Dates of       |
| Type of Outcome                | Instrument | Responsible | Administration |
|--------------------------------|------------|-------------|----------------|
| Classroom Process              |            |             |                |
| Student Learning Progress      |            |             |                |
| Social and Attitudinal Outcomes |          |             |                |
| Degree of Program Implementation |         |             |                |

*Chapter 3*

# Building Program Support

Successful implementation of innovative practices and programs depends on adequate knowledge about the design and implementation requirements of the program, the extent to which implementation can lead to achievement of desired improvement, as well as on support and expectations of success from all who are involved. Administrators need specific information in order to decide if the programs will meet their school and district needs, the extent to which implementation support needs can be met by the current district and school resources, and, what, if any, program constraints need to be addressed prior to implementation. Staff, parents, and others need to know how the program will affect them and student learning outcomes. Teachers, for example, need to know what changes the program will bring about in their classrooms and in teaching activities.

Planning for dissemination of information to involved groups is one of the most important initial activities for building program support. This planning is often not done well and, more often than not, is overlooked as an aspect of implementation planning. This early step in implementation planning is crucial, particularly for innovative programs such as adaptive education that require major rethinking and restructuring of delivery of instruction and related services. Program success requires staff willingness to make the necessary changes for effective program implementation and their later commitment to program continuation. Research of the 1970s and 1980s on effective schools has shown that innovative programs fail if they are not actively supported by school administrative and instructional staff and if external support (e.g., from the program developers) is withdrawn (Ellett & Wang, 1987; Fullan, 1985; Sergiovanni, 1990; Walberg & Keefe, 1988).

Thus, systematic planning for dissemination of information is a critical step in cultivating receptivity to innovative practices. This is especially important when implementation of an innovative program involves extensive changes in school organization and staff roles, which happens with adaptive education programs. Most schools are not optimally organized for the delivery of instruction that is closely matched to the needs of individual students. Although teachers generally attempt to adjust their instruction to provide for student differences, the systematic implementation of adaptive education is usually the exception, rather than the norm, for a variety of reasons, including a lack of organizational and resource support.

Adaptive education programs promote the development of new skills or the use of old skills in new ways among teachers and school staff. Implementation of adaptive education requires the school staff to coordinate and collaborate as a team to provide education and related services. Thus, a basic requirement for establishing staff commitment to change is the understanding that implementation of adaptive education is feasible because of the structural support among school staff. The restructuring and changes required in implementing adaptive education are worthwhile because of the potentially positive outcomes for their students.

The first step in building commitment is to develop awareness of the program benefits. This chapter aims to help persons who are responsible for the design, implementation, and evaluation of adaptive education programs to plan and deliver awareness presentations for various groups and individuals—district and school administrators, policymakers, teachers, parents, and students. First, the information needs are discussed. Next, an outline of recommended topics for awareness presentations is formulated.

## INFORMATION NEEDS OF INVOLVED INDIVIDUALS AND GROUPS

Many people are likely to be affected by educational innovation such as adaptive education. Teachers who are responsible for daily implementation of the program and students who are served by the program are most obviously affected. Specialist staff, district and building administrators, educational policymakers, parents, and other concerned members of the community also play key roles in successful implementation of innovative programs. The following sections describe the information needs of each of these groups for implementation of an adaptive education program.

### Classroom Teachers and Other Instructional Staff

Classroom teachers, specialist teachers, and instructional support staff are responsible for program implementation and student learning and outcomes. They need detailed information about the adaptive education approach, and their information needs are primarily practical. Although the history and theory of adaptive education are useful background information, the critical concern is how the theory is to be put into practice. They need to know what the components of adaptive education are and how these components are implemented in the classroom. Teachers and instructional staff tend to be concerned with the interface between the new program and the conventional instructional practices to which they are accustomed. They need to be assured that effective teaching under the new program will call upon the same teaching skills that good teachers already possess.

Teachers are also concerned about their roles and responsibilities in the program and how these will differ from their accustomed roles. Although differences between conventional and innovative programs should not be overly stressed, they should not be ignored. For example, if special services are to be integrated into the regular education program, both the general education teachers and specialized personnel need to know how this will be done.

Teachers need to know what kinds of changes are necessary in their teaching behaviors, in their relations with other teachers, and what new skills they will need. They need information about training and inservice support. They also are concerned about the effects of the new program on student achievement, behavior, and attitudes. Teachers who may be initially doubtful are often willing to try new ways of teaching if students are expected to benefit from the change.

It is important that information be presented to teachers in a noncoercive way. Questions should be welcomed and answered openly and honestly. Concerns should be accepted and dealt with realistically. For maximum cooperation and commitment, teachers must believe that their input is valued. It is important to convey to teachers that adaptive education programs are adaptive to teachers as well as to students, and many teaching preferences and styles can be accommodated within the conceptual and operational framework of adaptive education.

Above all, teachers are professionals whose ideas and suggestions are not only encouraged but actively solicited. Research and practical wisdom clearly suggest that the extent of staff support for implementation of an innovation is directly related to the extent that staff are involved in the planning process (Lieberman, Saxl, & Miles, 1988; Stein & Wang, 1988; Vaughan, Wang, & Dytman, 1987). Awareness sessions provide an opportunity for staff to be involved in the decision-making process from the beginning.

## Administrators and Policymakers

The decision to implement an innovative program that requires major restructuring generally rests with school and district administrators and policymakers. In most school districts, the superintendent and school board must approve any large-scale change, and successful implementation at a school requires the active support and participation of the school principal. In fact, principals are gatekeepers of change, and their support, or lack of support, for change efforts can determine the fate of an innovative program.

Administrators and policymakers need information about the adaptive education program in order to make informed decisions. They need to know the assumptions and components of the proposed innovation to decide how it relates to the philosophy, goals, and existing education program of the district and school. Awareness sessions provide an opportunity not only to communicate information about the instruction program to be implemented, but also to elicit information about district and school goals and needs and suggest how the program may help meet those goals and needs. Furthermore, it is important to acknowledge the limitations of the new program, and that it may not be appropriate for all educational contexts. The feasibility of the adaptive education program is closely tied to school and district resources and limitations. This should be emphasized in awareness presentations. The identification of resources and limitations becomes the database for the design of a school-specific delivery system by district central staff, building administrators, and school instructional staff.

A major concern of school administrators is accountability, both educational and fiscal, and awareness presentations must address this concern. Since administrators are responsible for ensuring that educational quality is maintained or enhanced, they are especially interested in data concerning the effects of an innovative program on staff time and functions and student learning outcomes. Administrators, for example, need to be sure that the proposed program will not place excessive demands on school budgets. The individualized instructional programs of the 1960s and 1970s tended to be expensive. Their management systems often involved high staff to student ratios, and the curricula required special materials and equipment. Now, new programs must operate within existing budgets unless they are externally funded. Therefore, a critical step in the preparation of awareness presentations is to show how reassignment of existing resources can support program implementation. It is important to show this group that extra expenses will not be incurred beyond start-up costs for training and for preparation of materials, for example, prescription sheets. Data concerning cost effectiveness of the proposed adaptive education program are helpful in the planning process, if available.

Policymakers at district and state levels are concerned that the proposed program conforms to state and local laws and policies. Each state has regulations governing the funding and implementation of education services for students with special needs. If the proposed adaptive program is expected to deviate from current practice (e.g., pre-referral intervention services provided by special education teachers as part of instructional teams in regular classroom settings), a way should be sought to achieve program goals within the existing legal structure. For example, many states recommend or mandate that special education students be educated in regular classrooms to the fullest possible extent, in some cases full time, provided that the required special services are available.

If full-time placement will not conform to state or local regulations, the school may risk losing resources needed for implementation. School administrators, therefore, should work with policymakers to explore strategies to implement coordinated and inclusive service to students with special needs in the proposed adaptive education program. Some states, for example, grant waivers of special education regulations for the operation of "experimental" programs for a limited time, and continuation usually depends on a thorough evaluation. Other states permit exceptions to certain laws and regulations if particular conditions are met. For example, a recent modification in Chapter 1 funding regulations allows those funds to support school-wide program implementation if over 75% of students in the school are eligible for Chapter 1 services. Administrators responsible for implementation planning need to be well versed in local laws.

School districts have district policies or guidelines that regulate aspects of education such as curriculum, student evaluation, and promotion, and the proposed program should comply with these policies. District policymakers and administrators need to know that program delivery plans conform to existing policies. This task is a major part of site-specific implementation planning. As with teachers, the early involvement of school officials in program planning increases the likelihood that they will support program adoption and continuation.

## Parents and Students

The effects of adaptive education are the primary concern of the consumers, students and parents. Parents are deeply interested in the quality of education and how this affects their children's learning. Therefore, data on learning under the innovative program need to be presented in a nontechnical, comprehensible form. Parents often express concerns about classroom discipline in relation to adaptive education. Parents may equate freedom of movement and choice of activities with a lack of order and discipline. Many parents have an aversion to the open classrooms of the 1970s, and they may perceive adaptive education and individualized instruction as a return to such unstructured learning environments. It is important to assure parents that the particular adaptive education program incorporates structured learning, direct instruction, systematic management, and much teacher–student interaction, while encouraging and teaching students to assume responsibility for managing their own learning activities under teacher supervision.

Parents have particular concerns when students with special needs are integrated in regular classes. Parents of general education students may fear that their children's academic progress will be hampered, while parents of students with special needs may fear that their children will not receive needed services and will not be accepted socially by their peers. Both groups of parents need information about how the adaptive education program can adequately accommodate the individual needs of their children. Discussions of features of the program design, particularly the individualized education planning that ensures education outcomes for every student, and a classroom management system that enables teachers to provide instructional support for highly diverse groups of students, are likely to increase understanding and lessen parent anxiety. In addition, parents of students with special needs should know how the program will utilize specialized professional personnel with classroom teachers to meet their children's needs. Presentation of data concerning outcomes from studies of adaptive education in integrated settings can be helpful in alleviating some of these concerns.

The discussion of parent concerns and fears is not meant to imply that parent opposition should be expected and to prepare to take a defensive posture. On the contrary, most parents trust the school officials and teachers to select and develop new education programs to enhance the quality of their children's education. Therefore, awareness presentations for parents should incorporate a positive approach to sharing information. Questions should be solicited and answered completely, and parent input should be encouraged during informational sessions as well as during actual program implementation. Parent–teacher organizations, newsletters, and other vehicles can be used for continuing communication. If parents feel that their input makes a difference, they are more likely to actively give the program support.

## AN OUTLINE FOR AWARENESS PRESENTATIONS

An outline of topics to be covered in awareness presentations for various groups is presented. The outline is based on extensive experience in working with local schools and staffs of regional and state education agencies to implement adaptive education programs in a variety of schools.

The suggested outline for awareness presentations is presented in Table 3.1. It is generally useful to begin an awareness presentation with a brief discussion of identified improvement needs of the school that are shared by the audience groups. This discussion generally leads to an explanation of adaptive education as an approach that has the potential to meet school improvement needs. Within this context, discussion of the history of the theory and practice of adaptive education, compared with traditional classroom teaching, should follow.

The theory and practice of adaptive education are presented in greater detail

**Table 3.1.**  Suggested outline and recommended emphasis of awareness presentations

| Topic | Recommended emphasis | | |
| --- | --- | --- | --- |
| | Teachers | Parents | Administrators |
| I. Background of Adaptive Education | | | |
|   A. History of adaptive education and this program and connections to current programming needs of staff | Brief | Very brief | Brief |
|   B. Examples of implemented programs | Brief | Brief | Brief |
| II. Program Rationale and Design | | | |
|   A. Major goals | Detailed | Detailed | Detailed |
|   B. Components and features | Detailed | Brief | Brief |
|   C. Staff roles | Detailed | Very brief | Detailed |
| III. Program Outcomes | | | |
|   A. Student learning and achievement | Detailed | Brief | Detailed |
|   B. Attitudinal outcomes | | | |
|     1. Peer preferences and interactions | Detailed | Brief | Detailed |
|     2. Attitudes (students and teachers) | Detailed | Brief | Detailed |
|   C. Classroom processes | Detailed | Very brief | Detailed |
|   D. Resource needs and cost | Very brief | Very brief | Detailed |

for teachers and school administrators than for others. The overview discussion of specific models and program implementations demonstrates that, although adaptive education is innovative, it is neither novel nor untested, and it rests on a solid research and development base (Glaser, 1977; Walberg & Wang, 1987; Wang & Walberg, 1986). This information is useful for all audiences, especially administrators who must be convinced that the program is not experimental.

Background information about adaptive education is generally followed by an explanation of goals, which is valuable information for all audiences. General goals, such as matching instruction to individual students, and goals particular to the setting, such as integrating students with special needs in regular classrooms, should be included in the discussion. The next topic in the outline deals with components of the specific program, which should be described differently for different groups. For example, brief descriptions in nontechnical terms of major components are usually sufficient for parents. Teachers, however, usually want detailed descriptions of all critical program features. Discussion of staff roles should be detailed for teachers and administrators and less so for parents. If the program will involve integration of regular and special education services, the relationships between general education teachers and specialized personnel can be explained at this point.

Everyone involved is interested in program outcomes, especially effects on student learning and achievement, and affective outcomes are of interest to teachers and parents. Classroom outcomes are of particular interest to teachers, and cost data are of primary interest to administrators. The outline in Table 3.1. provides a framework for discussing most of the relevant information and can be adjusted as needed. School administrators and staff should use their judgment and knowledge of the specific program to be implemented and the local environment to decide the information to be presented.

Awareness presentations should be supported with audiovisual materials and handouts. These materials can sometimes be prepared by school administrators or staff. In addition, brochures, other printed materials, slides, or videotapes may be available from program developers. Appendix 3.A provides questions and answers about adaptive education. Appendix 3.B is a sample of brochure text about a particular adaptive education program, which was prepared for administrators, policymakers, and teachers. Appendix 3.C is a sample of an outline of topics included in awareness presentations. Appendix 3.D contains abstracts of publications on the ALEM, which highlight specific issues in adaptive education approaches.

## INFORMATION ABOUT ADAPTIVE INSTRUCTION: A BIBLIOGRAPHY FOR AWARENESS PRESENTATIONS

Program specialists must be knowledgeable about adaptive education in general as well as the specific adaptive education program they plan to implement in order to prepare and deliver awareness presentations. Much of this necessary background information is provided in Chapter 1. The reader who wishes more comprehensive knowledge in this area can begin with the suggested readings listed in Chapter 1, and the bibliography at the end of this chapter of articles, books, and papers is relevant to topics for awareness presentations on adaptive education programs.

## SUMMARY

Effective dissemination of information about an adaptive education program to be implemented is an essential step in building support for the program. Program planners begin by identifying the information needs of teachers and instructional staff, administrators, policymakers, and parents, and they then plan awareness presentations geared to a specific group. Topics covered in awareness presentations include the background of adaptive education, the design of the particular program being implemented, and expected program outcomes. The amount of detail in the presentation of specific topics varies according to the targeted audience.

## REFERENCES

Ellett, C.D., & Wang, M.C. (1987). Assessing administrative leadership components of program implementation in an innovative ECE program. *Journal of Research in Childhood Education, 2*(1), 30–47.

Fullan, M. (1985). Change processes and strategies at the local level. *Elementary School Journal, 85*(3), 391–422.

Glaser, R. (1977). *Adaptive education: Individual diversity and learning.* New York: Holt, Rinehart & Winston.

Lieberman, A., Saxl, E.R., & Miles, M.B. (1988). Teacher leadership: Ideology and practice. In A. Lieberman (Ed.), *Building a professional culture in schools* (pp. 148–166). New York: Teachers College Press.

Sergiovanni, T.J. (Ed.). (1990). Adding value to leadership gets extraordinary results. *Educational Leadership, 47*(8), 23–27.

Stein, M.K., & Wang, M.C. (1988). Teacher development and school improvement: The process of teacher change. *Teaching and Teacher Education, 4*(2), 171–187.

Vaughan, E.D., Wang, M.C., & Dytman, J.A. (1987). Implementing an innovative program: Staff development and teacher classroom performance. *Journal of Teacher Education, 38*(6), 40–47.

Walberg, H.J., & Keefe, J.W. (Eds.). (1988). *Rethinking reform: The principal's dilemma.* Reston, VA: National Association of Secondary Principals.

Walberg, H.J., & Wang, M.C. (1987). Effective educational practices and provisions for individual differences. In M.C. Wang, M.C. Reynolds, & H.J. Walberg (Eds.), *Handbook of special education: Research and practice: Vol. 1. Learner characteristics and adaptive education* (pp. 113–128). Oxford: Pergamon.

Wang, M.C., & Walberg, H.J. (1986). Classroom climate as mediator of educational inputs and outputs. In B.J. Fraser (Ed.), *The study of learning environments 1985* (pp. 47–58). Salem, OR: Assessment Research.

## SELECTED BIBLIOGRAPHY

### a. General Expositions of the Theory and Practice of Adaptive Instruction

Clark, C.R., & Bott, B.A. (1991). Issues in implementing the Adaptive Learning Model. *Teacher Education and Special Education, 14*(1), 57–65.

Corno, L., & Snow, R.E. (1986). Adapting teaching to individual differences among learners. In M.C. Wittrock (Ed.), *Handbook of research on teaching* (3rd ed.). New York: Macmillan.

Glaser, R. (1977). *Adaptive education: Individual diversity and learning.* New York: Holt, Rinehart & Winston.

Reynolds, M.C., & Wang, M.C. (1981). Restructuring "special" school programs: A position paper. *Policy Studies Review, 2*(1), 189–212.

Sobehart, H.C. (1991, April). *Variables that are important to a high degree of implementation.* Paper presented at the annual meeting of the American Educational Research Association, Chicago.

Vaughan, E.D., Wang, M.C., & Dytman, J.A. (1987). Implementing an innovative program: Staff development and teacher classroom performance. *Journal of Teacher Education, 38*(6), 40–47.

Wang, M.C. (1980). Adaptive instruction: Building on diversity. *Theory Into Practice, 19*(2), 122–127.

Wang, M.C., & Lindvall, C.M. (1984). Individual differences and school learning environments. In E.W. Gordon (Ed.), *Review of research in education* (Vol. 11, pp. 161–225). Washington, DC: American Educational Research Association.

Wang, M.C., Rubenstein, J.L., & Reynolds, M.C. (1985). Clearing the road to success for students with special needs. *Educational Leadership, 43*(1), 62–67.

### b. Descriptions of Selected Model Programs

Center on Evaluation, Development and Research. (1986). *Adapting instruction to individual needs: An eclectic approach.* Bloomington, IN: Phi Delta Kappa.

Peterson, J., Heistad, D., Peterson, D., & Reynolds, M. (1985). Montevideo Individualized Prescriptive Instructional Management System. *Exceptional Children, 52*(3) 239–243.

Wang, M.C., Hill, J.H., & Sabo, K. (1991). *Pennsylvania Quality Education Initiative: Analysis of model programs.* Philadelphia, PA: Temple University Center for Research in Human Development and Education.

Wang, M.C., & Walberg, H.J. (Eds.). (1985). *Adapting instruction to individual differences.* Berkeley, CA: McCutchan.

### c. Outcomes of Adaptive Instruction

Manning, J., & Quandt, I. (1991, April). *The database for institutionalization of school-based innovation: Findings and implications.* Paper presented at the annual meeting of the American Educational Research Association, Chicago.

Sobehart, H.C. (1990). Implementing ALEM: An encouraging first year. In J.C. Lindle (Ed.), *Pennsylvania educational leadership yearbook 1990–1991* (pp. 12–19). Lancaster: Pennsylvania Association for Supervision and Curriculum Development.

VanLeuvan, P. (1991, April). *The evaluation design and preliminary findings of the imple-*

*mentation and outcomes for the QEI.* Paper presented at the annual meeting of the American Educational Research Association, Chicago.

Wang, M.C., & Birch, J.W. (1984). Comparison of a full-time mainstreaming program and a resource room approach. *Exceptional Children, 51*(1), 33–40.

Wang, M.C., Peverly, S.T., & Randolph, R. (1984). An investigation of the implementation and effects of a full-time mainstreaming program. *Journal of Remedial and Special Education, 5*(6), 21–32.

Wang, M.C., & Reynolds, M.C. (1985). Avoiding the "catch 22" in special education reform. *Exceptional Children, 51*(6), 497–502.

Wang, M.C., Reynolds, M.C., & Schwartz, L.L. (1988). Adaptive instruction: An alternative educational approach for students with special needs. In J.L. Graden, J.E. Zins, & M.J. Curtis (Eds.), *Alternative educational delivery systems: Enhancing instructional options for all students* (pp. 199–220). Washington, DC: National Association of School Psychologists.

Wang, M.C., & Walberg, H.J. (1983). Adaptive instruction and classroom time. *American Educational Research Journal, 20*(4), 601–626.

Wang, M.C., & Walberg, H.J. (1986). Classroom climate as mediator of educational inputs and outputs. In B.J. Fraser (Ed.), *The study of learning environments 1985* (pp. 47–58). Salem, OR: Assessment Research.

Wang, M.C., & Zollers, N.J. (1990). Adaptive instruction: An alternative service delivery approach. *Remedial and Special Education, 11*(1), 7–21.

Waxman, H.C., Wang, M.C., Anderson, K.A., & Walberg, H.J. (1985). Synthesis of research on the effects of adaptive education. *Educational Leadership, 43*(1), 26–29.

*Appendix 3.A*

---

# Questions Often Asked
# About Adaptive Education

***What kinds of students can be served by adaptive education?***
The adaptive education approach has been found to be effective in serving students with a wide range of learning characteristics from varied ethnocultural and socioeconomic backgrounds. A variety of adaptive instruction programs have been implemented by schools as a core education program for regular, academically gifted, and students with mild to moderate disabilities. The latter include students with learning disabilities, social and emotional disturbances, mental retardation, and visual impairments.

***In what grades has adaptive education been found to be effective?***
The most common adaptive education implementation settings thus far have been in preschool through elementary grades. Evaluations of the program in these settings have provided substantial evidence of the efficacy of the adaptive education approach for these grade levels. For example, implementing the Adaptive Learning Environments Model (ALEM) has shown the feasibility and effectiveness of the program. The ALEM has been rated by the Joint Dissemination Review Panel of the Department of Education as an exemplary early childhood program. The ALEM has also been implemented in some middle and high school classes, and evaluations of its efficacy in these settings have been shown to be positive.

***Is adaptive education effective in all kinds of schools and locales?***
Yes, provided the necessary staff development and implementation support are made available for program initiatives and maintenance. For example, ALEM has been successfully implemented in nearly 130 districts or sites across 27 states in public, parochial, and private schools. It has served as an educational model for the National Follow Through Program since 1968. In 1979, the ALEM was implemented as a full-time mainstreaming program funded by the Office of Special Education Programs of the U.S. Department of Education. It has also been used in school improvement efforts such as Chapter 1 and migrant education programs. Research on ALEM implementation has demonstrated that the program is effective with a wide range of age groups (preschool through elementary and middle school), in rural and urban schools in varied locations, and in schools with students from diverse socioeconomic and ethnocultural backgrounds.

***Does the design of adaptive education include group instruction?***
Yes. A hallmark of adaptive education is the utilization of alternative strategies. During the course of a school day, a teacher in an adaptive education classroom may use a variety of instructional groupings in order to adequately meet the learning needs of the individual students. For example, he or she may provide instruction in individual tu-

torials and in small- and large-group sessions. When some students are working independently, the teacher is able to instruct other groups of students.

### Are there class-size restrictions for implementing adaptive education?

Data from implementation of adaptive instruction in a variety of schools have shown its effectiveness in classes of varied sizes. The provision of adaptive education geared to the individual learning needs of each student in a variety of class sizes is facilitated through several specific design features. One design feature is instructional teaming. Additional instructional personnel can be available during basic skills instruction periods by systematically assessing and redeploying the personnel resources of the school, reorganizing staff teaching patterns, and carefully considering staff schedules. Under the adaptive education design, regular teachers are teamed with specialized program teachers (i.e., Chapter 1, math or reading specialists, and special education teachers).

Another design feature that allows for variable class size is the classroom management system. Instructional time of teachers and active learning time for students are increased because the system provides management support to teachers and fosters student self-management of their own learning. Peer tutoring is another program feature designed to facilitate program implementation in varied class sizes. Students in the program are encouraged, and taught, to be resources for each other in carrying out learning tasks and engaging in group projects.

### How do teachers maintain order and curriculum structure with adaptive education?

One of the design features of adaptive education is an instructional management system that facilitates the delivery of instruction by the teacher and other program staff while promoting student self-responsibility for learning. Some features of this system are:

1. Arrangement of furniture and materials for ready access and use by teachers and students
2. A flexible instructional grouping system to enhance instructional efficiency
3. A technique, interactive teaching, which enables the teacher to monitor students working independently, respond to requests for assistance, and periodically check the class as a whole
4. Coordination of program staff for the most efficient and effective use of available time and skills
5. Use of student prescription sheets that facilitates the management of students' tasks
6. The student Self-Schedule System, a hierarchy of learned self-management skills that enable students to take increasing responsibility for their own learning

A high degree of implementation of these design features, especially the instructional management system, helps to ensure smooth functioning of classroom activities, increased student time on task, and greater student success in learning.

### Do teachers need special training to use an adaptive education program?

Yes, and teacher training and support are seen as integral parts of program implementation. A comprehensive pre-implementation training program is conducted for teachers and other instructional personnel planning to work in adaptive instruction classrooms. In addition, ongoing staff development is provided throughout the school year. The staff development program includes individualized training that is targeted to the specific functions and training needs of each staff member. A unique feature of the program is a data-based approach that assists teachers in monitoring their own implementation efforts and helps identify staff development needs of individual teachers.

### Does implementation of adaptive education require the purchase of specially designed curricula?

No, most commercially published curriculum materials in use can be easily modified for individualized planning and instruction. Basal series in math and reading, for example, usually include explicit and carefully sequenced objectives, lessons that are closely tied to these objectives, and varied activities for each objective or lesson. These are all elements that are basic to an individualized curriculum. Therefore, in almost all cases, a school's current curricular resources can be modified and adapted to support program implementation. The assessment of available resources and the provision of strategies for adapting them for adaptive education classrooms are important parts of the site-specific implementation plan created for each school.

### How does the cost of implementing adaptive education compare with the cost of other special and general education alternatives?

A careful analysis and consideration of a school district's budget is the first step in the needs assessment phase of designing an implementation plan. Although the cost varies with the district, preliminary examination of the cost of implementing and maintaining adaptive education indicates that the program is a cost-effective education alternative. For example, the cost of installing and maintaining the ALEM as a full-time mainstreaming program in a school district was compared with the cost of maintaining both the district's general education program for regular students and its separate special education (resource room) program for mainstreamed students with mild disabilities. This comparison indicated that despite a considerable start-up cost (including, for example, the cost of curriculum revision and staff development), the integration of students with mild disabilities in ALEM classes could result in an appreciable reduction in the district's combined total spending for special and general education, even during the first year of implementation.

Implementing adaptive education as a core general education program has also been shown to be cost-feasible, although districts interested in adopting the program need to allocate funds to cover the normal start-up cost of implementing an innovative program. Such a cost varies from district to district, depending on the district's curricular preparedness, training requirements, and ability to redeploy current resources. After the first year, program implementation generally can be maintained by the district's general education budget.

### Do parents have a role in the adaptive education program?

Definitely, because learning occurs in the home as well as in school. An active program of family involvement to increase communication and cooperation between school and home is essential for complete success. Initial awareness activities are conducted to inform parents of the program's design and goals. As the implementation of the program progresses, parents receive frequent formal and informal reports regarding their children's progress. Parents are encouraged to participate in their children's learning, provide home instruction, and supervise homework, in consultation with teachers. Parents may also volunteer to be trained as instructional aides in adaptive education classrooms.

*Appendix 3.B*

---

# The Adaptive Learning Environments Model: Information for Administrators, Policymakers, and Teachers

The Adaptive Learning Environments Model (ALEM) is an educational program developed and field-tested under the direction of Margaret C. Wang, director of the Temple University Center for Research in Human Development and Education. Components of the program have been implemented by elementary schools in over 130 districts and sites across 27 states, serving as the core program for general or compensatory education or as a mainstreaming program for exceptional students.

The overall goal of the ALEM is to create school learning environments in which each student can acquire basic academic skills while becoming increasingly more confident in his or her ability to learn and to cope with the social and physical demands of the classroom environment. This goal is accomplished through the combination of two distinct, yet complementary, learning components. The first is a highly structured prescriptive learning component, which uses built-in diagnostic procedures that have come to be associated with the teaching of basic academic skills. The second learning component utilizes more open-ended exploratory learning approaches that are considered conducive to promoting processes of inquiry as well as to social and personal development in areas such as planning and management of learning.

An underlying assumption in the program's design is that the teaching of basic skills need not be sacrificed to an emphasis on fostering students' involvement in planning, making curriculum choices, and evaluating their own learning progress. Both objectives can be achieved through systematic programming and close monitoring of program implementation. The expected result for students is that they will become more competent and confident in their abilities to successfully acquire skills in academic learning and in management of the classroom environment. At the same time, teachers are expected to be able to spend increased amounts of time providing instruction, rather than having to manage students.

As a program that facilitates individualization of instruction, the ALEM is uniquely suited to accommodate a wide range of student characteristics and needs in regular classroom settings. Several features of the ALEM distinguish it as a program particlarly suited for serving special needs students in regular classes. These features include a comprehensive instructional delivery system that makes instructional provisions for meeting the needs of individual students; a built-in implementation support system that includes active involvement of school administrators, instructional support personnel, health professionals, and families; and use of a full-time rather than a shared-time approach to providing for the special education needs of regular and exceptional students.

In school districts where components of the ALEM have been adopted, research staff document and evaluate the degree of program implementation, student achievement in basic skills, classroom process effects (e.g., students' time on task and the settings and manner in which instruction and learning occur), attitudinal and social outcomes (e.g., students' sense of their own cognitive, social, and physical competence), staff development and administrative and organizational support requirements, and cost-effectiveness. The descriptions and data obtained from such evaluation research suggest the following scenario of a typical ALEM classroom in an elementary school setting.

Students are working in every area of the room, either in small groups or individually, at any given time. Teachers circulate among the students providing instruction and feedback to individuals and small groups as needed. Academic skills are taught directly, based on diagnostic test results, and every student is expected to make steady progress through the curriculum. Learning tasks are broken down into incremental steps, thereby providing frequent opportunities for evaluation. Each student's successes are recognized and acknowledged, momentary difficulties are pinpointed, and alternative instruction is provided before difficulties become learning problems. Under such conditions, individual differences are viewed by teachers and students alike as the norm rather than the exception. Student responsibility is emphasized. Students are taught to plan and monitor their own learning. They are expected to take responsibility for planning, managing, and completing all their teacher-prescribed and self-selected learning tasks within the time limits agreed on with the teacher.

Students in ALEM classrooms tend to exhibit comparatively higher rates of time on task than students in studies of conventional classrooms, and teachers spend more time on instruction than on managing students. Interactions among students, for the most part, are for sharing ideas and working together. The subdued, yet steady, sound of productive interaction between teachers and students and among students replaces the passive learning mode typically found in conventional classrooms. Distracted behavior by individual students is minimal and does not seem to interfere with the ongoing instructional-learning process.

Results from research on the impact of the ALEM on student achievement in basic skills and on student social behavior and attitudes have shown consistently positive trends. For example, analyses of standardized test results from school districts that participated in the National Follow Through Program, a nationwide compensatory education program sponsored by the Department of Education, show that ALEM students not only scored above estimated population norms for students from low-income families, but they also tended to score above the national norms established by the standardized tests. In addition, positive student achievement and attitudinal outcomes have been found in ALEM general education classrooms where students with disabilities or gifted students are integrated on a full-time basis. Results include reduced perceptions of differences among students, as manifested by students' self-ratings of their cognitive and social competence and measures of peer acceptance, as well as significantly increased decertification rates of mainstreamed students with disabilities.

From a fiscal perspective, the ALEM has been shown to be generally cost-effective. Despite start-up costs that might be greater than districts' ordinary basic education budgets, total installation and maintenance costs when averaged across 3 years have been shown to be reduced from the level of spending prior to implementation of the ALEM. At sites where the ALEM is used as a mainstreaming program for serving exceptional and nonexceptional students in the same regular classrooms, cost savings can be noted even in the first year, if the costs of maintaining separate regular and special education programs are considered.

Two major findings related to the feasibility and efficacy of the ALEM in accommodating diverse student learning needs and characteristics should be noted. First, there appears to be a sharp contrast with prevalent assessments in the literature regarding teacher expertise and student outcomes associated with instructional programs that aim to provide for student differences. Many researchers and practitioners believe that it is extremely difficult to reproduce what they view as the rare breed of teachers who can successfully implement such programs. Critics tend to attribute evidence of the effectiveness of adaptive education to unusual individual teachers and students. Data on the implementation and effects of the ALEM suggest, however, that with the support of a systematic and ongoing staff development program, a large percentage of public school teachers can effectively establish and maintain learning environments that are adaptive to the diverse needs of individual students.

The second major finding on the impact of the ALEM is that those desirable classroom processes identified in the research on teaching (e.g., high rates of time on task, increased instructional interactions with teachers) can indeed be obtained. Attainment of these outcomes appears to be made possible through the combination of a relatively structured curriculum and teacher-directed experiences; open-ended, student-initiated, and cooperative learning experiences; and large amounts of efficient, individually adapted instruction.

# An Outline of Topics Included in Awareness Presentations

I.  Background and Design of the ALEM
    A.  Goals
        1.  Creation of learning environments in which students systematically acquire basic academic skills
        2.  Development of students' ability to learn and to cope with the social and physical surroundings of the classroom while taking on increasing responsibility for their own learning and the learning environment
    B.  Design features
        1.  A comprehensive educational program for delivering "special" education services to all students through adaptive education
        2.  A highly structured prescriptive approach to instruction in basic skills, combined with exploratory activities for extension, reinforcement, enrichment, and student choice
        3.  Educational alternatives designed to generate inquiry, independence, and social cooperation
        4.  A management system that provides increased time for effective instruction
    C.  History of the ALEM
        1.  Product of over a decade of research conducted by Margaret C. Wang and her associates
        2.  Initial emphasis on individualized curriculum
        3.  Evolution of an innovative educational system implemented in over 130 school districts across 27 states
    D.  Major program components
        1.  Prescriptive learning component
            a.  Strong emphasis on basic skills (e.g., reading, math)
            b.  Use of diagnostic–prescriptive process to develop individual education plans for all students
            c.  Provision of a wide variety of learning activities for accommodating individual student learning needs
        2.  Exploratory learning component
            a.  The design of exploratory learning using the learning center strategy
            b.  Emphasis on activities that require students to learn alternative methods of communication, plan work appropriately, extend and apply basic skills, and express themselves creatively
            c.  Provision of opportunities for students to select certain learning activities

3. Instructional-Learning Management System: Self-Schedule System
   a. Purpose: Development of student self-management skills and facilitation of teacher management of the adaptive learning environment
   b. High level of teacher control of prescriptive learning tasks in basic skills
   c. Emphasis on student choice of sequence of learning tasks, types of exploratory activities, and workplace
   d. A highly structured system that promotes skills in taking on increasing self-responsibility
4. Data-Based Staff Development Program
   a. A system for monitoring the degree of implementation of the ALEM through classroom observations and other data
   b. Staff development activities based on implementation data and adaptive to individual staff needs
   c. Incorporation of three training levels:
      i. Basic training: An overview of the ALEM
      ii. Individualized training: Specific skills needed to implement the ALEM
      iii. Inservice training: Designed to maintain a high degree of program implementation

II. Recent Implementations of the ALEM
   A. College-School Collaborative Model for Personnel Preparation Project (1983–1986)
      1. Purpose: Explication and field testing of a college and school collaborative approach to preservice and inservice training
      2. Provision of an alternative training approach for systematic development of the professional knowledge and competencies required to implement innovative educational programs and practices
      3. Information sources (see Selected Bibliography): Clark and Bott (1991).
   B. Pilot Demonstration Project of Full-Time Mainstreaming of Special Education Students (1979–1982)
      1. A 3-year project funded by the Bureau for the Education of the Handicapped, U.S. Department of Education, and implemented in 4 districts in the Pittsburgh, Pennsylvania area
      2. Use of the ALEM for full-time mainstreaming of students with mild disabilities and gifted students in regular classes
      3. Positive classroom process and outcomes suggested by evaluation results
      4. Information sources (see Selected Bibliography): Wang and Birch (1984)
   C. Mainstreaming Project, New York City Schools (1982–1983)
      1. A project sponsored by the Division of Special Education, New York City Board of Education
      2. Use of the ALEM as a full-time mainstreaming program for students with mild disabilities in 28 regular classrooms in 5 schools
      3. Evidence of highly positive effects on classroom processes, achievement, and other outcomes
      4. Information sources (see Selected Bibliography): Wang, Peverly, and Randolph (1984); Wang and Reynolds (1985); Wang, Rubenstein, and Reynolds (1985)
   D. Project Follow Through (1968–)
      1. A compensatory education program for high-risk students from economically disadvantaged backgrounds
      2. Involvement of a wide variety of geographic and ethnocultural settings
      3. Information sources (see Selected Bibliography): Vaughan, Wang, and Dytman (1987); Wang and Birch (1984); Wang and Walberg (1983)
   E. Unified Instruction Project (1982–)
      1. Selected sites where the program is being implemented: Montevideo Public Schools, Montevideo, MN; New Orleans Parish, New Orleans, LA; Philadelphia School District, Philadelphia, PA

      2. Use of the ALEM to provide instruction in regular classes for students previously served by a variety of special and compensatory, categorical programs (e.g., Chapter 1, bilingual education, special education); emphasis on the coordination of general and special education services and personnel

      3. Information sources (see Selected Bibliography): Peterson, Heistad, Peterson, and Reynolds (1985); Sobehart (1990); Wang and Zollers (1990)

  F. Quality Education Initiative (1989–1992)

      1. Systematic documentation of the implementation and outcomes of 13 model programs in 75 Pennsylvania school sites

      2. Use of the ALEM at 12 school sites

      3. Information sources (see Selected Bibliography): Manning and Quandt (1991); Sobehart (1991); VanLeuvan (1991); Wang, Hill, and Sabo (1991)

III. Highlights of Findings on Program Implementation and Effects

  A. Improved implementation from fall to spring

  B. Increased student-initiated instructional interactions, constructive student–student interactions, and time on task

  C. Student achievement gains at least equal to, and sometimes exceeding, those in traditional programs

  D. Steady progress through the curriculum by general and special education students

  E. Positive attitudes toward school and taking responsibility in the classroom

  F. Positive teacher and parent attitudes toward the program and mainstreaming

*Appendix 3.D*

# Abstracts of Publications on the Adaptive Learning Environments Model

## THEORY AND PRACTICE OF ADAPTIVE INSTRUCTION

### The Rationale and Design of an Adaptive Beginning School Learning Environment: Curriculum Objectives

Margaret C. Wang
and Alexander W. Siegel

The focus of this article is on describing the rationale, goal, design, and the eight curriculum areas of the Adaptive Beginning School Learning Environment (ABLE) program. Developed and implemented in the early 1970s, the ABLE was designed to (a) be adaptive to the learning needs of the individual preschool child, and (b) teach learning-to-learn skills that are basic to effective functioning in school and extra-school environments. The paper includes discussions of the historical backgrounds and theoretical approaches of extant preschool programs as well as plans for future work. Although the ABLE is not a specific component in the current design of the ALEM, the principles and preschool instructional objectives of the earlier program are applicable today.

[LRDC Publication Series, 1975/1. Pittsburgh, PA: University of Pittsburgh, Learning Research and Development Center.]

### Adaptive Instruction: Building on Diversity

Margaret C. Wang

The rationale and the essential components for implementation of adaptive instruction are discussed. The components include diagnosis and monitoring of student learning progress, instruction in teaching self-management skills, and organizational supports such as multi-age grouping and instructional teaming (team teaching). The ALEM is described as a comprehensive program that combines aspects of prescriptive instruction that appear to be effective in ensuring basic skills mastery with aspects of informal education that are useful in generating attitudes and processes of inquiry, independence, and social cooperation.

[Theory Into Practice (1980), 19(2), 122-127.]

## Restructuring "Special" School Programs: A Position Paper

Maynard C. Reynolds
and Margaret C. Wang

The authors contend that changes in educational programming and policy provide an important opportunity to solve many long-standing schooling problems. The threefold purpose of the article is to (a) discuss the current context for school change, and, in particular, the need for educational provisions that serve students with special needs in regular classes; (b) describe the programmatic and policy requirements for restructuring current special and compensatory education programs; and (c) present an alternative approach for creating improved school learning environments for all students.

[Policy Studies Review (1983), 2(1), 189-212.]

## Provision of Classroom Instruction that is Adaptive to Student Differences

Margaret C. Wang

This module, designed for teacher educators, describes the theoretical underpinnings of adaptive instruction and summarizes research evidence related to its implementation and effects. The module contains three major sections. Section I, "Objectives, Needs Assessment, and Self-Assessment," is aimed at helping users to systematically assess their own professional development needs and the needs of their teacher-education programs. Section II, "Provision of Adaptive Instruction," consists of a review of relevant theory, research, and practice; a description of a conceptual model of program design, implementation, and evaluation; information on the design of appropriate personnel preparation programs; and a discussion of implications for future developments in personnel preparation. Finally, Section III, "Additional Readings on Adaptive Instruction," provides further reference materials on the topic.

[Module in the series entitled A common body of practice for teachers: The challenge of PL 94-142 to teacher education (1983). Washington, DC: American Association of Colleges for Teacher Education.]

## Individual Differences and School Learning Environments

Margaret C. Wang
and C. Mauritz Lindvall

This chapter provides a major review of the state of the art of research and practice related to differences in student learning. Topics include student learning characteristics (cognitive style, level of achievement, self-perception, and temperament); learning behavior (task involvement, energy deployment, autonomy, time-on-task, resource utilization, and decision making); learner achievement (adjustment and competence); and the implementation and evaluation of adaptive instruction (teachers' instructional expertise and substantive and utilitarian research). Implications are drawn for the theory and practice of adaptive instruction, and two major topic areas -- the role of the learner in the adaptive process, and instructional design research related to provision of adaptive instruction in school settings -- are prescribed and described as the subjects of future research.

[Chapter in E. W. Gordon (Ed.). (1984). Review of research in education (Vol. 11). Washington, DC: American Educational Research Association.]

## Learner Controlled Instruction

Margaret C. Wang

This short review article summarizes theory and research on the development of students' sense of control over their own learning and the effects on psychological and academic functioning. Programs designed with learner controlled features are described as being based on the premise that students who believe they can influence and control their learning and school environments tend to demonstrate more positive learning processes and outcomes than students who depend on teachers, other adults, or peers. Designs of educational programs and practices aimed at fostering students' sense of personal control are discussed, and implications are drawn for instructional design and school improvement.

[Chapter in T. Husen & N. Postlethwaite (Eds.). (1985). International encyclopedia of education: Research and studies. Oxford, England: Pergamon.]

## Avoiding the "Catch 22" in Special Education Reform

Margaret C. Wang
and Maynard C. Reynolds

The authors of this paper discuss a critical barrier to effective implementation of the "least restrictive environment" mandate of Public Law 94-142. A brief review of the major recommendations of the National Academy of Sciences (NAS) Panel on Selection and Placement of Students in Programs for the Mentally Retarded is followed by a discussion of the implications for actualizing the recommendations in the context of current policy and funding practice in special education. The conditions and decisions surrounding the institution and discontinuation of the ALEM as a mainstreaming program for mildly handicapped students are described to illustrate some of the major policy and implementation issues surrounding reform in this area. The authors maintain that solving the problems in special education requires revision of the classification system used to define special education and handicapped students, development of a more powerful mainstreaming system, and revision of current funding policies to permit and encourage change in the directions proposed by the NAS Panel.

[Exceptional Children (1985), 51(6), 497-502.]

## Adapting Instruction to Individual Differences

Margaret C. Wang
and Herbert J. Walberg (Eds.)

This book aims to provide a major review of the theory and practice of adaptive instruction from a variety of perspectives. It examines the design and implementation of several adaptive instruction approaches, theoretical and practical underpinnings, and implications for improving instruction and learning for increasingly diverse student populations. The 15 chapters, which were written by leading researchers and developers of adaptive instruction programs, are organized in three sections. The first section focuses on the theory and research associated with efforts to provide instruction that accommodates the learn-ing needs of individual students. The second section consists of chapters that describe the design, development, implementation, and evaluation of selected adaptive instruction programs and practices. The final section of the book includes retrospective highlights, as well as implications for future research and development, on topics such as views of learner differences and definitions of learning environments.

[Berkeley, CA: McCutchan (1985).]

## "Catch 22" and Disabling Help: A Reply to Alan Gartner

Margaret C. Wang
and Maynard C. Reynolds

This article responds to a critique of the 1985 Exceptional Children article by Wang and Reynolds entitled "Avoiding the 'Catch 22' in Special Education Reform." The authors reiterate their argument that broad-based reforms are required on two parallel fronts: the funding and delivery of educational services, and the adoption of demonstrably effective instructional approaches to the academic and social integration of students with special needs. They call for urban school systems to lead the way as testing grounds for innovative practices, and they note that several alternative instructional approaches have been cited as holding great promise for enhancing the quality of free public education services for general and special education students alike.

[Exceptional Children (1986), 53(1), 77-79.]

## Individual Differences and Effective Schooling

Margaret C. Wang

This article summarizes the knowledge base relevant to researchers and practitioners in creating school environments that effectively adapt to individual learning needs. Recent theoretical and substantive developments are traced in terms of their impact on how individual differences in learning are viewed, what types of information are examined and described, and how this information is used for instructional decision making. The discussion addresses implications of these developments in two areas: broadening the research base on individual differences and processes of learning and instruction in classroom settings; and improving schooling practice. The role of the school psychologist is highlighted, especially in identifying the learning needs of individual students, developing instructional alternatives for improving students' motivation and learning of basic skills, and working effectively with instructional and administrative staff as well as parents.

[Professional School Psychology (1987), 2(1), 53-66.]

### Adaptive Instruction: An Alternative Educational Approach for Students with Special Needs

Margaret C. Wang,
Maynard C. Reynolds, and Lisa Schwartz

This chapter examines an alternative approach to serving students with special needs in a broadly restructured general education system. The core of this approach is using adaptive instruction to achieve what has long been a goal of special education programs: identifying and accommodating individual learning characteristics and needs. In this discussion, the authors trace major developments that have set the stage for renegotiation and collaboration between special and general education. Then the rationale and concept of adaptive instruction as a key to effective schooling for both regular and special education students are presented. The design features and demonstrated effectiveness of a particular adaptive instruction program are summarized next. Finally, the implications of educational restructuring based on adaptive instruction in general education settings are noted, with special emphasis on the changing roles of school personnel.

[Chapter in J.L. Graden, J.E. Zins, & M.J. Curtis (Eds.). (1988). Alternative educational delivery systems: Enhancing instructional options for all students. Washington, DC: National Association of School Psychologists.]

### Adaptive Instruction: An Alternative for Accommodating Student Diversity through the Curriculum

Margaret C. Wang

The author discusses the research base and the design characteristics of adaptive instruction and its implications for school-based implementation as an alternative educational approach for accommodating diverse student learning needs. The discussion is based on the premise that certain variables related to student learning are alterable. The author briefly describes the adaptive instruction approach as involving two major tasks: the identification of student learning characteristics that are relevant for instructional planning, and the adaptation of the curriculum to the unique characteristics of individual students. Then she discusses the expanding research base on instructionally relevant learner characteristics and outlines some specific strategies for making appropriate curriculum adaptations. The chapter concludes with the implications of adaptive instruction for integrating special education students and their related service supports in regular education settings.

[Chapter in D.K. Lipsky & A. Gartner (Eds.). 1989). Beyond separate education: Quality education for all. Baltimore, MD: Paul H. Brookes.]

### Accommodating Student Diversity through Adaptive Instruction

Margaret C. Wang

This chapter discusses the rationale and design of the adaptive instruction approach, including a review of relevant research on its effectiveness in accommodating student diversity. Six different instructional models are described: Adaptive Learning Environments Model, Bank Street Model, Behavior Analysis Model, Individually Guided Education, Mastery Learning, and Team-Assisted Individualization. Well implemented programs that produce positive student outcomes and classroom processes depend on effective classroom management systems, a continuum of instructional and related services, and a supportive school-based delivery system. The latter includes awareness and implementation planning, needs assessment, curriculum development, effective management of resources and instruction, flexible organizational patterns, data-based staff development, and program evaluation.

[Chapter in S. Stainback, W.Stainback, & M. Forest (Eds.). (1989). Educating all students in the mainstream of regular education. Baltimore, MD: Paul H. Brookes.]

### Adaptive Instruction: An Alternative Service Delivery Approach

Margaret C. Wang and Nancy J. Zollers

This article provides a summary of the theoretical and research bases for the design and effects of programs using the adaptive instruction approach to maximize student learning. The authors discuss the salient features, implementation requirements, and effects of using a particular program, the ALEM, as an alternative service delivery approach for serving students with special needs in regular classrooms. Research on the outcomes and feasibility of school-based implementation of the ALEM suggests that a high degree of program implementation can be achieved in a variety of school settings when accompanied by systematic staff development and organizational support. Furthermore, when regular classroom teachers and specialized professionals work collaboratively to provide coordinated and inclusive instructional support in an integrated education system, all students can benefit.

[Remedial and Special Education (1990), 11(1), 7-21.]

# SUPPORTING RESEARCH RELATED TO THE DESIGN, IMPLEMENTATION, AND EFFICACY OF THE ALEM

### The Rationale and Design of the Self-Schedule System

Margaret C. Wang

The design of the Self-Schedule System, the instructional-learning management component of the ALEM, is described. The focus of the discussion is on the major behavioral objectives of the Self-Schedule System. These include development of students' ability to manage and control learning resources and the learning environment, to make choices and decisions with respect to the nature of the learning activities, and to take increasing responsibility for their own learning.

[LRDC Publication Series, 1974/5. Pittsburgh, PA: University of Pittsburgh, Learning Research and Development Center.]

### The Self-Schedule System for Instructional-Learning Management in Adaptive School Learning Environments

Margaret C. Wang (Ed.)

This monograph documents a series of research studies carried out during the develop-

mental stages of the Self-Schedule System. It includes (a) a brief description of the conceptual design of the Self-Schedule System; (b) documentation of the implementation process for field-testing the Self-Schedule System in school settings; (c) research findings on the effects of the Self-Schedule System on student and teacher classroom behaviors and student learning outcomes; and (d) an evaluation of the Self-Schedule System from the teacher's perspective.

[LRDC Publication Series, 1976/9. Pittsburgh, PA: University of Pittsburgh, Learning Research and Development Center.]

### An Investigation of Children's Concept of Self-Responsibility for Their School Learning

Margaret C. Wang
and Billie Stiles

This article reports findings from an investigation of the effects of the Self-Schedule System on development of young children's self responsibility for their school learning. Data collected for second graders from two schools consisted of perceptions of self-responsibility as assessed by a student interview and the Intellectual Achievement Responsibility Questionnaire, and weekly task completion rates that assessed the learning performance of each student. The results of the study indicate that the Self-Schedule System had significant positive effects on the subjects' perceptions of self-responsibility for their school learning as well as their rates of task completion.

[American Educational Research Journal (1976), 13(3), 159-179.]

## Individualized Early Learning Program

Margaret C. Wang, Gaea Leinhardt, and M. Elizabeth Boston

This paper provides a description of the early program development work and field research that help to form the foundation of the ALEM. The paper is organized into four major sections: an overview of the Individualized Early Learning Program (IELP), the earlier, less comprehensive version of the ALEM; the process of program development; field research activities; and insights gained while developing and studying the program. The field research focused on documentation of the degree of program implementation and the program's impact on student learning progress. The results reported in the paper support the program's feasibility and its positive effects on student achievement. The authors close the paper with a discussion of the implications of their IELP-related work for the development, design, and evaluation of innovative instructional programs in general.

[LRDC Publication Series, 1980/2. Pittsburgh, PA: University of Pittsburgh, Learning Research and Development Center.]

## Mainstreaming Exceptional Children: Some Instructional Design Considerations

Margaret C. Wang

Following a description of the rationale and design of the ALEM, data from a study in which the program was implemented in a multi-age primary classroom with mainstreamed low and high achievers are summarized. The results show that low-achieving students, as well as other students in the study's ALEM classroom, acquired the

ability to manage and complete assigned work. Their success is attributed to systematic instruction in self-management skills coupled with the ALEM's individualized diagnostic-prescriptive approach to teaching basic skills. The program's potential for providing quality education for both general and special education students is discussed.

[Elementary School Journal (1981), 81(4), 195-221.]

## Development and Consequences of Students' Sense of Personal Control

Margaret C. Wang

The twofold purpose of this chapter is to (a) examine the relationship between students' sense of personal control and their learning processes and outcomes, and (b) discuss the instructional design implications of the relationship for school programs aimed at maximizing student learning. A review of theories and research dealing with the consequences of students' perceptions of personal control, and the effects of educational practices designed to foster such perceptions, is followed by explication of a conceptual model for understanding the interrelationships among sense of control, teacher expectancy, classroom behavior, and student learning. Critical design characteristics of learning environments conducive to the development of a sense of personal control are discussed, and the ALEM is described as an instructional system incorporating these design features. Findings from evaluation of the efficacy of the ALEM are discussed to support the hypothesis that students' sense of personal control is important to school learning.

[Chapter in J. M. Levine & M. C. Wang (Eds.). (1983). Teacher and student perceptions: Implications for learning. Hillsdale, NJ: Erlbaum.]

## Analysis of the Design, Implementation, and Effects of a Data-Based Staff Development Program

Margaret C. Wang and Patricia Gennari

The rationale, design, and efficacy of the Data-Based Staff Development Program are discussed. The program is designed to improve the knowledge and skills of school staff for providing learning experiences that are adaptive to student differences. Results from analysis of data from 138 classrooms of 10 school districts are summarized. The three major findings discussed in the article are that (a) systematically collected and analyzed data on the degree of classroom implementation of the ALEM are useful in identifying staff development needs; (b) staff development activities designed on the basis of identified needs can be effective in improving the degree of implementation of specific program dimensions; and (c) teachers tend to improve their program implementation in areas where specific staff development work is conducted.

[Teacher Education and Special Education (1983), 6(4), 211-226.]

## Adaptive Instruction and Classroom Time

Margaret C. Wang
and Herbert J. Walberg

The study described in this article was designed to assess the implementability of the ALEM and determine the relation of the degree of implementation with efficient use of student time and other classroom processes. Results from the study show that 96% of the teachers (N= 156) were able to establish and maintain average to high degrees of program implementation, and that the degree of implementation was positively associated with students' use of learning time and with constructive classroom behaviors and processes.

[American Educational Research Journal (1983), 20(4), 601-626.]

## Time Use and the Provision of Adaptive Instruction

Margaret C. Wang

Implications of the theory and practice of adaptive instruction for time use by teachers and students are discussed. Findings from a study of program implementation, classroom processes, allocation and use of school time, and student achievement in 138 ALEM classes across 10 schools suggest that higher degrees of implementation are associated with more effective allocation and use of instructional-learning time

by both teachers and students. Of particular interest are the results showing that, in classrooms where the ALEM was implemented as a mainstreaming program for special needs students, teachers spent approximately equal amounts of time working with general and special education students.

[Chapter in L.W. Anderson (Ed.) (1984). Time and school learning. London: Croom-Helm, Ltd.]

## Effective Special Education in Regular Classes

Margaret C. Wang
and Jack W. Birch

The first of two articles on the ALEM published in Exceptional Children in 1984 summarizes major findings on the program's implementation and effects in 156 kindergarten through third-grade classrooms. Student populations in the classrooms included children from economically disadvantaged backgrounds, mildly to moderately handicapped students, and gifted students. Discussion in the article centers on the extent to which the ALEM could be implemented effectively across school sites with varying needs and contextual characteristics, as well as the relation among the degree of program implementation, classroom processes, and student achievement in reading and mathematics. Results suggest the overall implementability of the program and a relationship among favorable classroom processes, positive academic outcomes, and high degrees of program implementation.

[Exceptional Children (1984), 50(5), 391-398.]

## Comparison of a Full-Time Mainstreaming Program and a Resource Room Approach

Margaret C. Wang
and Jack W. Birch

This second Exceptional Children article on the efficacy of the ALEM focuses on a comparison of the program's effects as a full-time mainstreaming approach with the academic and social effects of a resource room approach. Data for the study reported in the article were collected on

179 general and special education students in ALEM classes and 71 students in non-ALEM classes. In all categories of outcomes, more positive effects were found for the ALEM students, including the mainstreamed handicapped students. Favorable outcomes included greater frequencies of on-task behavior and work in independent settings, as well as highly positive student perceptions of their own cognitive competence, social competence, and general self-esteem. Information on program cost is also reported to show the ALEM's cost-effectiveness over time.

[Exceptional Children (1984), 51(1), 33-40.]

## The Utility of Degree of Implementation Measures in Program Implementation and Evaluation Research

Margaret C. Wang,
Mehran Nojan, Charles D. Strom,
and Herbert J. Walberg

The dual focus of the study described in this article was on providing evidence to suggest both the utility of program implementation measures and the relationships among degree of implementation, classroom processes, and student achievement. The specific implementation measure used in the study was the Implementation Assessment Battery for Adaptive Instruction. Findings from 138 classes across 10 school districts indicate that a high degree of implementation of the ALEM was attained at all sites, and positive classroom processes and student achievement resulted. The authors recommend directions for future research on the measurement of program implementation as a means for program improvement and refinement.

[Curriculum Inquiry (1984), 14(3), 249-286.]

## An Investigation of the Implementation and Effects of a Full-Time Mainstreaming Program

Margaret C. Wang,
Stephen T. Peverly, and Robert Randolph

This paper reports a study in which the ALEM was implemented as a full-time mainstreaming program in 26 classrooms of five public schools of a large urban school district. Results of the study provide evidence of the feasibility and efficacy of the ALEM as a full-time mainstreaming approach for moderately handicapped students. Policy implications for the placement of special education students also are discussed.

[Remedial and Special Education (1984), 5(6), 21-32.]

## An Analysis of Program Design Implications for Teacher and Student Use of School Time

Margaret C. Wang

This chapter describes a program of research aimed at identifying and analyzing ways in which school time was allocated and used by ALEM teachers and students to maximize learning for individual students. A discussion of results from analyses of instructional processes and student activity in terms of time-based variables is followed by an exploration of the relationship between these variables and student outcomes. Findings indicate that the ALEM resulted in high rates of student time-on-task, teacher-student interactions, and time spent on individual tasks. The author discusses areas for future research on learning, classroom management, and time use.

[Chapter in C. Fisher and D. Berliner (Eds.). (1985). Perspectives on instructional time. New York: Longman.]

## The Adaptive Learning Environments Model: Design, Implementation, and Effects

Margaret C. Wang, Patricia Gennari,
and Hersholt C. Waxman

This chapter provides an overview of the program design and supporting research associated with the development, school implementation, and evaluation of the ALEM, and discusses implications of the research results for improving the provision of adaptive instruction in regular school settings. Findings from studies conducted at 11 ALEM sites over three years are summarized to provide evidence of the program's implementability, as well as the relationship among the degree of implementation, positive classroom processes, and student outcomes. The authors suggest areas for further research.

[Chapter in M.C. Wang & H.J. Walberg (Eds.). (1985). Adapting instruction to individual differences. Berkeley, CA: McCutchan.]

## Staff Development: A Key Ingredient of Successful Mainstreaming

Margaret C. Wang, Eva D. Vaughan, and Joan A. Dytman

The efficacy of a systematic data-based staff development approach is suggested by this article's description of findings from a study of the ALEM's implementation as a full-time mainstreaming program during 1982-83 in three districts of a large urban school system (five schools and 26 classrooms). The effectiveness of the mainstreaming program and the staff development approach is reflected in findings of high degrees of program implementation in the participating classrooms, positive academic and attitudinal outcomes for special education and general education students alike, and positive teacher attitudes. The authors suggest that it is time to shift attention from demonstrating the need for, and positive outcomes of, effective staff development programs to the study of how to implement such programs in a variety of school settings.

[Teaching Exceptional Children (1985), 17(2), 112-121.]

## Adaptive Education and Student Outcomes: A Quantitative Synthesis

Hersholt C. Waxman, Margaret C. Wang, Kenneth A. Anderson, and Herbert J. Walberg

This article presents results from a quantitative synthesis of studies comparing the effects of conventional (control) and adaptive education on students' cognitive, affective, and behavioral outcomes. A meta-analysis of 38 experimental and quasi-experimental published and unpublished studies yielded a total of 309 effect sizes. The mean weighted effect size was .45, suggesting that the average student in adaptive programs scored at the 67th percentile of the control-group distributions. The mean effect size appeared constant across grades, socioeconomic levels, races, private and public schools, and community types; the effect size also did not differ significantly across categories of adaptiveness, student outcomes, social contexts, and methodological rigor of the studies. The authors conclude that tailoring instruction to the learning characteristics and needs of individual students is an effective educational alternative for achieving intended social and academic outcomes.

[Journal of Educational Research (1985), 78(4), 228-236.]

## Classroom Climate as Mediator of Educational Inputs and Outputs

Margaret C. Wang and Herbert J. Walberg

This chapter reports findings from a study that examined the sensitivity of classroom climate measures to instructional programs and classroom processes and assessed the predictability of educational outcomes. The study was part of a broader research project designed to characterize the features and outcomes of exemplary adaptive instruction programs, and to increase understanding of how their features can be integrated into existing programs to promote more effective learning outcomes. The study sample was comprised of 65 elementary-grade classrooms in 13 schools. Eight model programs, including the ALEM, were represented. The study found differences in classroom climate measures among the model programs. There are significant relationships between students' subjective perceptions of social climate and objectively observed classroom characteristics. Measures of climate serve as predictors of important classroom outcomes, especially the assumption of self-responsibility among students.

[Chapter in B.J. Fraser (Ed.). (1986). The study of learning environments 1985. Salem, OR: Assessment Research.]

## Implementing an Innovative
## Program: Staff Development and
## Teacher Classroom Performance

Eva D. Vaughan, Margaret C. Wang,
and Joan A. Dytman

The study reported in this article examined the implementation of the ALEM by 42 teachers in four school districts during three years after the establishment of a systematic staff development program. Implementation of adaptive and program-specific features of the ALEM improved over the first two years, supporting the hypothesis that increased training support will lead to increased levels of implementation. The study also showed seasonal variations in implementation of program features, differences in rates of change and levels of implementation according to specific program features, and site variations in level and patterns of implementation. Implications for inservice and preservice teacher education are discussed.

[Journal of Teacher Education (1987), 38(6), 40-47.]

## Integrating Special Needs
## Students in Regular Classes:
## Programming, Implementation,
## and Policy Issues

Margaret C. Wang, Stephen T. Peverly,
and Rita Catalano

This chapter illustrates the possibility of overcoming the inadequacies of many present educational delivery systems, and realizing the vision of the "least restrictive environment" principle. It focuses on selected research on the ALEM as a comprehensive system of adaptive instruction and on implementation support mechanisms. In addition to a descriptin of the major design features of the program, the chapter summarizes findings from three studies that were conducted as part of the ongoing research on the implementation and effectiveness of the ALEM. The authors conclude with policy, administrative, and programming steps that should be taken to achieve effective integration and productive collaboration between general and special education.

[Chapter in J. Gottlieb and B.W. Gottlieb (Eds.). (1987). Advances in special education (Vol. 6). Greenwich, CT: JAI Press.]

## Teacher Development
## and School Improvement:
## The Process of Teacher Change

Mary Kay Stein and Margaret C. Wang

This article reports the results of a study that investigated teachers' motivational processes while implementing an innovative instructional program for the first time. The teachers' performance, self-perceptions, and attitudes were measured at several times during the year through behavioral observations, interviews, and questionnaires. Significant increases were observed in both teachers' levels of success and their perceptions of self-efficacy. The timing of the most significant increases suggests a natural progression of improvement in teachers' implementation of an innovation leading to an increase in their perceptions of self-efficacy.

[Teaching and Teacher Education (1988), 4(2), 171-187.]

# TRAINING MATERIALS

## The Primary Education Program
## (PEP)

Margaret C. Wang
and Lauren B. Resnick

This set of nine manuals describes procedures for implementing the Primary Education Program (PEP), an adaptive early learning curriculum. Incorporated as part of the preschool/primary grades curriculum component of the ALEM, PEP emphasizes the development of basic academic and social skills. Its specific elements are curricula in classification and communication skills, quantification skills, and exploratory learning. The PEP manuals describe implementation procedures for designing the learning environment, using the PEP diagnostic tests and learning materials, and managing the processes of learning and instruction. Effects of PEP on students' achievement and use of school time also are reviewed.

[Johnstown, PA: Mafex (1978).]

## Establishing and Managing Adaptive School Learning Environments: The Self-Schedule System

Margaret C. Wang

This manual is designed to help teachers implement the Self-Schedule System, the instructional-learning management component of the ALEM that enables students to take increasing responsibility for their learning time and task management. The manual provides detailed explanations of the rationale and design of the Self-Schedule System, step-by-step guidelines for its implementation, and brief discussions of research findings related to its effects.

[Johnstown, PA: Mafex (1979).]

## Training Manual for the Implementation Assessment Battery for Adaptive Instruction Vols. 1 and 2

Margaret C. Wang,
Rita Catalano, and Erika Gromoll

This manual provides information for use by school personnel in monitoring and refining implementation of the 12 critical design dimensions of the ALEM. Training focuses on the rationale and procedures of the Implementation Assessment Battery for Adaptive Instruction, scoring and analysis of the resultant data, and use of the results to design staff development activities to improve program implementation. The manual consists of two volumes. Volume 1 includes an overview of the theory and practice of adaptive instruction and the ALEM's design and operationalization, as well as a general description of methods and procedures for administering the Battery. Volume 2 describes training procedures for use of the Battery and includes necessary training materials.

[Philadelphia, PA: Temple University Center for Research in Human Development and Education (1986).]

*Chapter 4*

# Curricular Resources for Implementing Adaptive Education

This chapter provides a practical guide for teachers and school personnel responsible for curriculum development and implementation. The chapter includes detailed information on developing expertise in analyzing and modifying available curricular resources, techniques for adapting resources for group and individual work, and instructional management procedures for effective use of curricular resources to implement adaptive education programs.

## CURRICULAR RESOURCES FOR IMPLEMENTATION OF ADAPTIVE EDUCATION IN REGULAR CLASSROOM SETTINGS

Every class has students with individual interests, talents, and learning needs who learn in different ways and at different rates. The traditional teacher-directed approach of whole-group instruction geared to the average student is often too difficult for some students in the class and too easy for others.

Programs that effectively provide instruction that meets the learning needs of students utilize varied instructional methods based on individual student learning characteristics. Each student's knowledge of subject content is assessed when beginning a unit of instruction and again during the course of instruction. This information is used to determine further learning activities and to modify the student's curriculum. The variety of instructional strategies and alternative learning paths include systematic and structured lessons for the development of basic literacy skills, as well as learning experiences that require student initiative and exploration. Alternative learning paths are built into a program for students who require greater than usual instructional support and for those who proceed at an accelerated rate with minimal teacher intervention. In addition to the development of basic literacy skills, implementation of an adaptive education approach emphasizes student ability to be self-directed in instruction. Self-direction develops when classroom learning environments give students opportunities to use their knowledge and skills to solve problems and assist others, and provide cooperative learning activities and options that require the application of their knowledge and skills across subject boundaries and in new situations. Thus, the adaptive education process may be viewed as a cycle of activities that provides continuous monitoring and adaptation of instruction and learning activities to the varied needs of the students to ensure learning outcomes.

Implementation of programs with these features generally requires some modification of existing curricular resources, which are generally teacher-directed activities designed for group rather than individual needs. This chapter focuses on the preparation of curricular resources that provide learning experiences responsive to the characteristics and needs of individual students and opportunities for students to develop and use self-instruction processes in learning.

Because reading and mathematics are subject areas essential to other school subjects, particularly in elementary and middle schools, preparation of curriculum materials for these two subjects is illustrated in this chapter. The techniques for analyzing and preparing curricular materials and resources for reading and mathematics can be readily applied to other subjects, such as social studies and natural sciences. It is assumed that readers have a working knowledge of the school curricula and experience with at least one published curriculum or basal series in reading and one in mathematics. For the reader who does not have a working knowledge of the school curriculum, a thorough examination of at least one basal series for each subject, including student texts and teacher manuals, is strongly recommended prior to using this chapter.

## The Instructional Cycle in Implementation of Adaptive Education

A diagram of the instructional cycle for implementing an adaptive education approach is shown in Figure 4.1. As the figure shows, the cycle consists of a recurring sequence of instructional activities, beginning with diagnosis and continuing through prescribing, teaching, monitoring, assessing, and returning to diagnosis. In each phase of the cycle, the teacher utilizes a variety of curricular

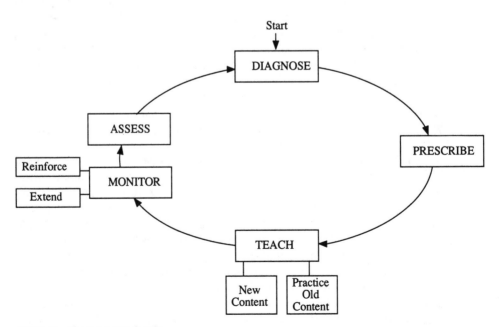

**Figure 4.1.** The instructional cycle.

resources, which are listed in Table 4.1. The components of the cycle and the use of the corresponding resources are discussed below.

Diagnosis refers to determining each student's level of understanding, functioning, and learning needs with respect to a particular curriculum objective or to the general goal of the curriculum unit so that instruction can be specific to the student's needs and targeted learning goals. Diagnosis may be based on results from curriculum-based placement tests, which identify the student entry levels; diagnostic tests designed to pinpoint specific learning competencies and difficulties; unit pre-tests; curriculum-embedded tests; or informal means such as student work samples.

When a student's level of functioning (e.g., knowledge base, level of performance, and understanding of prerequisite skills) is assessed and specific learning needs have been diagnosed, the teacher prescribes appropriate learning activities to meet those needs, including group and individual instruction and independent assignments. The teacher selects activities for each student based on available curricular resources and on the student's specific learning task, individual interests, and learning style. Given the diversity of student abilities, interests, and ways of functioning in most classrooms, a variety of learning options is made available to all students, including those who require greater than usual instructional support. Suggestions for activities for group and individual work may be found in curriculum guides and teacher manuals, and may include cooperative learning groups, individualized assignments, teacher tutoring, or peer tutoring. These activities may involve a variety of materials, including textbooks, workbooks, worksheets, computerized exercises, and other materials such as learning kits, games, and exploratory projects developed by teachers and students.

The next phase in the instructional cycle is teaching students the knowledge and skills needed to carry out their learning tasks. Small-group instruction is the most efficient form of teaching when a group of students has similar learning needs. Instruction is likely to involve individual tutoring by teachers or peers when an individual student has unique learning needs. Occasionally, in-

**Table 4.1.** Curricular resources for the instructional cycle

| Phase | Appropriate resources |
|---|---|
| Diagnose | Placement tests<br>Diagnostic tests<br>Pre-tests<br>Work samples<br>Informal teacher observation of task performance (process and outcomes) |
| Prescribe, teach, and monitor | Curriculum guides<br>Teacher manuals<br>Textbooks<br>Workbooks<br>Skill sheets and worksheets<br>Other available learning materials such as kits, games, computer-assisted instruction or practical exercises, and teacher-constructed learning tasks |
| Assess | Skill sheets, worksheets, and other work samples<br>Teacher observations of student performance of learning tasks<br>Unit or lesson post-tests<br>Level tests<br>Teacher-constructed tests |

struction may involve the whole class. In any of these methods, instruction may introduce new content or reinforce and extend old content, depending on the curriculum objective and student needs.

As students carry out their assigned learning tasks, their progress is monitored by the teacher who checks their work and progress through informal observations or formal tests. A central program feature of adaptive education programs is "interactive teaching," which is an instructional process used by teachers that provides individualized instructional intervention by focusing on the immediate needs of students as they carry out their learning tasks. By circulating among the students as they work independently and by briefly checking their work, the teacher reinforces and extends the students' learning through feedback and immediate instruction at the time when attention is needed and is most effective. The teacher can modify the student's learning plan or prescription if a student is having difficulty with a prescribed task or has successfully completed it.

Assessment of student learning is next in the instructional cycle, and both formal (unit or lesson post-tests, level tests, teacher-constructed tests) and informal (work samples or observations of student performance) means determine if and to what extent each student has achieved the objectives of his or her prescribed work. If assessment reveals that the student has not yet attained mastery, he or she is given additional instruction (reteaching), followed by a prescription of additional practice activities and reassessment. If assessment shows that the objective has been reached, the student moves on to new content, unless the teacher decides to prescribe or encourage the student to select extension and enrichment activities. In either case, assessment provides diagnostic information as a basis for the teacher's next prescription or assignment, and thus, the instructional cycle begins anew.

A curriculum suitable for use in an adaptive education program has clearly defined objectives arranged in a logical sequence. If the subject has a hierarchic structure such as mathematics, the prescribed learning sequence is based on an analysis of the curriculum objective to ensure mastery of the initial skills before advanced skills are taught. The curriculum consists of a variety of learning activities that provide for the learning needs of individual students. It includes a curriculum-based diagnostic and assessment system so that teachers can monitor student mastery of curriculum objectives.

Prior to the 1960s and 1970s, few published curricula included all, or even most, of the features described above. During these decades, however, a number of individualized curricula specifically designed for implementing the adaptive education approach were developed and field tested (cf. Glaser, 1977; Wang & Walberg, 1985). These individualized curricula and the associated research had a profound effect on curriculum development in general. As a result, published curricula generally include a well-defined sequence of objectives, varied curriculum-embedded and adjunct practice activities, and procedures for assessing mastery of objectives of lessons, units, and levels. Since commercial curricula include many of the components needed for adaptive education, schools planning to implement an adaptive education program can continue to use their curricular resources in most cases, and the purchase of special materials is rarely required. It will, however, be necessary to adapt curriculum materials and prepare adjunct materials, such as prescription sheets, to allow students to enter the curriculum at different points, to receive assignments tailored to their unique needs, and to proceed at their own pace. A discussion of the analysis and preparation of materials to support the delivery of adaptive education follows.

## CURRICULUM ANALYSIS AND PREPARATION

### Identification of Available Curricular Resources

The first step in curriculum preparation is to inventory and assemble relevant resource materials available in the school. Figure 4.2. provides the Instructional Components Checklist that may be useful for this purpose. The resources that form the curriculum core are basic components. A school is unlikely to possess all of the listed components, but not all are needed for a well-designed adaptive curriculum. There must be sufficient materials to provide a variety of practice and related activities and to enable teachers to assess student progress.

The basic teaching and learning resource for teachers and students is generally the student textbook. District curriculum guides (if any) and teacher manuals are important resources for planning and delivering instruction. Student workbooks or comparable materials, such as sets of worksheets, provide activities for practice and extension of skills.

As discussed in the previous section, tests are used for diagnosis, placement, and assessment of mastery of objectives. Therefore, a systematic assessment program closely matched to the curriculum is essential. Although teacher-constructed tests, assessment measures, and informal observations may serve some of the functions listed above, placement tests and unit or lesson post-tests (incorporated in commercial textbooks) are strongly recommended.

Other resources include enrichment materials and activities, either as part of a particular basal series or from other sources such as published sets of reproducible exercise materials or manipulatives. These resources are not essential, but they are useful for providing opportunities for additional practice of

---

Basic components
_____ District curriculum guides
_____ Student textbooks
_____ Teacher manuals or teacher edition of student texts
_____ Student workbooks
_____ Duplicating masters or other worksheets
_____ Placement tests
_____ Unit or lesson pre-tests
_____ Unit or lesson post-tests
_____ Cumulative tests (level tests)

Supplementary components
_____ Additional duplicating masters or worksheets
_____ Commercially available learning kits, games, books, and computerized learning
               materials (list or describe) _____
_____ Audiovisual materials such as film strips, and audio- and videotapes (list or describe) _____
               scribe) _____
_____ Teacher-constructed learning activities that can be coordinated with the basic curriculum (describe) _____
               riculum (describe) _____
_____ Teacher-constructed tests (list or describe) _____
_____ Other (describe) _____

---

**Figure 4.2.**   Instructional components checklist.

targeted skills. They reinforce retention and application and extend students' ability to utilize their knowledge and skills in problem solving.

The category "Supplementary" in the Instructional Components Checklist includes a variety of materials that teachers and schools tend to accumulate. Some of these are regularly used, while others sit on closet shelves. These materials may be available in the school and district libraries, from local libraries and museums, or from the business community. Such resources are particularly useful for exploratory or additional practice activities related to curriculum objectives, for providing alternative modes of learning according to student abilities and preferences, and for offering both teachers and students a greater choice of learning activities related to basic skills.

Curriculum materials for the instructional components are inventoried and assembled for each grade level implementing the adaptive education program. It is recommended that curriculum materials be prepared for at least one grade level below the lowest participating grade and one or two grade levels above the highest participating grade to accommodate students working below and above grade level. For example, if the program is to be implemented in third grade classes, materials for grades two, three, four, and five should be assembled, analyzed, and prepared, and if implementation is for grades one through four, materials should be prepared for kindergarten through sixth grade.

## Analysis of Curricular Resources and Their Organization into Instructionally Meaningful Sequences

The purpose of analysis of curricular resources is to organize curriculum objectives in instructional clusters and into manageable lessons, appropriately sequencing objectives, identifying learning activities from various resources, and developing curriculum-based assessments and tests for monitoring and evaluating student progress and mastery.

Segmenting the curriculum into meaningful and manageable lesson units is somewhat arbitrary and may vary from one situation to another. The structure and organization of a district curriculum guide usually provides a basis for lesson units. Teacher manuals for the basal series should be consulted as well, especially if the curriculum is expected to follow the basal sequence. Curriculum guides and teacher manuals often provide lesson plans or other structural aids helpful to curriculum analysts, not only for segmenting the curriculum but also for identifying objectives and appropriate learning activities for each lesson. If lessons are indicated in the curriculum guide or the basal materials, these sequences should be used with modifications needed for individual students.

If the curriculum is not divided into lessons, the following guidelines for segmenting the curriculum into lessons may be used. In reading, a story or a set of short selections with accompanying activities is usually appropriate for a lesson. In mathematics, a lesson generally includes one new concept or procedure, part of a new procedure if it is complex, or review of a previously learned procedure. The teacher or curriculum revision team should begin curriculum preparation by deciding the amount of material appropriate for a group instruction session plus subsequent individual work.

## An Inventory System for Organizing
## Curriculum Materials and Activities: The Prescription Sheet

The next step in curriculum analysis is development of an inventory system for organizing curriculum materials and activities that can be easily used by teachers for planning and prescribing specific assignments for individual students. An organizational system for this purpose should provide teachers with a list of available curriculum materials and activities, efficiently communicate assignments to students and team teachers, and provide an accurate record for monitoring student progress.

Figure 4.3. shows a sample of a recording system that provides an inventory of curriculum materials and activities for a given unit of instruction.This inventory recording system, known as the prescription sheet, was developed as part of a curricular delivery system for organizing learning materials and activities and for communicating assignments to students (Wang, 1980). Prescription sheets are printed forms that list standard curriculum options and other learning activities, and they include space for specific assignments and recording progress. As successive lessons, objectives, instructional management tasks, and related learning activities are identified, they are entered on the prescription sheet. Prescription sheets can be handwritten or generated from a computerized instructional management system, and the prescription sheet shown can easily be adapted to a computerized format.

Prescription sheets provide a systematic and efficient way to make assignments and record student progress. The sheets are an information source about the curriculum and learning options, and they enhance effective communication between students and teachers. Prescription sheets display curriculum options and supplementary curricular resources available for each objective and level of the curriculum. Perhaps more important, prescription sheets provide information about students' specific assignments and help to organize curriculum options, thus providing support that enables students to become increasingly responsible for monitoring their progress and making curricular choices.

The simple format of the sample prescription sheet in Figure 4.3. has been found useful and manageable by teachers. Each horizontal row corresponds to one lesson, and the learning activities associated with the lesson are entered in appropriate columns.

Prescription sheets are prepared and printed as part of the curriculum preparation task. The actual typing of the prescription sheet can be done by parent volunteers, school clerks, classroom assistants, student teachers, or other support personnel. The appendix contains additional examples of prescription sheets and includes of one page of a set prepared for Level $3-2^2$ of the Macmillan Reading Program (1989) and one page of a set prepared for Level 4A, Unit 1, Section 2 of the Macmillan Mathematics Series (1987). Other formats may be used for preparing prescription sheets, and an example of a mathematics prescription sheet using an alternate format is also provided in the appendix. In this case, each horizontal row corresponds to part of one objective. This example was developed by a school staff with much experience in implementing an adaptive education program. It is recommended that schools preparing to begin implementation use the format shown in Figure 4.3. because it is simple and can be easily adapted to fit a variety of subjects and curricula. The decision to use this

Name: Alan Schwartz
Textbook: Landscapes
Level: Macmillan 10-P5

| Curriculum objective | Story title | Workbook | Skill practice | Reteaching | Other activities | Test | Comments |
|---|---|---|---|---|---|---|---|
| | "A Trunk Full of History" pp. 220–235 | pp. 64–67 | pp. 43–45 | Masters pp. 17–18 pp. 23–24 pp. 29–30 | Map activity | | TG p. 280 Chart 70–74 |
| Comparisons | "Picture the Past" pp. 250–255 | pp. 73–77 | pp. 49–51 | Masters pp. 19–20 pp. 25–28 | | Spelling | TG p. 320 Chart 80–83 |
| Context clues | "The WK Man Unplugged the TVs" pp. 18–28 | pp. 1–5 | pp. 1–3 | Masters pp. 3–4 pp. 7–8 pp. 11–12 | Activity A: Sequencing events | | TG p. 6 Chart 1–4 |
| | "Pippi Finds a Spink" pp. 32–40 | pp. 6–9 | pp. 4–6 | Masters pp. 1–2 pp. 7–8 pp. 11–12 | Write article: Use "Vocab Treasures" | Unit test | TG p. 26 Chart 5–11 |
| | | | | | | | |
| | | | | | | | |

**Figure 4.3.** Sample prescription sheet.

or other formats, however, should be made by the teacher or instructional team. Some guidelines for preparing prescription sheets are presented below:

1.  One prescription sheet is prepared for each unit of instruction based on the result of step 1 of the curriculum analysis.
2.  Each horizontal row on the prescription sheet represents a "dedicated space" for listing materials and activities for one lesson. For example, in Figure 4.3., the first column lists curriculum objectives and the second column lists the specific titles of the lesson. In this example of a prescription sheet for a reading curriculum, the titles of the stories in the basal series are listed in the second column.
3.  Each column of the prescription sheet is designed to record materials or activities of a curriculum component or curricular resource.
4.  Pages in the student workbook corresponding to each lesson are also listed on the prescription sheet. (Workbook pages are listed in column 3 of Figure 4.3.) If the workbook (or comparable resource) contains several distinct types of exercises, different types may be entered in different columns. For example, in the sample prescription sheet for the Macmillan Reading Program (see appendix), exercises related to understanding cause and effect are listed in several columns depending on whether they are in the workbook or used for skill practice.
5.  A column should be reserved for listing curriculum-based assessment tasks, and tests or checklists such as a vocabulary list are entered in the appropriate space.
6.  The number of columns in the prescription sheets is determined by the content and nature of the subject matter and student needs. For example, columns can be used for resources and curriculum-related information such as enrichment and review activities. Column headings may refer to a certain type of activity (e.g., enrichment activities), or to the source of the activity (e.g., workbook). The guidelines are that all the curricular resources and options identified for inclusion in a given lesson are listed and that clear criteria be established for distinguishing and categorizing activities. The column headings of the prescription sheets in the appendix provide additional illustrations of formats.

*Entering Lesson Titles and Objectives*    When column headings have been determined for the prescription sheet, the next step is to enter titles and objectives for each lesson in the unit in each row of the prescription sheet. The curriculum guides of the school district and the teacher manuals of the basal series are the basic resources for this task. Lesson plans and descriptions in guides and manuals usually list the content and objectives of each lesson, and titles and objectives can generally be transferred in order to the appropriate rows of the prescription sheet, one lesson per row. If a list of objectives is not included in a curriculum guide or in adjunct materials, objectives should be identified by the curriculum analyst to help teachers and students focus on targeted skills and information. Identification of objectives requires thorough examination of curriculum materials for each lesson, with a view to what exactly the student is expected to be able to do. The identified objectives are then listed in appropriate order.

Curriculum objectives entered on prescription sheets need not (and should not) be restricted to those in the curriculum guide or basal series. Students require varying amounts of instruction and learning support, and a variety of supplementary activities and materials may be needed for selected students. Additional objectives and available activities may be identified by the curriculum analyst based on student needs and implementation requirements. If time for curriculum analysis is limited, however, it may be advisable to start with those included in the extant curriculum and add supplementary or alternative materials as the need arises.

It is also helpful to number the objectives. In some curriculum guides and basal series this has already been done and, if not, the analyst can assign numbers. Objectives are best numbered sequentially throughout the level. Objectives are numbered to facilitate record keeping of student progress through the curriculum and to identify activities related to specific objectives, which will become evident in the next section.

**Identifying and Entering Learning Activities and Tests**    Next, learning activities from the various curriculum components are matched to the lesson content and objectives and entered on the prescription sheet. Curriculum guides and basal teacher manuals are invaluable aids. Lesson plans and descriptions usually indicate the content and objectives of each lesson, as well as associated textbook and workbook pages and other activities. This information can be transferred to the prescription sheet for a particular lesson.

In some cases, certain learning activities have been numerically keyed to particular curriculum objectives, and these numbers should be included in the listing on the prescription sheet. Numerical codes facilitate the matching of activities and exercises to objectives. If the curriculum in use does not have such a feature, a numbering system that matches activities to objectives should be developed.

It is generally easier to enter materials and activities listed in the curriculum guides and teacher manuals on prescription sheets before entering the supplementary activities, such as trade books, kits, flash cards, games, and teacher-constructed activities. Teachers working on curriculum preparation and revision may decide not to use any supplementary materials, at least initially, if time is short and learning activities already included in the lesson guide provide a sufficient range of options to begin the program. For example, if booklets in reading kits are to be prescribed for extended reading, their readability level should be determined in order to appropriately match them to the specific objective or lesson.

Every space on the prescription sheet does not need to be filled. Activities included in some curricular components may not be appropriate to individual students. In other cases, resources may be identified or developed by teachers as the school year progresses. Sufficient space should be allowed in columns for extension and enrichment activities so that teachers can enter assignments for individual students. Sometimes, activities cannot readily be entered into particular cells on prescription sheets because they are suitable or adaptable to many levels of student ability, or because they integrate several objectives or subject areas. They can be listed at the bottom of the prescription sheet. They serve an important function, however, by providing students with options and alternative assignments that extend the individual student curriculum.

***Checking for Accuracy and Completeness*** The last step in preparation of prescription sheets is checking for accuracy and completeness. This important step is often overlooked, but it is worthwhile, because problems in implementation due to inadequacies or errors on prescription sheets are prevented. If possible, the review should be done by someone other than the analyst and by teachers who are familiar with the curriculum. A review should ensure that:

> All required lessons are included in the correct order.
> Objectives within lessons are complete and properly sequenced.
> All relevant textbook pages, workbook pages, exercises, and activities listed in curriculum guides or teacher manuals are included in the appropriate lessons.
> Supplementary materials are matched to the correct level, and materials related to specific objectives are placed in lessons that teach those objectives.
> Each test corresponds to the objective that the test is designed to measure.

At least one learning activity should be included for each corresponding objective. Even if at least one learning activity per objective has been included, it does not necessarily mean that the curriculum is adequate for implementation of adaptive education. The diversity of learning needs and styles in most classes requires a variety of alternative learning activities for each objective. In addition, extension of learned skills and practice in new and varied contexts can both strengthen the skills and make learning more interesting for students. For example, reading and language skills can and should be extended by various creative writing exercises. Similarly, mathematics skills can be extended by activities involving applications in new contexts and mathematical puzzles. Identification and preparation of such extension and enrichment activities constitute the subject of the next section.

## Identification and Preparation of Supplemental Materials and Activities

An environment rich in learning activities and curriculum materials, both commercial and teacher-constructed, provides many pathways for accommodating unique student abilities, learning styles, and interests. A variety of learning options gives students opportunities to experiment, to become more aware of their own interests and abilities, and to learn to plan, monitor, and evaluate their own work. In addition, flexibility in adapting to the needs of students in heterogeneously grouped classes is increased when activities vary in level of difficulty and type (e.g., written versus manipulative). Examples of nonbasal types of activities that promote desirable educational goals are:

> Trade books, both fiction and nonfiction, provide opportunities for students to extend their reading skills and to use reading for further learning.
> Educational games and challenging puzzles on computers or in other forms help students to generalize learned skills to a variety of situations and contexts. For example, mathematical and verbal puzzles require that students apply skills in contexts different from those in which they were acquired.
> Learning activities can promote the integration of subject areas. For example, a science activity in which students measure and graph the out-

come of an experiment integrates science and math, and an assignment
to write and present a play or skit integrates writing with dramatics.

Learning activities that involve students working cooperatively or independently in building, constructing, drawing, writing, discussing, or making presentations promote creativity and interest, as well as enhance
motivation, thinking, and problem solving.

Even this limited list may lead the program implementor or teacher to de-
clare, "Help! How can I ever find time to create all these types of activities?"
Fortunately, not all such extension and enrichment activities need to be created
"from scratch." Most schools already possess suitable materials and activities, as
well as components from which others can be constructed. A thorough inventory of available resources is likely to yield useful supplies such as books, kits,
games, assorted duplicating masters, and audiovisual materials. Moreover, identifying and creating additional learning activities need not occur all before
school starts, and it should be a continuing process throughout the school year.
Teachers and support personnel who implement adaptive education programs
are generally ingenious at finding time and resources to create exploratory activities. The availability of a rich variety of materials and activities also enables
teachers to continually update their learning centers and make meaningful, systematic changes as instruction shifts, student interests change, or the usual options become tiresome.

Suggestions for constructing activities can be found in many places. In
many cases, school districts or nearby universities maintain resource centers
where materials can be borrowed, copied, or constructed. Teachers can make use
of their own interests or hobbies; for example, a teacher who collects stamps may
devise activities in which students read about stamps, bring in unusual stamps,
and design their own stamps. Teachers can share resources and ideas. Ideas may
be obtained from professional journals, magazines, and books, as well as from
regional and local resources such as museums, public libraries, or resource centers maintained by the state education agencies, such as the Intermediate Units
in Pennsylvania or the Bureau of Cooperative Educational Services (BOCES) in
New York.

A few general guidelines for selection and construction of curriculum materials and resources are:

1.  Although each activity does not have to be related to a specific instructional
    objective, all activities should provide meaningful learning experiences.
2.  Tasks related to a particular skill area should range from simple to complex
    to accommodate the levels of students. Each student should be able to find
    activities that he or she can do, yet are challenging. Students acquire the
    skills needed to carry out more complex activities by completing simple
    activities.
3.  Manipulative, written, and computerized tasks should be available, which
    enable teachers to accommodate student learning styles and needs. In addi-
    tion, learning opportunities and self-direction are enhanced if students are
    permitted to choose media that match their interests and desire for variety
    and choice.
4.  Some activities should be designed for individuals working alone and others
    for cooperative learning in groups of two or more. Group activities encour-

age constructive learning interactions, cooperation, and sharing of ideas and resources.

5.  Each activity should have a clear purpose, even if it does not result in a particular product or outcome. For example, reading a book or building with blocks in a construction area for 20 minutes, although purposeful, does not necessarily have a specific product or outcome. If, however, a task does have a desired outcome, this should be made clear to students. This not only helps them organize their work, but also provides a standard by which they can judge their progress.

6.  In order to maximize student self-direction and minimize the need for teacher intervention, directions for carrying out each activity should be simple, explicit, and geared to the students' level. If the teacher must be consulted, a script to explain the task should accompany the material.

7.  Activities should be packaged so that students can easily find all components, use them, and return them to their proper places.

8.  It is also useful to develop activities that require or teach students to evaluate their own work. Some tasks result in immediate knowledge of successful completion, such as games and puzzles, but in other cases, it may be possible to provide answer keys or other means for self-checking. The result is the student's appreciation of his or her creativity and ingenuity.

9.  Teachers should also maintain an inventory of materials and activities that have not been entered on prescription sheets, including those in the classroom and in storage, to keep track of available options. New activities can be added and activities that wear out or are inappropriate can be removed. Keeping such a list enables a teacher to change activities periodically and to quickly identify activities appropriate for particular students.

## Recording Student Progress Through the Curriculum Using Prescription Sheets

Teachers and students are both accountable for student progress through the curriculum in an adaptive education program. Teachers are accountable for diagnosing individual student needs, making appropriate assignments as necessary, and assessing student mastery of objectives. Students are accountable for completing assigned tasks on time, having them checked, and mastering the objectives. Structured methods for recording student progress through curricula are vital. At a minimum, records should show the specific objectives, sets of objectives, and tests that have been mastered by each student, as well as the dates on which mastery criteria were met.

One example of such records is the prescription sheet described above. These records are useful not only for summative evaluation purposes such as how fast or how well a student is progressing in the reading curriculum, or if most students are mastering the mathematics curriculum at an appropriate rate, but for instructional planning as well. For example, if a teacher notes that students are having difficulty with a particular objective, he or she may decide to assemble them for small-group instruction. If records show that a certain student is progressing more rapidly or slowly than other students in his or her reading or mathematics group, the teacher may decide to change the student's group assignment. When prescription sheets are used as a record system for student progress, they provide a database for fine tuning instruction to maximize student progress.

Another example of progress records is a profile sheet that records student progress for the entire class in the curriculum. Standard record-keeping forms for individual students and the whole class are usually available from the school or basal text publisher. If record forms are available and judged to be suitable, they should be used. Available forms, however, sometimes are not sufficiently detailed.

The task of classroom record keeping is usually the responsibility of teachers, students, other teaching staff, or classroom assistants. They can enter information on printed forms or into a computerized database. A sample form for recording curriculum progress is shown in Figure 4.4. Columns correspond to pre- and post-tests and objectives of successive units. A color code can be used to record dates so that when a student has mastered a particular objective or test, the teacher fills in the block with a color indicating that month, or records the actual date. A format similar to that shown in the figure is recommended because teachers have found it easy to use and students and others find it easy to understand.

Classroom record keeping can also be computerized, and should be implemented whenever possible to save time and to facilitate easy information retrieval. A classroom computer management system allows teachers to enter data and to retrieve information about individual or group performance quickly.

The time constructing printed forms or computerized systems for record keeping and maintaining records throughout the school year pays off hand-

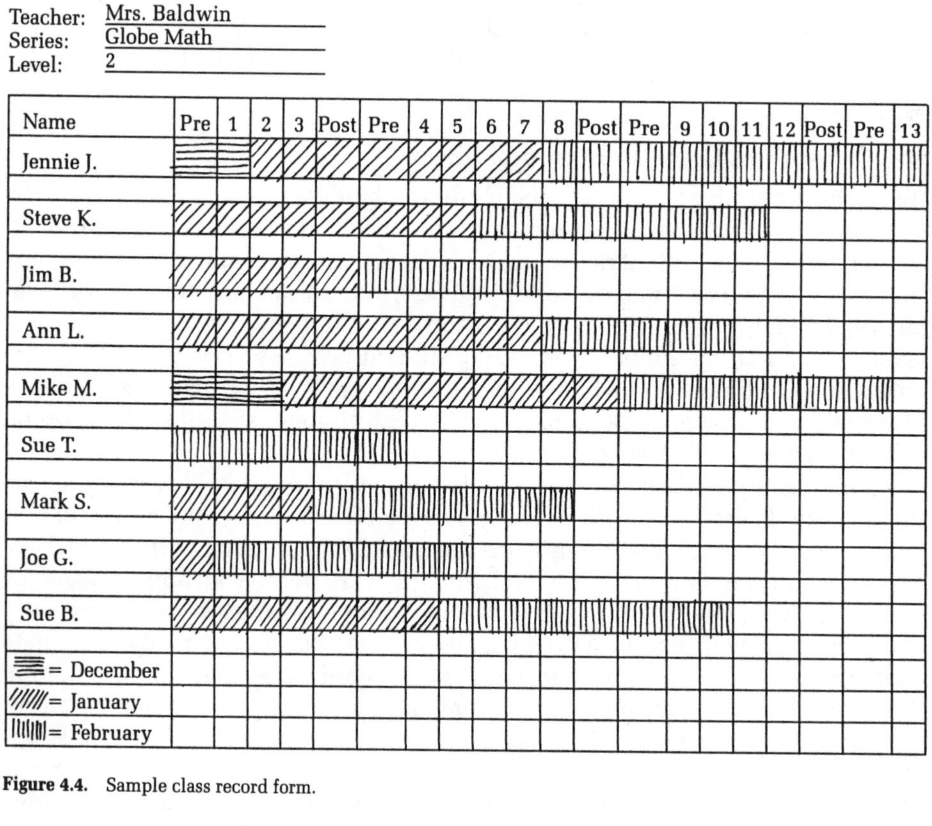

Teacher: Mrs. Baldwin
Series: Globe Math
Level: 2

Figure 4.4.   Sample class record form.

somely in alleviating some management tasks that consume much precious instruction time. Simple and efficient methods for recording, reviewing, and updating daily, weekly, and monthly student progress should be discussed and decided by the participating regular and specialist teachers prior to program implementation. Accurate, comprehensive, and up-to-date records are invaluable, not only for management and instructional planning, but also as reinforcement for students and as a database for program evaluation.

## MANAGING CURRICULUM PREPARATION

Refinement and preparation of the curriculum for implementing adaptive instruction can be a time-consuming task, depending on the curriculum materials already in place. It is suggested that curriculum preparation for implementing adaptive education be undertaken by teams of program teachers, although the program coordinator generally coordinates the process of curriculum preparation. The involvement of teachers in curriculum preparation promotes feelings of ownership of the program and gives teachers a sound knowledge base for implementation of the curriculum in the classroom.

Preparation of prescription sheets and development of record-keeping procedures should take place well before implementation of the adaptive education program, because the prescription sheets and other materials developed during these sessions must be typed and copied before the program begins.

Time needed for curriculum development depends largely on the number of levels to be prepared. Experience suggests that curriculum preparation for elementary grades requires 3–5 days of work by two people who are able to analyze between four and six grade levels of one subject. The number of individualized curriculum components, such as diagnostic tests and individualized assignment forms, also influences the time and staff required for the task. Another important factor is if the basic school curriculum is organized around a single basal series or utilizes a combination of series or other materials. If a combination of materials is used, analysts need to consider sets of materials and several different guides or manuals during curriculum preparation, so the task will involve more time. Time for identification and development of supplementary materials and activities prior to implementation may be limited so that material development should be planned to continue throughout the year.

Pre-implementation curriculum analysis and preparation work can be divided depending on available people and resources and on the preferences of the analysts. For example, the entire curriculum preparation group may work on the reading curriculum until it is completed, and then work on the mathematics curriculum, or part of the group may work on reading while others work on mathematics. Although it is often more efficient to work in teams, some analysts prefer to work individually, and such decisions are best left to the participating analysts.

Arrangements should be made well in advance for office or classroom space for curriculum development and for necessary staff and curricular resources. Curriculum preparation is a start-up cost that a school district planning to implement adaptive education needs to allocate in addition to staff development, which may not be an additional cost to the school, depending on the existing allocation for staff development. Many schools involved in this aspect of planning have found it practical and feasible to recruit retired school staff to devote time, for example 2, weeks in the summer, to curriculum preparation before program implementation.

## CLASSROOM IMPLEMENTATION OF THE CURRICULUM

This section provides those responsible for staff development and program implementation with information to assist teachers in using the curriculum materials and activities. This section does not aim to tell teachers how to teach, either individually or in groups, but for a review of recent research concerning effective instructional practices and teacher expertise in managing classroom instruction and related roles, see Brophy (1986), Reynolds (1989), U.S. Department of Education (1986, 1987), Wang, Haertel, and Walberg (1990), and Wittrock (1986). The discussion in this section focuses on the instructional delivery process and strategies for regulating the flow of classroom activities.

### Instructional Delivery Process

The adaptive education approach utilizes a wide variety of instructional options, including small-group instruction, individual work by students, whole-group meetings, and individual tutoring by teachers, aides, or peers. Instructional groupings are flexible to meet both teacher and student needs. (Scheduling and utilization of the various grouping options are discussed more fully in chap. 5, this volume.) A brief description of the purpose of group and individual work is included in the context of prescription sheets.

In adaptive education programs, small groups are formed based on student performance on placement tests, diagnostic tests, and other assessment methods. Group placements are flexible so that students may move from one group to another depending on individual needs and rate of progress. Groups may vary in size and consist of as few as 2 or 3 or as many as 9 or 10 students. Moreover, not all members of a group need to attend every group meeting. Based on the teacher's judgment, some students may be assigned to do individually what other students do as a group.

Groups usually include students working at approximately the same level. This does not mean, however, that all students in the group need to have identical abilities. In reading, for example, a student functioning at a higher or lower reading level than most of his or her peers can participate in group meetings for oral reading and other skills development, and receive appropriate individual reading assignments. In addition, students working below the level of their group can be given additional individual help by the teacher, other students, or resource personnel.

In implementing adaptive education programs, as in traditional programs, group lessons are usually used to introduce new concepts or skills, to review material that several or all students require, and to engage in learning activities that are social such as discussion of a reading passage. Student textbooks are basic materials used in small-group instruction, but worksheets, workbooks, and other exploratory learning materials can provide additional skills instruction, guided practice, and review. Group lessons may be used for timed tests or drills, for creative and extended activities, or for enrichment activities. In both adaptive and traditional instruction, individual seatwork is assigned for practice and enrichment and extension activities. In adaptive education programs, however, seatwork assignments vary widely depending on student needs and interests.

## Strategies for Regulating the Flow of Classroom Activities

Adaptive education includes many options for grouping students and for sequencing activities. This section describes a strategy for combining various curricular options and grouping arrangements to provide for individual differences. Examples are included of ways that prescription sheets can be used to design individual learning plans and to regulate the flow of activities that occur simultaneously in classrooms where the adaptive education approach is implemented.

An example of the daily use of prescription sheets by teachers and students is presented in Figure 4.5., which is a flow chart showing a strategy for using curricular options for a given lesson to create individualized learning plans for students. As shown in the flow chart, a student begins a new lesson or series of lessons with Activity A, a group meeting in which the teacher presents new content and directs group activities. These activities may include guided practice in a textbook, workbook, and other exercises such as writing or computer-assisted instruction. As shown, if a student requires additional instruction, he or she may be assigned extra tutoring with the teacher, individually or in a small group. If no additional instruction is needed, the student is assigned Activity B, which consists of independent tasks in the textbook or workbook listed in the prescription sheet for the curriculum unit. If a student needs additional help to perform these tasks, tutoring sessions with the teacher can be scheduled.

After a student has successfully completed the work assignments (Activity B), he or she may move to a prescribed activity of choice or to another teacher-prescribed assignment. For example, the flow chart shows that the pupil's next task (Activity C) is supplementary activities, which may be listed on the prescription sheet or selected by the teacher or the student. Supplementary activities are individually prescribed for each student. Students who need additional practice can be assigned remedial activities (e.g., Activity C.1. as shown in Figure 4.5.) such as additional worksheets, kits, or tutoring by a peer. Other students may be assigned a variety of enrichment and extension activities (e.g., Activity C.2.). Thus, activities are prescribed based on student interests and abilities and vary according to individual needs.

With a systematic record of curricular options available such as is provided in prescription sheets, students can be informed of suggested learning activities and can choose a set of supplementary activities. Ideally, all activities for a day should be prescribed at the same time so that the student is aware of all assignments and can plan his or her time accordingly. If the teacher discovers during the course of instruction that a student needs more practice with particular skills, additional tasks or activities should be assigned.

The flow chart indicates that a student may need additional help in completing his or her supplementary activities. Help can be provided through individual tutoring sessions, as the teacher circulates among the students, or in a small-group session if several students need the same kind of help. After students complete the supplementary activities, the teacher may schedule a group meeting for the next lesson as listed on the prescription sheet (Activity A).

To illustrate teacher and student use of prescription sheets to monitor progress and to regulate activities, an example is given based on a reading curricu-

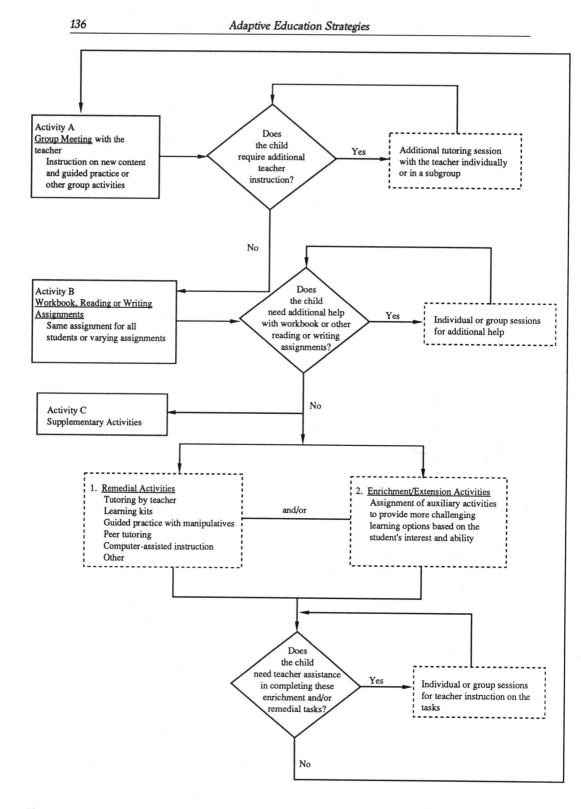

**Figure 4.5.** Strategy for using curricular options for individualizing instruction. (Solid line = assignment required for all students in a group, dotted line = individualized assignment.)

lum, and methods for curriculum analysis in other subjects are similar. In this example, the work of Jenny, a second grade student, is described over several days. The reading curriculum used at Jenny's school is based on the Macmillan Reading Program (1987). Jenny's prescription sheet for reading is shown in Figure 4.6. As her prescription sheet shows, she is working on Level 1–2$^2$ of the Macmillan Program. Jenny's reading group began a new lesson on October 18, and the prescription sheet shows Jenny's assignments from the 18th through the 20th.

As shown in the figure, Jenny's reading assignment on October 18 included reading "That's What Friends Are For" pages 10–19 and completing workbook pages 1–4. The teacher indicated this on the prescription sheet by circling the assigned work. The "x" and the date written after the page number indicate that the assignment was completed and checked by the teacher on that day.

The next day, October 19, Jenny was assigned Skill Practice pages 2, 3, and 4 for practice on curriculum objectives related to the main idea and details. Based on results from pre-testing and other performance indicators, the teacher decided that Jenny did not need to complete Skill Practice page 1. Jenny was also assigned pages 43–48 for reteaching. On October 20, Jenny was assigned pages 330–331 from Word Work and Activity 3 from the Exploratory Writing Center. Jenny's satisfactory completion of work for the 19th and 20th is shown on the prescription sheet.

A group lesson was scheduled on October 20 for additional instruction related to one or more lesson objectives. The meeting may have included all or some members of Jenny's group. During the meeting, the teacher assessed Jenny's progress and made an additional assignment. Examples of such additional activities include making a crossword puzzle with the vocabulary words from the last reading story, performing an instructional activity on the computer that identifies main ideas, or peer tutoring.

On October 21, Jenny's group began the lesson "Animals of Freedom." During the group meeting, the teacher prescribed the relevant studybook and skillpack exercises, and the cycle began again. As with the previous lesson, certain assignments were given to all students, and other assignments were matched to student needs. If, for example, Jenny had not yet mastered the objective of identifying the main idea, one or more of her supplementary assignments may have involved continuing to work on this objective. Conversely, if Jenny had mastered some new objectives or mastered them before the rest of her group, she may have been assigned enrichment and extension activities, or have begun independent work on the next lesson objectives.

## SUMMARY

To summarize, a variety of curricular options that include teacher-prescribed and student-selected exploratory learning activities constitute the building blocks that effectively provide for student diversity in adaptive education.

The chapter contains ideas for constructing learning materials and supplementary activities to meet student needs for a wide range of learning options and experiences. It also details how to develop a systematic process for organizing and preparing existing curriculum materials to support classroom implementation of adaptive education programs. One such system is the use of prescription

Name: Jenny  
Grade: 2  
Level: Macmillan 1–2²  
Friends Aloft

| Curriculum objective | Story title | Workbook | Skill practice | Reteaching | Other activities | Test |
|---|---|---|---|---|---|---|
| Understands main idea and details | "That's What Friends Are For" pp. 10–19 *10/18* *(Group Lesson)* | pp. *(circled)* *10/18* | pp. 1 *(circled)* *10/9* | pp. *(circled numbers)* *10/9* | Word Work pp. 330–331 *10/20*  *Activity 3/From Exploratory Writing Center 10/20* | |
| | "Animals of Freedom" pp. 20–27 | pp. 5, 6, 7, 8 | pp. 5, 6, 7 | pp. 45, 46, 49, 50, 51, 52 | Word Work pp. 332–333 | |
| | "The Bremen Town Musicians" | pp. 9, 10, 11, 12 | pp. 8, 9, 10, 11 | pp. 53, 54, 55, 56, 57, 58 | Word Work pp. 334–335 | |

**Figure 4.6.** A prescription sheet for an individual student.

sheets as an information source for teachers and students to effectively manage their learning activities. Prescription sheets provide printed lists of standard curricular options and other available activities. They make it possible for teachers to easily use the curricular resources to meet the needs of students with a wide range of abilities, talents, learning styles, and interests; to communicate expectations and progress of student work on a systematic basis; and to provide a planning guide for communicating student needs to teachers and specialist support staff who work as a team with students. For the student, the prescription sheet permits independent management of assignments and provides an ongoing record of work accomplished.

In addition to suggestions of how to organize and revise existing curricula for classroom implementation of adaptive education, specific suggestions on the use and management of curricular options are also described in detail. It is hoped that by using the procedures described in this chapter, readers will be able to adapt and expand their existing curricula with minimal time and effort to efficiently prepare and use auxiliary materials that are essential in supporting the effective delivery of adaptive education programs.

## REFERENCES

Brophy, J.B. (1986). Research linking teacher behavior to student achievement: Potential implications for instruction of Chapter 1 students. In B.I. Williams, P.A. Richmond, & B.J. Mason (Eds.), *Designs for compensatory education: Conference proceedings and papers* (Vol. IV, pp. 121–179). Washington, DC: Research and Evaluation Associates.

Glaser, R. (1977). *Adaptive education: Individual diversity and learning.* New York: Holt, Rinehart & Winston.

*Macmillan Mathematics Series.* (1987). Riverside, NJ: Macmillan.

*Macmillan Reading Program.* (1989). Riverside, NJ: Macmillan.

Reynolds, M.C. (1989). Children with special needs. In M.C. Reynolds (Ed.), *Knowledge base for the beginning teacher* (pp. 129–142). Oxford: Pergamon.

U.S. Department of Education. (1986). *What works. Research about teaching and learning.* Washington, DC: Author.

U.S. Department of Education. (1987). *What works. Research about teaching and learning* (2nd ed.). Washington, DC: Author.

Wang, M.C. (1980). Adaptive instruction: Building on diversity. *Theory into Practice,* 19(2), 122–127.

Wang, M.C., Haertel, G.D., & Walberg, H.J. (1990). What influences learning? A content analysis of review literature. *Journal of Educational Research,* 84(1), 30–43.

Wang, M.C., & Walberg, H.J. (Eds.). (1985). *Adapting instruction to individual differences.* Berkeley, CA: McCutchan.

Wittrock, M.C. (Ed.). (1986). *Handbook of research on teaching* (3rd ed.). New York: Macmillan.

*Appendix 4*

# Sample Prescription Sheets

Name: _____
Grade: _____
Level:  Macmillan 3–2²
Friends Aloft

| Curriculum objective | Story title | Workbook | Skill practice | Reteaching | Other activities | Test |
|---|---|---|---|---|---|---|
| Understands cause/effect | "Skating for a Gold Medal" pp. 84–91 | pp. 26, 27, 28, 29 | pp. 23, 24, 25 | pp. 43, 44, 49, 50, 63, 64 | Word Work pp. 342–343 | |
| | "Kate Can Skate" pp. 92–103 "Skating Song" pp. 104–105 | pp. 30, 31, 32, 33 | pp. 26, 27, 28, 29 | pp. 47, 48, 49, 50, 59, 60 | Word Work p. 344 | |
| | "Buster's Job" pp. 108–117 | pp. 34, 35, 36, 37 | pp. 30, 31, 32 | pp. 51, 52, 57, 58, 61, 62 | | |

Name: _____
Grade: _____
Level:  Macmillan 4A–p1

| Curriculum objective | Textbook | Workbook | Duplicating master | Enrichment | Tests | Comments |
|---|---|---|---|---|---|---|
| Decimal system<br>Numeration<br>  Identify place value<br>  to hundred thousands | pp. 26–27<br>pp. 34–35 | p. 9<br><br>p. 12 | | p. 391<br>p. 392 | Pre-test<br>Math program<br>assessment<br>September | |
| Use zero as a place holder | p. 27 | | Worksheet<br>Zero as a Place Holder | | PMET | |
| Relationships<br>  Write numbers to ten<br>  thousands and hundred thousands | | | | | | |
| Reading numbers to ten thousands and<br>  hundred thousands | p. 36<br>p. 38 | | | Unit Review<br>p. 43<br>pp. 1–28 | | |
| Rename hundred thousands as ten<br>thousands, thousands, hundreds, tens, and<br>ones | | | | | PMET | |
| Rounding<br>  Determine value to nearest tens and<br>  hundreds | p. 30, 31 | p. 11 | Judy/Instruction work-<br>sheet #10 | p. 391 | | |
| Determine value to nearest thousands and<br>  nearest ten thousands | p. 36, 37 | p. 13 | Sound off and round<br>off | | | |

Assignment Sheet

Name _____

Pre-test date _____     Post-test date _____

Level 2 Chapter 6

1—Add 2 digits, no regrouping
2—Add 2 digits, regrouping
3—Story problems, 2-digit addition

**Pre-test Score**

| 0 | 1 | 2 | 3 | 4 | 5 | 6 |
|---|---|---|---|---|---|---|
| 0 | 1 | 2 | 3 | 4 | 5 | 6 |
| 0 | 1 | 2 | 3 | 4 | | |

Unsatisfactory Score | Satisfactory Score

**Post-test Score**

| 0 | 1 | 2 | 3 | 4 | 5 | 6 |
|---|---|---|---|---|---|---|
| 0 | 1 | 2 | 3 | 4 | 5 | 6 |
| 0 | 1 | 2 | 3 | 4 | | |

Unsatisfactory Score | Satisfactory Score

**Re-test Score**

| 0 | 1 | 2 | 3 | 4 | 5 | 6 |
|---|---|---|---|---|---|---|
| 0 | 1 | 2 | 3 | 4 | 5 | 6 |
| 0 | 1 | 2 | 3 | 4 | | |

Unsatisfactory Score | Satisfactory Score

| Obj. | Date | Student page | Enrichment worksheet | Reteaching Text page | Set | Basic wkst | Date | Supplementary activities |
|---|---|---|---|---|---|---|---|---|
| 1 | | 135, 136 | 43 | 306 | 12 | 43 | | |
| 2 | | 137, 138 | 44 | | | 44 | | Group meeting |
| 3 | | 139, 140 | | | | | | |
| 2 | | 141, 142 | 45 | 307 | 13 | 45 | | |
| 2 | | 143 | | | | | | |
| 3 | | 144 | | | | | | Group meeting |
| 3 | | 145, 146 | | | | | | |
| 3 | | 147, 148 | 46 | | | 46 | | |
| 3 | | 149, 150 | 47 | | | 47 | | |
| 2 | | 151, 152 | 48 | | | 48 | | |
| | | | | | | | | |
| | | | | | | | | |
| | | | | | | | | |
| | | | | | | | | |
| X | | 153 | Chapter checkup | | | | | |
| X | | 154 | Chapter project | | | | | |
| X | | 155 | Chapter review | | | | | |
| X | | 156 | Chapter challenge | | | | | |

# Chapter 5

# Instructional Management

A visitor to a well-run elementary classroom implementing adaptive education observes a beehive of activity. Teachers and students are busy with a purposeful task, yet many different activities are occurring at the same time. A teacher is conducting a reading lesson with a group of six students at a large, round table. Seven other students are working on reading or mathematics assignments, and the materials in front of them are of different types and from different levels of the reading and mathematics curricula. Two students are engaged in an experiment about light and optics at a science center, one student is putting together a puzzle map of North America, another is recording on a tape recorder a poem she has written, and another student is curled up in the library corner reading a book.

In a distant part of the room, four students are rehearsing a play, which they will present the next day. A classroom assistant (a volunteer or a paraprofessional) is circulating about the room. During a period of 5 minutes, he or she is observed checking one student's completed assignment, assisting another student who signaled for help, and interacting briefly with three others as he or she passes their way.

The classroom is not silent. The teacher, a special education teacher, the classroom assistant, and several students are talking in low voices so there is a pervasive hum, but no one is raising his or her voice. Although students occasionally walk from one place to another as they change tasks or get or return materials, the movement is purposeful, not distracting or disruptive. Occasionally a student may be observed daydreaming, wandering, or otherwise unengaged in learning, but such behaviors are infrequent and of short duration.

All of these activities are part of a systematic plan. Without a well-organized and efficient management system, teachers would be hard pressed to meet the demands for effective classroom implementation of adaptive education practices. In fact, the lack of such a system has often prevented teachers from implementing adaptive education. This chapter provides specific suggestions on procedures to plan and implement classroom management systems to support adaptive education programs.

This chapter focuses on specific suggestions for:

1. Effective and efficient management of space, facilities, and instructional materials

2. Time and task management
3. Coordination of regular classroom teachers and specialized professional staff
4. Student self-management
5. Utilization of a time management system known as the Self-Schedule System
6. Fostering motivation and discipline

Both static (space and materials) and dynamic (time and task) dimensions of instructional planning and delivery are addressed.

## MANAGEMENT OF SPACE, FACILITIES, AND INSTRUCTIONAL MATERIALS

In adaptive education programs, activities occur in a variety of instructional groupings. Sometimes students work in groups, with or without the teacher; at other times they work alone. Group sizes vary depending upon the activity. The classroom facilities—furniture and instructional materials—must be arranged (and rearranged) to accommodate all of these instructional groupings. Besides working in a variety of instructional groupings, it is likely that different students work simultaneously on different tasks and use different materials, depending on the levels of skill, learning styles, and interests. Under these circumstances, distribution of materials by the teacher would be time consuming and inefficient. Therefore, materials must be stored and arranged for easy access by students with minimal teacher or other staff intervention.

The following sections provide suggested guidelines for arranging space and facilities for effective classroom implementation.

### Guidelines for Storage of Materials

The variety of materials required for effective implementation of adaptive education programs and the need for access by students and teachers make efficient storage of these materials a high priority. Access and use are greatly facilitated if materials are clearly labeled and stored in readily accessible containers that require little effort for students to take out and return, and if all materials for a particular aspect of the curriculum are stored in a single area. The storage area for a given subject is best determined by the space and material requirements of the subject. For example, an area near a sink (if one is available) is designated for art activities because of easy access to water for mixing paints, washing hands, and cleaning paintbrushes, and a science activity area, which generally requires ample working space and electrical equipment, has a large table and is located near outlets. Each activity area should include storage space that can accommodate all materials to which students have direct access. A mathematics area, for example, should include space for workbooks, as well as a variety of manipulative materials and tools such as rulers, protractors, calculators, and computers. An art area needs storage space for paper, paints, scissors, and other art materials.

Activity and storage areas should be labeled and accessible. Labels can be words, letters, numbers, colors, or other codes appropriate to the materials and student levels. Management and maintenance of activity areas are facilitated by clear boundaries between adjacent areas, such as bookshelves, pegboards, or other functional partitions. Labels and boundaries make it easier for teachers to monitor the activity flow and students, and they facilitate the students' ability to locate and replace materials.

Commercial materials such as kits and games are usually packaged and labeled for ease of student use. Appropriate packaging is needed, however, for teacher-constructed activities and some commercial supplemental materials. Games or other activities with many small parts or pieces should be stored in appropriately labeled boxes, plastic bags, or other containers so that pieces are less likely to be scattered or lost. Containers should be large enough so that students can put materials in and take them out with ease.

It is useful to code or number activities within each learning area so that teachers and students can easily refer to particular activities, such as "Activity #4 in the Art Area." If materials consist of sequential sets, such as worksheets corresponding to successive objectives of the mathematics curriculum, materials should be stored in the proper order and sequentially coded. Teachers should check periodically to ensure that materials are complete and in good condition.

## Arranging Student Work Spaces and Other Facilities

Student desks traditionally are lined up in rows and separated from one another. Although this arrangement may be the choice of some teachers who are implementing adaptive education, it may not be as functional or facilitative as other arrangement possibilities. For example, to encourage instructional interactions among students, it may be preferable to arrange desks in clusters or to use tables seating two or more students instead of individual desks. Some desks can be kept separate while clustering others. In fact, this is probably advisable because some students work best in a quiet area or may need to work away from other students on occasion. No arrangement needs to be permanent. Teachers may decide to rearrange student work spaces frequently or infrequently depending on the instructional activities, the learning needs of the individual students, and teacher preference.

Program designers and teachers must decide whether students will be required to do all or most of their work at permanently assigned places or if they will be permitted to change their workplaces according to their activities. The decision should be carefully made, based on program and curriculum requirements, the available learning activities, and teacher preference.

If students are permanently assigned to work spaces, it is important that their desks or tables be located so that all have easy access to learning materials and activities. If students are permitted to change their work spaces depending on the activity or subject, it is best to cluster work spaces near materials. For some subjects or activities, such as reading, small rugs or cushions may be more appropriate than desks or tables.

If students are not assigned permanent desks or tables, each student needs a personal space for his or her belongings. This may be a desk to which the student is assigned for whole-class activities, or it may be a shelf, bin, or cubbyhole. Students may use their space to store personal belongings, as well as workbooks, notebooks, and folders.

The teacher's desk is preferably located near the door, which is easily accessible to students and visitors entering the room and permits teachers and visitors to enter and leave without disturbing students. The teacher's personal belongings and materials not directly for student use should be stored in facilities close to the teacher's desk.

For small-group instruction, the teacher needs a table or similar area suitable for working with as many as 8–10 students. The location of the table should allow the teacher a good view of the room so that he or she can see the rest of the class, especially if no other adult is in the classroom. A small table reserved for individual tutoring and testing should be located in a remote area of the room, such as a corner far from the door and away from traffic and noise.

Many alternatives for arranging materials and furniture in adaptive education classrooms are possible. Room designs of two classrooms are illustrated in Figure 5.1. and Figure 5.2., which are based on a "learning center" approach. Each curriculum subject or area has its own center, which includes both materials for that subject matter and work spaces for students using the materials. Figure 5.1. shows a floor plan for a primary grade classroom, and single desks are grouped together to promote group activities, peer help, and interaction among students working in the same activity area. Extra desks and furniture have been removed from the classroom to create more work space for students. Supplies and equipment for mathematics, science, and social studies are located in the same general area to encourage integration of these activities, and the construction area is located at some distance from academic areas. A large space in the center of the room is available for students to work with materials from various areas either on the floor or rugs, which encourages student interaction and integration of activities.

Figure 5.2. is a floor plan for a seventh grade classroom in a middle school. The room includes learning areas for English and writing, mathematics, science, civics, history, and geographic studies, as well as centers for listening, creative writing, supplemental mathematics, science, and current events activities. Most desks are arranged in clusters of four to encourage students to work interactively, although a few individual desks are located against a wall. Tables in the reading and math areas are used for small-group instruction, and can serve as additional student work spaces.

These figures represent only two of many possible plans, and suggest some alternative ways of designing primary and intermediate classrooms. Teachers should design their own classrooms, considering room size, available furniture and equipment, age of students, learning activities and materials, the curriculum requirements, and their personal teaching styles. Flexibility and efficiency are the important considerations in classroom design. Classroom arrangement should provide support to teacher and student curricular activities, to teacher and student preferences, and to responsible student functioning and behavior.

## TIME AND TASK MANAGEMENT

The variety of instructional activities that take place simultaneously in adaptive education classrooms mandates management procedures that facilitate the flow of activities with minimal confusion and interruption. An important planning task is coordinating the schedule and work assignments of all involved staff (classroom teachers, classroom assistants, and other resource personnel) and their students. Concurrently, the teachers have the task of developing schedules

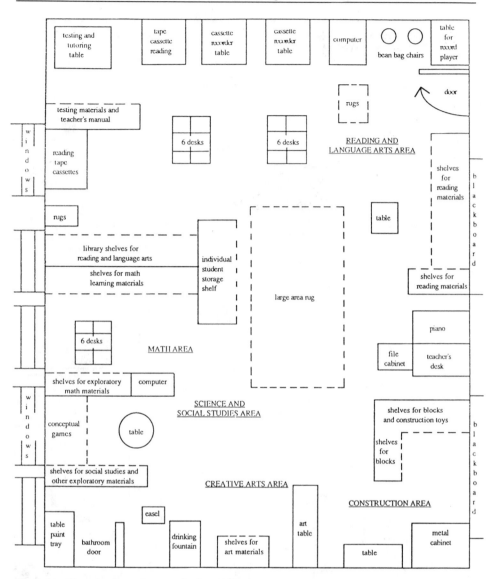

**Figure 5.1.** Floor plan for a primary grade classroom.

that include ample time for required group lessons and individual activities, as well as procedures for monitoring and managing these activities. All of these aspects of time and task management are discussed in the following sections.

## Scheduling

The school day in most schools is divided into six to eight periods of 30–60 minutes, and, within a class, each period is usually allocated to a particular subject. This kind of scheduling does not lend itself well to the implementation of adaptive education programs. More appropriate is some form of modular scheduling, with large blocks of time that teachers can use flexibly to meet instructional needs. At minimum, if individualized instruction is planned only for reading, language arts, and mathematics, half the school day (2½–3 hours)

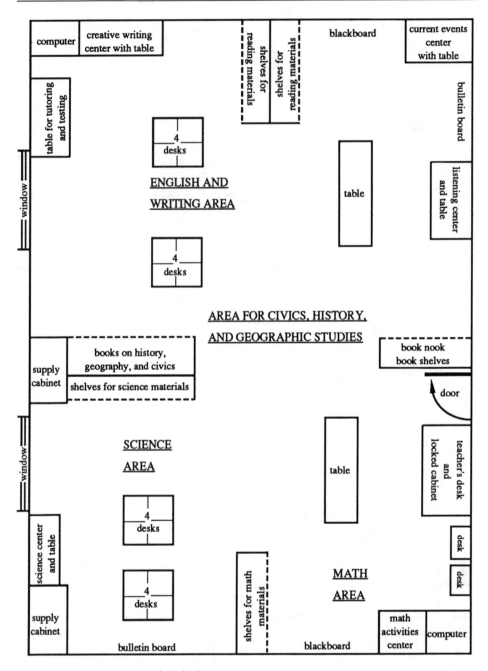

**Figure 5.2.**  Floor plan for a seventh grade classroom.

should be allocated to these subjects, and the remainder of the school day used for other subjects in more traditional group instruction. If the adaptive education program is to be implemented in most classes, teacher schedules and curriculum requirements can generally be accommodated best by arranging the school master schedule so that half the classes have an individualized basic skills instruction block in the morning, and the other half in the afternoon.

Another consideration in designing a master schedule is the availability of classroom assistants or volunteer paraprofessionals. If at all possible, each program classroom should have a classroom assistant for basic skills subjects. If available classroom assistants or volunteers are fewer than the program classes, the scheduling of basic skills subjects such as reading and mathematics requires more planning. One way to solve this may be to schedule basic skills subjects at different times so that the scheduling of classroom assistants accommodates class needs. Classroom assistants are assigned on a rotating basis to different classrooms during the basic skills block. For example, for six program classes and three classroom assistants, three classes can be scheduled for basic skills instructions in the morning and three in the afternoon, with each classroom assistant assigned to spend the morning in one classroom and the afternoon in another. If individualized instruction is planned for other subjects, the allocated block of time needs to be lengthened accordingly, and appropriate time should be scheduled for special subjects such as physical education and art.

School administrators need to set aside a weekly conference time of 40–60 minutes for program staff to meet, discuss common concerns, share ideas, and attend specific staff development sessions. This is generally done by scheduling common preparation time for particular instructional teams (e.g., all second grade teachers and relevant specialists). It is also important to schedule school-wide meetings for staff at least once a month. If a single meeting for all program staff cannot be arranged, times should be scheduled for meaningful subgroups of the staff (e.g., all primary grade teachers). Coordination of the scheduling needs discussed above may require considerable juggling. School administrators and others responsible for overseeing program implementation need to work together well before the start of the school year to develop an appropriate master schedule for the school.

## Instructional Grouping

Within the block of time allocated to individualized basic skills instruction, classroom teachers can use the time according to their preferences, the needs of the students, the curriculum, and school policy. Scheduling possibilities range from assigning specific portions of the time to particular subject areas to making the entire block available for several subject areas. It is, however, recommended that the teacher and class progress systematically from relatively rigid, teacher-controlled scheduling to more flexible, student-controlled scheduling as students acquire the skills needed to manage their own learning. Regardless of the rigidity or flexibility of scheduling, however, adequate time must be provided for group and individual work for all students.

Scheduling needs to accommodate a variety of types of instruction that depends on the student needs and curriculum objectives. For example, research on effective teaching has shown that direct instruction by the teacher promotes achievement in basic skills (Brophy, 1986). Direct instruction is efficiently delivered in group settings. In adaptive education programs, direct basic skills instruction takes place primarily in small groups that are based on diagnosed student needs. In contrast to a common impression that students spend most of their time working alone, research has shown that students in adaptive education programs spend about the same proportion of their time working in groups as do students in more traditional programs (Wang & Walberg, 1983, 1986).

Instructional grouping, especially for reading, is not new to most teachers. Elementary classes in traditional settings usually have their "robins," "blue jays," and "thrushes" (or, for the more adventurous, "pirates," "bandits," and "raiders"). The instruction offered in such groups is essentially the same as in adaptive education classes. The purpose of placing students in smaller instructional groups is to provide for their diverse needs. In reading, small-group instruction is used for such instructional outcomes as familiarization with vocabulary and concepts in new stories, group discussion of story content and assigned exercises, oral reading, skills development and guided practice, discussion of work assignments, review, and other reading-related group activities. Similarly, in mathematics, small-group instruction is used for introducing concepts and procedures, skills development, guided practice in new procedures, skills practice and maintenance drills, review of completed work, problem-solving activities, application of math skills, and other mathematics-related group activities.

The number of reading and mathematics groups appropriate for a class depends on student learning needs and available time. In a typical single-grade classroom, three or four reading groups and two or three mathematics groups are usual, and a larger number would probably be unmanageable. If two teachers are teamed for reading instruction for two classes, for example, the number of reading groups may increase to more adequately respond to student diversity and the teachers may form six different student groups.

Assigning students to groups should be a flexible and ongoing process. Reassignment becomes appropriate if a student's rate of progress or other evaluation indicates that his or her learning needs would be better met in another group. Sometimes it may be appropriate to combine groups or to divide a large group into smaller ones. If some students in a class are below the lowest group level, above the highest group level, or between two levels, for example, they can still participate in group activities while receiving additional, independent instruction and individualized assignments. Because ongoing assessment of student progress and instructional intervention are the core of effective implementation of adaptive education, changes in groupings based on student needs, availability of resources, and teacher time are perceived as the norm, and students do not feel stigmatized by changes in group assignments.

Heterogeneous grouping practices, such as multi-age grouping and classes that include mainstreamed students with special needs, provide an organizational structure that allows flexibility for directing resources and expertise to accommodate differences among students. This is in contrast with homogeneous organizational structures such as ability-tracked classes, special education classes that include only students labeled as "learning disabled" or "socially and emotionally disturbed," and tracking systems that segregate high- or low-achieving students in separate classes. Heterogeneous grouping practices are viewed as a responsive alternative to tracking practices, a typical school response to student diversity (Braddock & McPartland, 1990; Oakes, 1985). Heterogeneous grouping is based on an adaptive mode of instruction in contrast to the selective mode that predominates in homogeneous organizational structures. When adaptive education is implemented in heterogeneously grouped classes, all students benefit, including those who tend to make unusually slow or fast progress.

Through the integration of students who are at different developmental and academic achievement levels, the heterogeneous group organizational structure provides opportunities for spontaneous and planned peer modeling and peer tutoring (Allen, 1976; Jenkins, Pious, & Jewell, 1990; Villa & Thousand, 1988). Aside from socialization functions attributed to heterogeneous grouping practices, cooperative learning and peer tutoring situations have been found to contribute to the school achievement, and the motivation of tutors and tutees have increased teacher efficacy (Fogarty & Wang, 1982; Johnson, Skon, & Johnson, 1980; Slavin et al., 1985).

Some spontaneous peer tutoring and modeling might occur in homogeneously grouped classrooms. However, the greater age and ability span in heterogeneously grouped classrooms generally tends to result in a wider range of student talents, skills, and interests. When viewed as instructional resources, individual differences among students can be an asset in expanding instructional and learning time. In addition, the spontaneous or planned occurrence of peer tutoring in homogeneously grouped classrooms allows teachers to spend more instructional time with students who need extra assistance.

Obviously, establishing and revising schedules and student groups to accommodate all levels of reading and mathematics competency, while also arranging group and individual work for all students, may require considerable juggling as well as trial and error. The key is flexibility. For example, younger students generally need more frequent, but shorter, group meetings than older students and short individual assignments between group meetings. At higher grade levels, some groups may need daily meetings, while others meet two or three times a week with other assignments on intervening days.

Moreover, every student may not need to attend every lesson scheduled for members of his or her group. The teacher may decide to meet with two or three members of a subgroup more frequently for additional instruction. In addition, subgroups of students who have quickly mastered objectives or who have special interests and talents may meet with the teacher for individualized activities. The teacher may also decide to work with students on an individual basis, while more independent work is given to students who do not require as much teacher intervention. No student, however, should spend a disproportionately large amount of time in either individual or group settings, and group and individual activities should be balanced.

Table 5.1. presents an example of a plan of instruction for one reading group at the second grade level. The teacher has allotted 25–30 minutes on Mondays

**Table 5.1.** Plan of instruction for a reading group at approximately second grade level

| | Activity | | | |
|---|---|---|---|---|
| Day | Oral reading and vocabulary comprehension | Skills development | Individual tutoring | Group review and/or discussion |
| Monday | 25–30 minutes | 20–30 minutes | 25–30 minutes* | |
| Tuesday | | 25–30 minutes | 20–25 minutes* | 25–30 minutes* |
| Wednesday | 25–30 minutes* | | 20–25 minutes* | 25–30 minutes |
| Thursday | 25–30 minutes | | 20–25 minutes* | 25–30 minutes* |
| Friday | 25–30 minutes* | 25–30 minutes* | 20–30 minutes* | |

\* = optional time used if needed.

and Thursdays for oral reading and vocabulary comprehension, and 25–30 minutes on Tuesdays for skills development exercises, with optional time for group review and/or discussion and individual tutoring. If, for example, a student or small group needs additional help in developing oral reading or decoding skills, the teacher can establish a daily individual or small-group session as an optional activity.

## Management Techniques for Teacher Efficiency

In any educational program, the teacher's job has many dimensions and is often complicated by unpredictable events that require immediate attention and alterations in plans and schedules. In adaptive education programs, the complexity is increased by the need to coordinate the activities of groups and individuals, and without careful planning, the demands on teachers could quickly lead to information overload and frustration. This section describes daily—and minute-to-minute—management procedures that reduce demands on teacher time for management purposes, increase the efficiency of instructional delivery, and ease the flow of activities in the classroom.

A management system can support effective implementation by allowing each student to enter a program curriculum at any point commensurate with level of performance and to proceed at an individual rate. In this section, techniques are discussed that facilitate the management of student progress in the curriculum and enhance student productivity.

*Prescribing Assignments and Monitoring Student Progress* A support for teachers is the use of prescription sheets. Prescription sheets facilitate efficient use of student and teacher time by communicating individual assignments to students on an ongoing basis without interrupting instruction and learning routines.

Group instruction sessions are held to introduce students to using prescription sheets, and they are taught routines for using prescription sheets, just as they are taught routines for other instructional activities. When students have learned to follow their prescription sheets, teachers can usually prescribe work for a day for a curriculum unit, or a week, when students can self-monitor long-term assignments. Assignments for the next day or the next assignment are made while teachers move about the room, monitoring student work. Teachers with experience in implementing adaptive education programs indicate that they usually can prescribe the next assignments for most students in this way. At the start of each day (or at the end of the day when student work is checked, feedback received, and new assignments made by the teacher), students can locate their prescription sheets and begin work on their assignments without the teacher's immediate attention, and the teacher can proceed to group instruction, individual tutoring, or whatever else is scheduled without having to spend time telling students what to do.

Management of prescribed work is considerably facilitated if each student is provided wth a pocket folder for each subject of his or her individual curriculum. The student's prescription sheet and loose materials for completing assignments are kept in the folder. In addition to updated daily prescriptions, teachers can insert assigned worksheets directly into the folders. The student does not need to ask for worksheets, and the teacher does not need to interrupt activities to get the requested materials.

***Managing Student Requests for Individual Help***　Students often need help, feed-back, or evaluation while the teacher is busy with other students. A management system should enable students to request assistance without interrupting the teacher and to continue working while waiting for help.

An example of such a management technique designed to facilitate class-room implementation of adaptive education programs is the use of "teacher call signals" or "teacher calls." Teacher calls are sturdy, brightly colored objects, with sides that are two different colors. By placing the call on one side, the stu-dent signals to the teacher or others that "I need help," while the other side with a different color signals "No help is needed at this time." Teacher calls can be easily and inexpensively constructed from a variety of materials by students and classroom assistants, and sample teacher calls are shown in Figure 5.3.

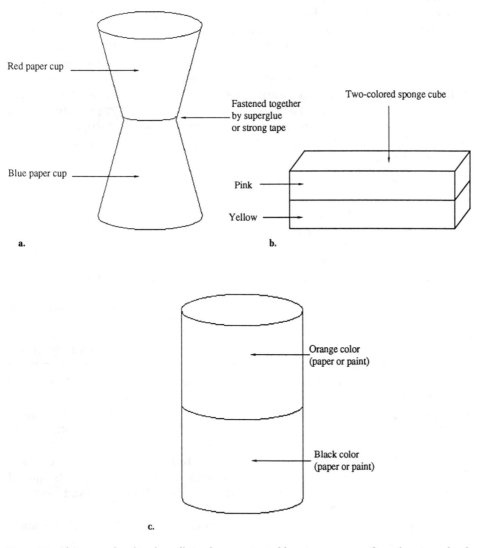

**Figure 5.3.**　Three examples of teacher call signals: **a.** constructed from two paper cups, **b.** cut from two-colored sponge cube, **c.** constructed from juice can.

Each work area can be provided with teacher calls and the number of calls in each area can signal the maximum number of students the area can accommodate, which manages overcrowding. By scanning the room periodically, the teacher can quickly note the students who need help, acknowledge their requests, and respond to them. Students may need to wait before receiving assistance. "Wait-time tasks" ensure that students use their time constructively. Wait-time tasks are useful activities that students can complete independently without help from the teacher. Recommended wait-time tasks include reading a book, reviewing exercises on previously learned skills, or completing enrichment activities. A set of wait-time task materials should be centrally located so that they are readily accessible to students.

*Monitoring Student Work: Interactive Teaching*   Research in conventional classrooms has shown that effective teachers do not stay at their desks while students are doing seatwork, but move about the room and interact with students to provide feedback and to monitor student performance and progress. In adaptive education classrooms, such monitoring of individual work is especially important. Interactive teaching enables the teacher to systematically monitor students who are working independently, respond to requests for assistance, and periodically check the class as a whole. The teacher engages in interactive teaching when group meetings or individual tutoring sessions are not in progress. The teacher moves about the classroom in a predetermined path that ensures that all parts of the room where students are working are seen. The teacher stops to interact briefly with individual students, although not necessarily every student. The types of interactions that may occur include:

1. Assisting students who requested help
2. Diagnosing learning difficulties
3. Teaching new content or reinforcing old content
4. Checking completed assignments
5. Revising or updating prescriptions
6. Monitoring student progress
7. Assessing individual learning by asking what the student is trying to accomplish and how
8. Providing feedback to students about their task performance and work progress

Interactive teaching enables teachers to gather important information regarding each student's learning needs and working styles, to respond to these individual differences immediately, and to check students' work in their presence and provide immediate feedback. Teachers can schedule individual tutoring sessions or small-group meetings if they identify students who require more extended tutoring. Frequent checking of students' work in their presence is important, because potential learning problems can be identified before they become serious. Frequent checking indicates to students that performance standards must be met before they can go on to other assignments. Students should not begin a new assignment without completing the previous one and having it checked.

Teachers or classroom assistants can usually check completion of assignments in primary grades quickly while circulating about the room. Such immediate checking is not always possible in higher grades. Under these circumstances, a classroom assistant or designated student may be assigned to certify completion or direct the student to seek teacher assistance before continuing; a teacher may briefly check assignments, leaving complete checking for a later time; or students can be directed to check their own answers with scoring keys, and correct errors or request help if they cannot.

Since the need to conduct group instruction and to tutor individual students may leave the classroom teacher little time for interactive teaching, it is helpful to have other personnel monitor individual students. For example, classroom assistants or specialist teachers on the team can circulate about the room helping individual students while the regular classroom teacher is otherwise engaged. If two classroom teachers have developed arrangements for an instructional team, one can circulate among students while the other conducts group meetings. Principals, special education teachers, Chapter 1 reading or math teachers, and other resource personnel are likely to find interactive teaching a good way to assess the progress of individual students and the class as a whole. If student teachers or classroom volunteers are assigned to the classroom, their participation in interactive teaching removes some instructional management responsibilities from the classroom teacher and also provides the student teacher with invaluable experience in diagnosing and prescribing for individual needs.

## COORDINATING THE WORK OF PROGRAM STAFF

Contrary to expectations and perceptions, implementation of an adaptive education program generally does not require more staff. The number and type of staff, as well as the ratio to students, are basically the same as in more traditional educational programs, although smaller teacher to student ratios may increase instructional time. The main difference between adaptive education and traditional programs (and/or less effective implementation of adaptive education programs) is in how staff resources are utilized. Some realignment of roles and increased coordination of the work of staff members are required for efficient and effective implementation of adaptive education programs. Coordination and teaming are particularly critical if students with special needs are integrated in regular classes. Classroom teachers and specialist staff need to work together closely as a team to effectively provide the needed instructional and related services for these students in regular classroom settings.

Paraprofessionals as classroom assistants are essential for effective implementation of adaptive education, given the demands of providing small-group and individual instruction on the classroom teacher. Ideally, an assistant is assigned to each program classroom during the time block for individualized basic skills instruction. Because the time block is often only ½ of the school day, one half-time classroom assistant per program class is usually sufficient. Parents and other volunteers can learn to perform many functions of paraprofessionals. Classroom assistants can perform these tasks under teacher supervision:

> Helping students with their seatwork while the classroom teacher conducts group lessons or works with other students
> Tutoring individuals
> Checking completed student work
> Trafficking students in and out of activity areas

Constructing learning materials
Photocopying and other clerical tasks

It is recommended that teachers meet briefly with their classroom assistants each day to discuss duties and other matters, such as instructional concerns about individual students. Above all, teachers need to learn to use the extra help in their classrooms to benefit themselves and their students. Management of personnel resources is both an art and a science. If teachers do not use the personnel effectively, teacher assistants or parent volunteers may be a burden rather than a help.

## Instructional Teaming

Two types of teaming are effective in classrooms implementing adaptive education programs: teaming between two (or more) classroom teachers who share responsibility for students in the combined classes, and teaming between classroom teachers and resource personnel (e.g., special education teachers, Chapter 1 teachers, or specialist teachers) to deliver special services in regular classrooms.

By working together in instructional teams and by sharing talents and resources, classroom and specialist teachers can greatly increase their efficacy in providing options and individual alternatives to students. A wider variety of instructional alternatives and teaching styles is available to support instruction and learning. Instructional teaming between regular classroom teachers and specialized personnel are especially critical to instructional support and related services for students with special needs who are integrated in regular classrooms. Compared to students in self-contained classrooms, students in classrooms with instructional teaming have been found to spend more of their school time receiving instruction. In addition, studies have found significant differences in student achievement, self-concept, and attitudes toward school in classrooms with instructional teaming (Pugach & Johnson, 1989; Schmuck & Runkel, 1985; Witt & Martens, 1988).

Teaming between two classes at the same grade level or between successive grade levels increases efficiency and helps to manage the delivery of instruction in a number of ways. First, reading and mathematics groups can be formed by combining students from both classes. The reading and mathematics skill levels of both classes probably overlap so the learning needs of all students can be met by a smaller number of groups than would be needed for the two classes separately. Second, while one teacher is instructing a group or an individual, the second teacher can engage in interactive teaching with other students. Third, by giving students access to the learning materials and resources of both classrooms, options for learning and individualized instruction are increased. Instructional teaming is particularly helpful if the school is unable to provide enough classroom assistants, because a full- or part-time classroom assistant may be sufficient to help two classes rather than one class.

In traditional educational settings, resource personnel such as reading specialists, special educators, speech and hearing specialists, compensatory education (Chapter 1) teachers, English as a Second Language (ESL) teachers, psychologists, and social workers tend to function relatively independently of regular classroom teachers. It is common practice for resource personnel to "pull out" students from their regular classes and provide the services in a resource room. These support staff have not been shown to improve student outcomes as expected (Jenkins, Pious, & Jewell, 1990; Oakes, 1985; Wang, Reynolds, & Walberg, 1988). Even if these pullouts are infrequent and brief, they tend to interrupt the flow of classroom activities and deprive students of classroom instruction. In addition, the special treatment sets these individuals apart from other students and defines them as different, generally in a negative way.

In adaptive education programs, this segregation of students is discouraged. First, since basic skills instruction is individualized for all students, students with special needs do not perceive themselves nor are perceived by others as different. Second, special services can usually be integrated into regular classroom activities, which reduces or eliminates the need for pullouts. It is clear that classroom teachers and resource personnel in adaptive education programs need to work as a team, coordinating their activities and roles flexibly to plan and deliver appropriate instruction to each student. These professionals, as well as the students they serve, benefit by such team effort and collective expertise.

Instructional teaming by regular classroom teachers and resource personnel requires major rethinking and restructuring of roles, scheduling, and resource allocation (Reynolds, Wang, & Walberg, 1987). The role of resource personnel includes, for example, provision of support services to regular classroom teachers and direct instruction of students. Special educators and other resource personnel can support the work of regular classroom teachers by providing special materials, offering advice on teaching methods to meet individual student needs, and helping to solve instructional problems.

The establishment of cooperative and integrative links between regular teachers and specialized resource personnel must be a key component in the design of programs that aim to institutionalize the educational restructuring required to effectively respond to the diversity of needs of students in regular classroom settings. In particular, the roles of classroom teachers, specialist teachers, principals, school psychologists, and other related personnel must be redefined to achieve an effective interface among all of those whose work is directly or indirectly related to enhancing student learning.

In adaptive education classrooms, regular teachers are expected to implement complex instructional procedures for diverse student populations, and are responsible for serving all students in the mainstream. The increased instructional demands of this approach, however, are offset considerably by support from specialist teachers and other professionals who are members of the instructional team in regular classes. Under these conditions, the work of the regular teacher can be demanding, yet rewarding. In working with specialists, regular teachers have the support of a powerful team of colleagues who possess a full understanding of the curriculum and instructional planning.

## STUDENTS AS RESOURCES FOR MANAGEMENT AND INSTRUCTION

Students themselves are an important resource for time and task management in the classroom, because a major goal of adaptive education is that students take on increasing responsibility for managing their own learning. Students can contribute to classroom management by helping with routine classroom management tasks, peer tutoring, and by scheduling and monitoring their own activities. Besides taking on routine classroom duties and helping each other, students can be taught to take on responsibility for managing their own learning and behavior. Development of student self-management abilities benefits both teachers and students. Teachers, freed from some management responsibilities, have more time to teach. Students, given greater responsibility for their own learning, develop an increased sense of personal control. A student's sense of personal control has been shown to be related positively to efficiency in learning and problem solving (Wang & Palincsar, 1989; Zimmerman, 1986). For these reasons, it is recommended that designers of adaptive education programs for schools incorporate systematic procedures for developing student self-management skills.

In every classroom, routine noninstructional and instructional tasks must be carried out on a regular basis, and teachers can save time and provide practice in self-management by teaching students to perform these tasks. Students can also be instructional resources for other students. For example, if a student needs a drill or a test on a rote learning task, another student can be responsible for administering the drill or test. Students can be encouraged to help each other with tasks in peer tutoring. Not only is the teacher freed for other instructional activities, but both the tutor and the tutee benefit from the interaction (Cohen, Kulik, & Kulik, 1982; Fogarty & Wang, 1982; Jenkins, Pious, & Jewell, 1990).

Adaptive education programs have made different kinds of provisions for student self-management. For example, the Team-Assisted Individualization Program (Slavin, 1983) uses cooperative groups in which students provide help and instructional support for their peers. Teachers in programs such as Behavior Analysis (Ramp & Rhine, 1981) use techniques such as contingency contracting, which is a systematic arrangement of reinforcing events in order to strengthen or weaken specific behavior. The Adaptive Learning Environments Model (ALEM) incorporates a system, the Self-Schedule System, for student self-scheduling of teacher-prescribed and self-selected tasks (Wang & Stiles, 1976). Teachers in adaptive education programs can incorporate a combination of techniques, depending on student grade levels, school policies, and teacher preferences. For illustrative purposes, the Self-Schedule System is described below.

## The Self-Schedule System

The Self-Schedule System was designed to serve two purposes: to help students develop self-management skills to effectively function in adaptive education classrooms, and to increase the amount of time teachers can spend in providing instruction rather than in managing students. In the Self-Schedule System, self-management refers to students' ability to manage their time and the tasks they are expected to complete. The Self-Schedule System is designed to support students in developing management skills for making choices and decisions about, for example, the order in which their assigned tasks are completed, the optional activities they choose, and how to manage their time so that they can complete their tasks in a specified time.

Specific skills students acquire under the Self-Schedule System are:

1. Ability to follow instructions
2. Knowledge of the learning resources (e.g., materials and activities in the learning centers and activity areas) as well as rules regarding selection and use

3.  Ability to locate, manage, use, and store all learning materials and equipment with little or no teacher supervision
4.  Ability to know when and where to get help
5.  Knowledge regarding transition from one activity to another

The Self-Schedule System is based on three assumptions about self-management abilities. The first assumption is that self-management abilities are learned sets of skills, and students do not develop self-management skills automatically with increased age. The second is that the cognitive and social demands of assuming responsibility for school learning require a variety of abilities. For example, choosing which of two teacher-prescribed tasks to do first and completing both tasks in 1 hour is simpler than selecting two of five optional activities, deciding in what order to do these in addition to teacher-prescribed tasks, and completing all tasks in 3 hours. The third assumption is that development of self-management skills is a gradual process, and that students need to be guided through a progression beginning with few demands of responsibility and working up to a more demanding level of responsibility.

A series of objectives for developing self-management skills in adaptive education classrooms, arranged in order of complexity, is shown in Figure 5.4. At the bottom are relatively simple skills (levels A and B) that involve deciding the order of completion of two or more tasks of a single type and completing them. Skill levels A and B are prerequisites to Skill level C (deciding on the order of two or more teacher-prescribed and self-selected tasks and completing them), and Skill level C is a prerequisite to Skill level D. The number of tasks to be completed and the amount of time increase from levels A, B, and C (two tasks, less than ½ of the school day) to D (½ the school day) to E (1 school day) to F (5 school days). The student who has attained Skill level F can schedule a week's activities (teacher-prescribed and self-selected) on Monday and complete all of the tasks by the end of the day on Friday.

The hierarchy in Figure 5.4. may also be interpreted as a sequence of objectives for the instruction of self-management skills. As with any other skill, students will progress through the hierarchy of self-management skills at different rates. The highest level achieved is also likely to vary among students. Most primary grade students will probably not exceed level D, although some may reach level E or even F. Most older students can reach level D and beyond, but some may not get past level C. At any given time, therefore, some students in a class may be working on mastering objective B, others on C, and still others on D. Some students may benefit from a simple description of the system while others require repeated practice through role playing and assigned tasks at each level. Above all, training of self-management skills must be adapted to individual differences in the same way as instruction in reading and mathematics.

Helping students become proficient self-managers requires organizational and instructional support, and students and teachers need a system for recording scheduled teacher-assigned and self-selected activities, and procedures for checks to ease teacher monitoring of student task completion and movement in and out of activity areas. Two examples, the self-schedule sheet and the self-scheduling board, are discussed.

The self-schedule sheet is a record in which the teacher and the student enter planned tasks, and the teacher records task completion. The forms are designed by the teacher based on the available learning activities and learning

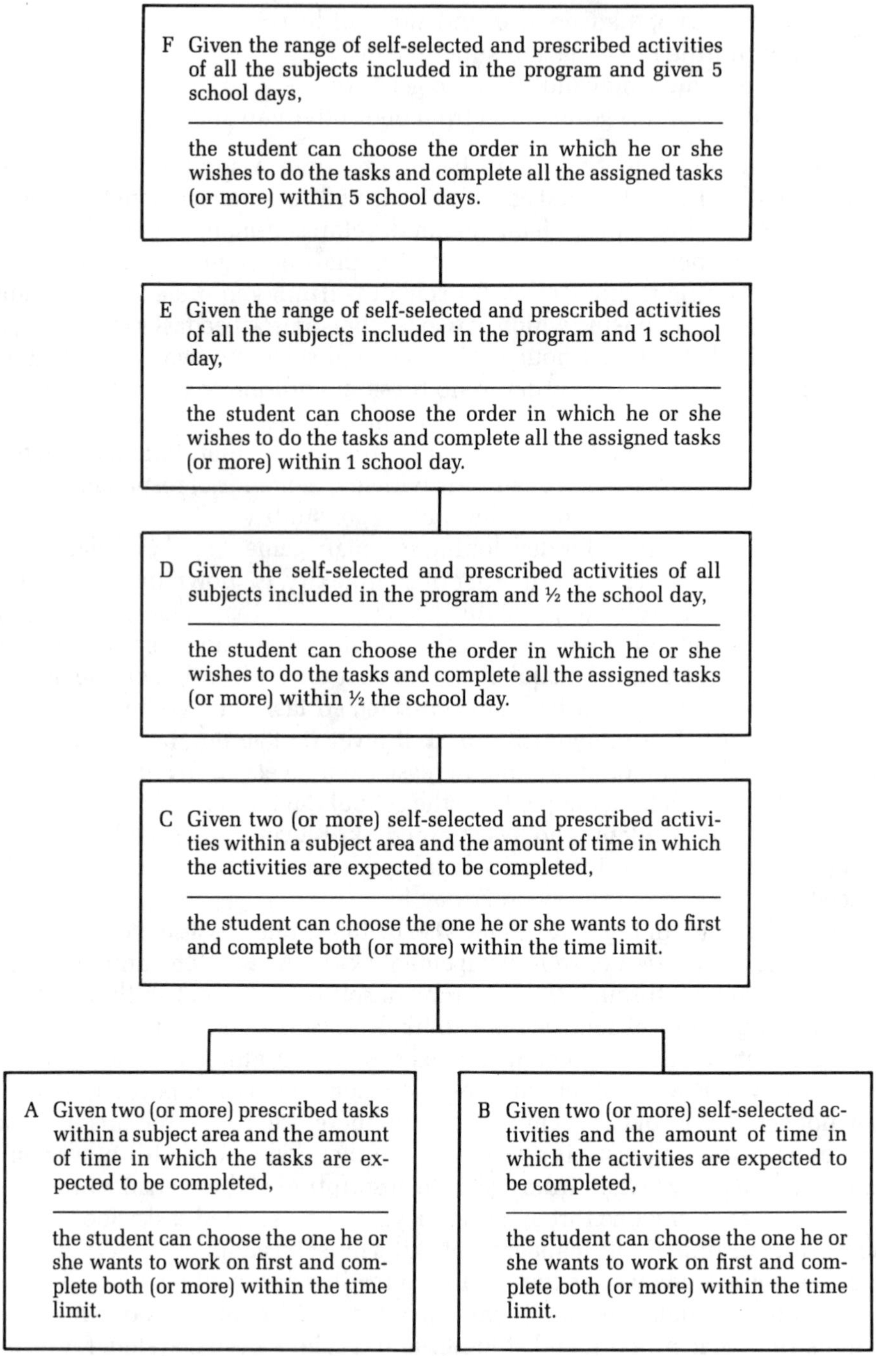

F  Given the range of self-selected and prescribed activities of all the subjects included in the program and given 5 school days,

the student can choose the order in which he or she wishes to do the tasks and complete all the assigned tasks (or more) within 5 school days.

E  Given the range of self-selected and prescribed activities of all the subjects included in the program and 1 school day,

the student can choose the order in which he or she wishes to do the tasks and complete all the assigned tasks (or more) within 1 school day.

D  Given the self-selected and prescribed activities of all subjects included in the program and ½ the school day,

the student can choose the order in which he or she wishes to do the tasks and complete all the assigned tasks (or more) within ½ the school day.

C  Given two (or more) self-selected and prescribed activities within a subject area and the amount of time in which the activities are expected to be completed,

the student can choose the one he or she wants to do first and complete both (or more) within the time limit.

A  Given two (or more) prescribed tasks within a subject area and the amount of time in which the tasks are expected to be completed,

the student can choose the one he or she wants to work on first and complete both (or more) within the time limit.

B  Given two (or more) self-selected activities and the amount of time in which the activities are expected to be completed,

the student can choose the one he or she wants to work on first and complete both (or more) within the time limit.

**Figure 5.4.** A hierarchy of objectives for the development of student self-management skills.

needs of the students. A sample self-schedule sheet for a third grade class is shown in Figure 5.5. A slash in a block indicates that the subject or activity was assigned to or selected by a student on that day. Teachers also write the student's scheduled group meetings for that week, as shown in the figure. The time that a

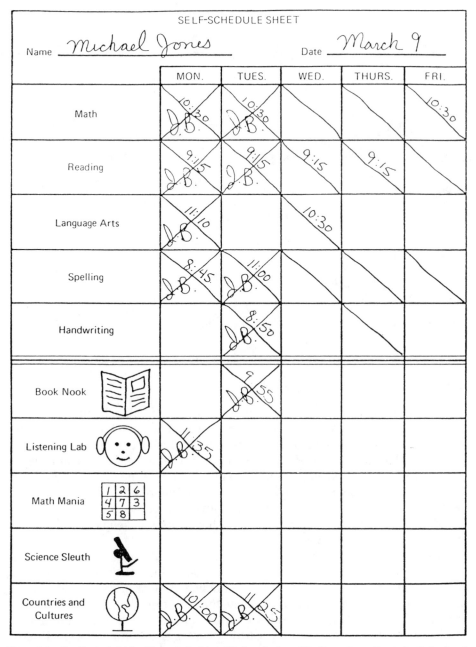

**Figure 5.5.** A self-schedule sheet for a student in a third grade class. (The figure shows the student's sheet as it would appear at the end of the day Tuesday.)

student begins an activity is entered in the block by the teacher or student. When the activity is completed, it is checked by the teacher who crosses the slash and initials the block. Thus, the self-schedule serves as a daily and weekly planning guide for the student and as a record of tasks completed for both student and teacher. Figure 5.6. shows an example of a self-schedule sheet for a seventh grade student.

SELF-SCHEDULE SHEET

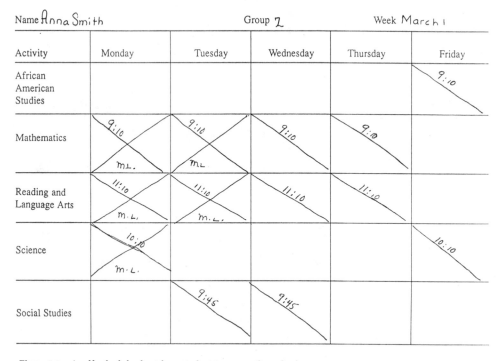

Name Anna Smith                    Group 7                    Week March 1

| Activity | Monday | Tuesday | Wednesday | Thursday | Friday |
|---|---|---|---|---|---|
| African American Studies | | | | | 9:10 |
| Mathematics | 9:10 / mL. | 9:10 / mL | 9:10 | 9:0 | |
| Reading and Language Arts | 11:10 / m.L, | 11:10 / m.L, | 11:10 | 11:10 | |
| Science | 10:10 / m.L. | | | | 10:10 |
| Social Studies | | 9:45 | 9:45 | | |

**Figure 5.6.** A self-schedule sheet for a student in a seventh grade class.

Teachers need to revise the format or content of self-schedule sheets as changes are made in classroom learning resources. Each student in the class receives a copy of the self-schedule sheet each week. Teacher assignments are usually entered for the entire week, while student choices are made on a daily basis.

The self-schedule sheet is used in conjunction with the prescription sheet. The prescription sheet is used to keep track of student progress through the curriculum, including lessons covered and workbook pages assigned and completed, for each subject. The self-schedule sheet is used to keep track of student time spent in various activities.

The self-scheduling board is a technique for monitoring student movement in and out of learning centers and activity areas, and is a large board, such as a bulletin board, to which tags or cards are attached. A block of space is labeled for each learning center, and students indicate the center in which they are working by inserting name tags or cards, or hanging tags on hooks. If the teacher limits the number of students working in a learning center at one time, the pockets or hooks are equal to the allowed maximum. Additional hooks or pockets provide storage for name cards or tags when they are not in use.

When a student selects a particular learning center, the student places his or her name card or tag in the appropriate place before going to the chosen center. If all of the pockets or hooks for the desired center are already in use, the student must make another choice. After completing the activity and having it checked, the student moves his or her marker to the next center or stores it. The self-scheduling board provides daily practice for students in making choices, identifying options, and responsibility for materials.

*Implementing the Self-Schedule System* A management system such as the Self-Schedule System is new to most students and needs to be implemented gradually. For example, at the start of a school year, students generally are assigned specific workplaces and specific tasks to be completed at specific times. During the initial days and weeks, the teacher then gradually introduces instruction in the use of prescription sheets and carrying out prescribed tasks, demonstrates activities in each learning center, describes and demonstrates the use of materials in each center, provides opportunities for each student to try out activities, explains the use of the self-schedule sheet and self-scheduling board, and provides guided practice in their use.

When students are able to use their self-schedule sheets and the self-scheduling board and to complete activities under supervision, the teacher can begin to implement student self-scheduling. For example, teachers may institute a 40-minute block of time for a subject, and students can decide which of two teacher-prescribed assignments to complete first (objective A, Figure 5.4.). Similar blocks of time are allocated to self-chosen activities, and students may select two activity areas and complete their tasks in any order (objective B in Figure 5.4.). The teacher monitors students to ensure that they use their prescription sheets and self-schedule forms appropriately, indicate their choice of learning centers on the self-scheduling board, obtain materials for each task, undertake the activities in an orderly manner, use teacher calls or other signals to request teacher assistance or checking of work, and complete both activities within the time limit. When students do all of these things, the teacher extends the blocks of time for teacher-prescribed and self-selected tasks. Teachers experienced in implementing adaptive education programs have found that a reasonable goal for most classrooms is that at least 80% of the students are working at the level of objective D or beyond by the end of the first semester.

Implementors of adaptive education programs often are questioned by teachers and administrators about a motivational or disciplinary system, or what to do if a student consistently exhibits a learning or behavior problem. Although some adaptive education programs may incorporate a particular motivational system such as a token economy, many leave such matters to the discretion of individual teachers within the guidelines of school or district policy.

A basic premise in effective classroom management is to arrange the classroom environment so that problems are unlikely to arise. Students who perceive a high level of personal control over their own behavior are more task oriented and use problem-solving strategies more efficiently to mediate their learning (cf. Levine & Wang, 1983; Zimmerman, 1986). Consequently, motivation and discipline problems are less likely to arise. The management system described in this chapter is designed to foster conditions that promote self-management as a preventive rather than remedial measure. For example, the individualization of assignments to match the abilities and needs of individual students tends to decrease the likelihood of frequent failure, a condition often associated with off-task and disruptive behavior. Teaming classroom teachers with specialist staff increases resources for developing problem-solving strategies, and the emphasis on student self-management tends to shift the responsibility for appropriate behavior from the teacher to the students. Thus, students are expected to monitor their own behavior rather than expecting that the teacher control behavior through disciplinary actions.

Guidelines for promoting motivation and discipline that are applicable to conventional and adaptive educational settings include:

1.  If the school motivational and disciplinary policies and practices work satisfactorily, they should be followed and enforced consistently.
2.  If such policies do not exist, fair and workable policies should be developed and implemented.
3.  Motivational and disciplinary policies and practices of the school and district should be clearly communicated to school staff, students, and parents.

At the classroom level, guidelines include:

1.  Rules governing appropriate classroom behavior should be explained to students from the first day of class.
2.  Routines for dealing with recurring events (e.g., requesting permission to leave the room or using special equipment) should also be established early.
3.  Students should be systematically taught to work within the classroom rules and routines.
4.  Teachers should establish a positive classroom climate by clearly communicating expectations for successful performance, praising student accomplishments, showing an interest in student work, and showing respect and personal regard for each student and his or her instructional or motivational problems.
5.  Teachers should adopt a problem-solving approach that involves their knowledge and experience and possibly other resources to define the problem, plan and implement appropriate interventions, evaluate their effects, revise the plan if necessary, and continue until the problem is solved.

## SUMMARY

This chapter provides guidelines for planning and implementing management systems to support classroom implementation of adaptive education. Among the factors to be considered in designing such a management system are the arrangement of space and materials, scheduling and monitoring student work, coordination of the work of program staff, restructuring and redefining staff roles, and development of student self-management abilities. By using the suggested guidelines in this chapter, in combination with information about the school's human and material resources, program implementors and instructional leaders can design an instructional management system optimally suited to the needs of the particular school, its teachers, and its students.

## REFERENCES

Allen, V.L. (Ed.). (1976). *Children as teachers: Theory and research on tutoring.* New York: Academic Press.

Brophy, J.E. (1986). Research linking teacher behavior to student achievement: Potential implications for instruction of Chapter 1 students. In B.I. Williams, P.A. Richmond, & B.J. Mason (Eds.), *Designs for compensatory education: Conference proceedings and papers* (Vol. IV, pp. 121–179). Washington, DC: Research and Evaluation Associates.

Braddock, J.H., & McPartland, J.M. (1990). Alternatives to tracking. *Educational Leadership, 47*(7), 76–79.

Cohen, P.A., Kulik, J.A., & Kulik, C-L.C. (1982). Educational outcomes of tutoring: A meta-analysis of findings. *American Educational Research Journal, 19*(2), 237–248.

Fogarty, J., & Wang, M.C. (1982). An investigation of the class-age peer tutoring process: Some implications for instructional design and motivation. *Elementary School Journal, 82*(5), 451–469.

Jenkins, J.R., Pious, C.G., & Jewell, M. (1990). Special education and the regular education initiative: Basic assumptions. *Exceptional Children, 56*(6), 479–491.

Johnson, D.W., Skon, L., & Johnson, R. (1980). The effects of cooperative, competitive, and individualistic goal structures on student achievement on different types of tasks. *American Educational Research Journal, 17,* 83–93.

Levine, J.M., & Wang, M.C. (Eds.) (1983). *Teacher and student perceptions: Implications for learning.* Hillsdale, NJ: Lawrence Erlbaum Associates.

Oakes, J. (1985). *Keeping track: How schools structure inequality.* New Haven: Yale University Press.

Pugach, M.C., & Johnson, L.J. (1990). Meeting diverse needs through professional peer collaboration. In W. Stainback & S. Stainback (Eds.), *Support networks for inclusive schooling: Interdependent integrated education* (pp. 123–137). Baltimore: Paul H. Brookes Publishing Co.

Ramp, E.A., & Rhine, W.R. (1981). Behavior Analysis Model. In W. R. Rhine (Ed.), *Making schools more effective: New directions from Follow Through.* New York: Academic Press.

Reynolds, M.C., Wang, M.C., & Walberg, H.J. (1987). The necessary restructuring of special and regular education. *Exceptional Children, 53*(5), 391–398.

Schmuck, R.A., & Runkel, P.J. (1985). *Handbook of organization development in schools* (3rd ed.). Palo Alto, CA: Mayfield Publishing Company.

Slavin, R.E. (1983). *Team-assisted individualization: A cooperative learning solution for adaptive instruction in mathematics.* Baltimore: Johns Hopkins University Center for the Social Organization of Schools.

Slavin, R.E., Sharan, S., Kagan, S., Hertz-Lazarowitz, R., Webb, C., & Schmuck, R. (1985). *Learning to cooperate, cooperating to learn.* New York: Plenum Press.

Villa, R.A., & Thousand, J.S. (1988). Enhancing success in heterogeneous classrooms and schools: The powers of partnership. *Teacher Education and Special Education, 11*(4), 144–154.

Wang, M.C., & Palincsar, A.S. (1989). Teaching students to assume an active role in their learning. In M.C. Reynolds (Ed.), *Knowledge base for the beginning teacher* (pp. 71–84). Oxford: Pergamon.

Wang, M.C., Reynolds, M.C., & Walberg, H.J. (1988). Integrating the children of the second system. *Phi Delta Kappan, 70*(3), 248–251.

Wang, M.C., & Stiles, B. (1976). An investigation of children's concepts of self-responsibility for their school learning. *American Educational Research Journal, 13*(3), 159–179.

Wang, M.C., & Walberg, H.J. (1983). Adaptive instruction and classroom time. *American Educational Research Journal, 20*(4), 601–626.

Wang, M.C., & Walberg, H.J. (1986). Classroom climate as mediator of educational inputs and outputs. In B.J. Fraser (Ed.), *The study of learning environments 1985* (pp. 47–58). Salem, OR: Assessment Research.

Witt, J.C., & Martens, B.K. (1988). Problems with problem-solving consultation: A re-analysis of assumptions, methods, and goals. *School Psychology Review, 17*(2), 211–226.

Zimmerman, B.J. (Ed.). (1986). [Special issue]. *Contemporary Educational Psychology, 11*(4).

# Chapter 6

# Pre-implementation Staff Training

Pre-implementation training is used to refer to training activities that occur prior to program implementation, but that is only the first stage of a process that continues to provide support to staff throughout the program. In the context of this chapter, staff development might be a more appropriate term than training. Staff development more accurately characterizes the process of providing systematic, ongoing professional development opportunities to help school staff become progressively more effective in their program implementation roles.

Staff development for the implementation of innovative programs has two major phases: pre-implementation training and implementation training support. The focus of this chapter is the first stage: pre-implementation training. Design and provision of continued staff development support after initial implementation is the subject of Chapter 7.

Nothing is more crucial to successful implementation of an innovative educational program than systematically designed and implemented staff development based on the information and technical needs of the staff. Studies of the implementation and outcomes of innovative programs have shown that effective staff development is a major variable in successful program implementation and institutionalization (Ellett & Wang, 1987; Fullan, 1990). The implementation of innovative school improvements in the 1970s and 1980s has pointed to the crucial role of systematic staff development in supporting effective program implementation (cf. Joyce, 1990; Reynolds, 1989; Vaughan, Wang, & Dytman, 1987; Wang, Haertel, & Walberg, 1990). Effective training provides teachers and staff with knowledge and techniques, and enables staff to be directly involved in the program planning process. Staff development activities allow staff to define the problems inherent in starting a new program, develop a process for resolving the problems, and discuss concerns related to implementation. Thus, staff development can be seen as an opportunity to involve the school staff in determining their own training needs, which fosters program ownership and commitment to implementation.

This chapter focuses on the design and delivery of pre-implementation training that is adapted to the needs of the school, district, and individual participants and provides participants with the information, skills, and materials needed to initiate implementation of adaptive education programs in their schools. This chapter is of particular interest to district and school administrators, instructional leaders, and others responsible for planning and maintaining program implementation, and consists of three major sections. The first discusses the goals and design of a data-based approach to staff development. The second focuses on planning pre-implementation training. The third section describes the content and delivery of pre-implementation training.

## A DATA-BASED APPROACH TO STAFF DEVELOPMENT

The purpose of staff development prior to implementation of innovative programs is to provide teachers and school staff the opportunity to retool and develop knowledge, attitudes, and expertise to effectively bring about program implementation that ensures positive student outcomes. Thus, a major goal of this staff development is to provide continuing professional development and technical help to assist teachers in initiating and maintaining the implementation of adaptive education. Staff development activities associated with innovative instructional programs are expected to promote staff expertise and positive attitudes toward program implementation. Staff development is a process that calls for substantial time and personal investment on the part of school staff. According to Hall and his associates (Hall, Loucks, Rutherford, & Newlove, 1975), adoption of an innovative program generally involves progression through a series of levels.

As Figure 6.1. shows, the three levels of use that are characteristic of individuals who have not yet used the innovation are nonuse, orientation (awareness), and preparation. After program implementation begins, the stages continue: mechanical use, routine, refinement, integration, and renewal. Although change is assumed to follow this order in all cases, all levels are not necessarily attained. This is the importance of staff development: The support of a well-designed staff development program enables staff to progress to true expertise.

The role of pre-implementation training, as discussed in this chapter, is to help school staff move relatively quickly from nonuse to orientation and preparation and set the stage for the shift to mechanical use in the early months of implementation. At that point, the ongoing support component of staff development takes over to facilitate a high degree of program implementation, refinement, institutionalization, and renewal (see chap. 7, this volume.).

A staff development program that successfully promotes teacher growth from nonuse to renewal must possess certain characteristics and be rooted in and flexible to daily implementation needs of school staff. The common practice of providing one-shot lectures or workshops that often do not address immediate classroom needs is seldom effective in producing lasting change. In this chapter, staff development activities based on specific day-to-day implementation needs of individual staff are referred to as a data-based approach to staff development.

In the staff development model described in this chapter, pre-implementation training and continued professional development support are data-based, and the content and delivery of the training are guided by data concerning school and staff resources, implementation needs of the staff, and constraints. Continued training support and technical assistance during implementation is based on the assessed level of implementation attained by individual staff and the school as a whole. In both cases, staff development is designed to meet the par-

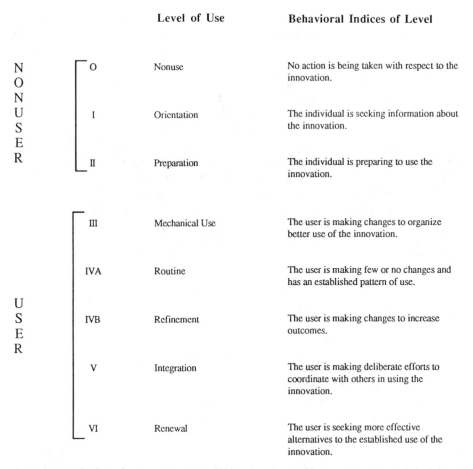

| | Level of Use | Behavioral Indices of Level |
|---|---|---|
| **NONUSER** 0 | Nonuse | No action is being taken with respect to the innovation. |
| I | Orientation | The individual is seeking information about the innovation. |
| II | Preparation | The individual is preparing to use the innovation. |
| **USER** III | Mechanical Use | The user is making changes to organize better use of the innovation. |
| IVA | Routine | The user is making few or no changes and has an established pattern of use. |
| IVB | Refinement | The user is making changes to increase outcomes. |
| V | Integration | The user is making deliberate efforts to coordinate with others in using the innovation. |
| VI | Renewal | The user is seeking more effective alternatives to the established use of the innovation. |

**Figure 6.1.** Levels of use of an innovation: Typical behaviors. (Reprinted by permission. Copyright by the American Association of Colleges for Teacher Education. Marsh, D.D., Knudsen, D.J., & Knudsen, G.A., The role of staff development in implementing the Bay Area Writing Program. *Journal of Teacher Education, 38* [Nov.–Dec. 1987]: 37.)

ticular professional development needs of staff, as suggested by the needs assessment and implementation data.

## PLANNING PRE-IMPLEMENTATION TRAINING

Just as a good lesson plan provides a teacher with a structured framework that allows for student input and variation, a good staff development plan provides trainers with a framework for helping teachers develop knowledge and expertise required for program implementation and allows for and encourages input and revisions. Pre-implementation training development involves assessment of training needs and design of activities to meet these training needs of individual staff.

Needs assessment identifies the gap between existing school programs and practices and those to be implemented and guides decisions about how training can best help staff to bridge the gap. Needs assessment provides information about existing human and material resources that can be utilized in the design and delivery of the staff development program. Information of this type is generally obtained as part of the district and school needs assessment process that is carried out many months before implementation (see chap. 2, this volume). Information about current teaching policies and practices and the training and experience of participating teachers and staff is particularly relevant to the design of pre-implementation training. For example, a different training emphasis and content might be needed in a school that already utilizes an individualized instructional approach in reading or math than in a school that does not.

If program staff vary widely in their training, experience, or teaching practices, pre-implementation training may need to be more individualized than if these aspects were less varied. Moreover, if the needs assessment reveals that staff members have training or experience in an adaptive education program, their expertise can be utilized for delivery of training. By considering such site-specific factors, planners can design training suited for meeting program implementation requirements and the training needs of the staff.

Although pre-implementation training can be conducted at any time prior to implementation, the best time is just before the start of the school year. This timing is less likely to disrupt vacations or other activities, and the newly acquired knowledge and skills can be used immediately and reinforced, thus enhancing staff motivation and enthusiasm about the program. In addition, if training takes place just before the start of school, it is possible to link training with teacher preparation for classroom implementation.

Three to five full days are needed for pre-implementation training for classroom teachers and other staff members who bear primary responsibility for program implementation, and adjunct staff, such as district administrators, classroom assistants, and itinerant teachers, require less time. Three to five days are generally sufficient for discussion of important program components and staff concerns, and to develop an implementation plan for individual teachers that is responsive to their readiness and their specific implementation needs and helps them to prepare their classrooms for program implementation. When pre-implementation training has been scheduled, planners need to ensure that necessary resources will be available and participants have been notified, and they need to arrange for adequate space.

Pre-implementation training may be delivered by external consultants, local experts, or a combination of both, depending on the program and factors such as cost and availability. If the program has been developed by a person or group outside the school or district, it may be advisable to have the developers conduct, or at least supervise, the training. Since program developers often have experience working with local administrators in implementation planning, arranging pre-implementation training is usually not difficult. Using outside program developers or their representatives as trainers, however, is not always feasible. Generally, it requires that the training staff travel, which is costly and means that later on-site assistance may not be readily available. An alternative is to establish a collaborative relationship between the district adopting the innovative program and education faculty from a local college or university. Through their own research and contacts with program developers, college faculty develop expertise in implementing a particular program and can offer this to the collaborating school district.

Regardless of whether the program has been externally or locally developed, teachers with experience in adaptive education programs should be considered for use as trainers. Research has shown that teachers prefer job training that is delivered by other teachers to training by outsiders (Little, 1981; Showers, 1990; Stein & Wang, 1988). If the innovative program is already implemented in a school or district close by, it may be possible to arrange for staff from that location to conduct at least part of the training. This course of action has potential benefits for both the trainers and trainees. Providing training furthers the professional development of the visiting teachers, and collegial relationships between schools and districts are enhanced.

The expertise of local individuals should not be overlooked. If the needs assessment has identified a local teacher or administrator with relevant experience or skills, that person should be called on to help deliver training. For example, a teacher who has used a management system similar to that in the innovative program might be asked to conduct a session, perhaps with a program expert, on the program's management system. By utilizing local resources in this way, program planners not only increase the efficient use of resources but also promote a feeling of program ownership in the local staff. Such a feeling of ownership can be a major factor in successful implementation.

To ease initial implementation, some program developers have recommended that innovations be implemented sequentially (stepwise) rather than all at one time. In stepwise implementation, a limited number of program components are introduced initially and others are added later. For example, a school might implement a new program curriculum first and wait until it is established before implementing the management system. In integrated implementation, all aspects of the new program are introduced at the same time.

Stepwise implementation requires fewer initial changes from previous practices. Furthermore, pre-implementation training can focus on components to be implemented first. Stepwise implementation, however, also poses some serious problems. First, the components of a complex educational program are rarely self-contained and are usually mutually interdependent. It may be difficult or impossible, for example, to implement a new curriculum properly without the accompanying management system. Trying to do so is like teaching someone to drive a car by first moving the gearshift lever to the required positions without using the clutch, then adding the clutch in the teaching process. Of course, it is possible to describe the gearshift positions independent of use of the clutch, but if one tries to move (implement) the gearshift lever without depressing the clutch, the car will not go. Similarly, it is often possible to describe various components of an educational program separately, but the components must be implemented together for the entire system to work. Stepwise implementation is sometimes referred to as a piecemeal approach, and this has often served as a reason for nonimplementation of programs that call for a comprehensive restructuring, such as adaptive education.

A second problem related to stepwise implementation is a practical one. When the school year is underway and teachers and staff are occupied with the delivery of instruction, time for training and preparation may be difficult to arrange. For these reasons, it is advisable to develop a plan that calls for implementing all aspects of the program in an integrated manner, rather than implementing them as separate components.

If integrated implementation is planned, all major components of the program must be considered in pre-implementation training, but all program features do not need to be covered equally. Planners need to set priorities for skills needed by school staff to begin the program. Additional training can be incorporated in support activities later in the school year.

## DELIVERY OF PRE-IMPLEMENTATION TRAINING

### A Model for Data-Based Pre-implementation Training

Figure 6.2. presents a model for delivery of data-based pre-implementation training that divides training into three major stages. The content of each stage depends on relevant needs and resources of the school and of individual participants.

The first stage, awareness training, provides a knowledge base about the program as discussed in Chapter 3. The second stage, in-depth training, addresses the acquisition of skills for effective implementation. The difference between awareness training and in-depth training is similar to that between declarative and procedural knowledge in the acquisition of cognitive skills. Declarative knowledge is "knowing that" and procedural knowledge is "knowing how." Program participants learn about program components in awareness training, and during in-depth training they learn how to implement these components in classrooms.

In-depth training is divided into the substages of training differentiated according to staff roles and individualized training. Training according to roles emphasizes what all persons in a particular role (e.g., classroom teacher) need to know and be able to do, and training sessions generally include all persons in that role. In the course of this training, differences among the needs of individual staff members become evident. For example, in sessions on the diagnostic–prescriptive process, some teachers may quickly develop the skills to write student prescriptions while others need more help. Information about differences in the needs of individual program participants is used to design and deliver individualized training suited to those needs.

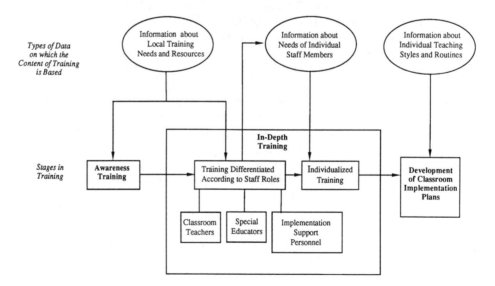

**Figure 6.2.** A model for data-based pre-implementation training.

The last stage of pre-implementation training involves development of classroom implementation plans. The plan developed for a particular classroom is individualized because it depends not only on program needs but also on the teacher's particular teaching styles and routines. A teacher's classroom implementation plan specifies the steps and schedule for implementing the new program over the first weeks of school and provides a transition between pre-implementation training and actual program implementation in the classroom.

Guidelines for conducting training in each stage are presented below. In the discussion, the person delivering training is referred to as "the trainer," and those receiving training are referred to as "participants."

**Awareness Training** Awareness training begins as soon as participants receive information about the innovative program. Even if the staff level of awareness is relatively high, it is wise to begin pre-implementation training with a review of awareness information to ensure that all participants have a common base for the next phases of training. This stage can generally be carried out in a single session that all participants attend, because the information needs of all school and district staff are similar.

It is useful to begin awareness training with an overview describing the major features of the innovative program and giving participants a general idea of the program. A site visit to a school implementing the program is ideal. Because pre-implementation training usually takes place just before school starts, such a visit is rarely possible at this time, so staff may have visited a site during the previous school year. In lieu of a visit, the first session might include a film, videotape, or slide presentation of the program in action. Film or videotape is best for showing classroom interactions and slides are well suited to illustrating static features such as arrangement of classroom facilities.

After a program overview, each major component of the program can be described in detail, and roles of individual staff members in implementing each component are delineated briefly. Discussion of staff roles is important because the delivery of adaptive education often requires changes from accustomed roles and the ways in which people interact. In particular, if mainstreaming of students with special needs in regular classes is a program objective, awareness training needs to address ways in which regular and special education teachers will work together and the responsibilities of each. Although most information to be disseminated is suited to a lecture and demonstration format, time for comments and questions from participants is essential. When participating staff have the opportunity to ask questions and make comments and decisions, they develop a sense of ownership of the program. Comments and questions often reveal certain misconceptions that can be dispelled immediately. Questions and concerns should be dealt with as honestly and as completely as possible, although it is perfectly appropriate to point out that a given question will be more fully addressed in a later session.

During this first phase of training, teachers often express concern about the differences between adaptive education and traditional practices. It is understandable that teachers who have taught in traditional programs for many years are uncomfortable about the changes they must make to implement adaptive education. A good way to deal with these concerns is to point out that a basic characteristic of adaptive education programs is the use of a variety of practices to address student diversity, and many of the effective practices traditionally used by teachers are also used in the adaptive education approach. The adaptive education approach provides a structure that facilitates consistent use of effective practices that good teachers have always employed. For example, all good teachers accommodate instruction to student needs as much as possible, and features of adaptive education such as prescription sheets provide a structural support that makes individualizing instruction more feasible.

*In-Depth Training*   By the end of the first stage of pre-implementation training, participants should have a reasonably good idea of an adaptive education program and their roles in implementing it, although they may not know how to put their knowledge into practice. The second and major stage of training provides staff with the technical knowledge to implement the program. Participants receive more detailed information about their roles, work with curriculum materials, prepare adjunct materials, and arrange their classrooms in accordance with their teaching styles and program implementation requirements.

Staff members have training needs specific to their program roles. Thus, classroom teachers responsible for classroom implementation need intensive training in daily curriculum implementation and management. Special educators need to learn to coordinate their services with the activities assigned by classroom teachers. Implementation support personnel (administrators and others responsible for monitoring implementation) need ongoing training in schoolwide program management and in planning and delivery of staff development.

Most of the in-depth training concerning staff roles can be delivered in group sessions that include all persons in that role. In areas where training needs overlap, as in the interaction of regular classroom teachers with special education teachers, the two groups should meet for relevant discussions. In-depth role training usually involves more active training activities. These include examination of materials, and preparation and design of additional materials. Other techniques, such as role playing, may also be useful.

*Training for Classroom Teachers*   Classroom teachers, who bear primary responsibility for classroom program implementation, need in-depth training in all program components of adaptive education: the diagnostic–prescriptive process, design of classroom facilities and materials, instructional processes specific to the program, and the classroom-learning management system. Classroom teachers must also learn to coordinate and integrate the program components to provide instruction that meets individual student learning needs.

Training in the diagnostic–prescriptive process generally centers around the use of prescription sheets, which have been discussed in Chapter 4. Prescription sheets should be distributed to the participants and the format explained. Training in the diagnostic–prescriptive process includes guidelines for teaching students how to use their prescription sheets. The trainer can provide examples for their use, and participants should practice prescribing.

A useful technique is to present participants with information about a hypothetical student and ask what they would do next (e.g., Brian has correctly completed Activity Sheets 22, 23, and 24. What are the options for his next prescription? For another example, Alice scored 5 out of 10 on the unit test for Unit VI, and the criterion score is 8. What would you do now?) A few exercises of role playing teacher and student parts also provide a realistic opportunity to practice skills of diagnosing and prescribing.

Classroom teachers with mainstreamed students in their classes are often concerned about prescribing for these students. This provides an opportunity for trainers to emphasize that the process of prescribing is basically the same for mainstreamed and regular students because, in both cases, the teacher makes judgments based on immediate learning needs, and classroom teachers and special educators work as teams to diagnose student needs and to deliver appropriate instruction when mainstreamed students need special help.

Training to design classroom facilities and materials should prepare teachers to arrange furniture and equipment according to program requirements and their preferences; store basic skills curriculum materials; and select, create, and maintain supplemental instructional materials.

Arranging space for storage of materials and classroom activities can usually be quickly discussed in a group session. If the specific adaptive education program has requirements for classroom arrangement, such as learning centers, guidelines are provided during this training session, and the training includes suggesting sample floor plans. Since spatial configurations and facilities vary from one classroom to another, further guidance in arrangement of space and facilities is best left to later individualized training.

In discussing selection, creation, and maintenance of supplemental instructional materials, training may begin with guidelines for appropriate activities. Teachers should be encouraged to think about ways to utilize resources they already possess, as well as ideas for developing new ones. Activities devised by teachers at other sites to meet particular objectives may be shown and participants asked to suggest other possibilities. Discussion typically develops quickly to a lively exchange of ideas among participants, who may wish to design some appropriate activities in the session.

Although teachers are primarily responsible for the materials in their own classrooms, they should also be aware of other facilities and materials in the school available for their use. For example, special education teachers often have materials that they may be willing to share with classroom teachers, and the school probably owns equipment, such as movie projectors, that is accessible to staff. Participants should be made aware of all of these opportunities for expanding their classroom materials and facilities.

The instructional process, consisting of techniques teachers use to instruct, motivate, and interact with students, requires little discussion during pre-implementation training. With the exception of a few programs, there is nothing inherently different between the instructional process in adaptive and conventional education. In both cases, teachers explain, demonstrate, model, and provide opportunities for practice. Unless the program dictates specific instructional processes, teachers will be relieved to know that they do not need to learn new instructional skills and behaviors. This does not mean, of course, that all teachers utilize instructional techniques equally well. In any kind of education program, most teachers can improve their skills with proper help and support. Improving teaching skills, however, is best left to the ongoing staff development component.

Although instructional processes are similar in adaptive and conventional education, the setting of instruction is often different. Teachers need training in the program procedures for providing basic skills instruction, assigning students to groups, scheduling group meetings, and managing group and individual activities that occur simultaneously. Teachers unfamiliar with the adaptive education approach are often particularly concerned about their ability to orchestrate this variety of classroom events. This aspect of the training should provide guidelines, give examples (e.g., sample schedules for small-group instruction), and suggest ways that teachers can monitor all students in the classroom while working with a group.

One way to reduce the management load on individual teachers, as well as enhance student opportunities to learn, is by forming instructional teams of two (or more) regular teachers at the same or successive grade levels and of relevant specialized professionals. Discussion of instructional grouping during pre-implementation training provides an opportunity to discuss possibilities for teaming.

A critical design feature of adaptive education programs is the classroom management support that fosters students' self-responsibility for managing their own behavior and the classroom learning environment. Many adaptive education programs incorporate particular systems for developing student self-responsibility. In such cases, teachers need systematic training in system components and implementation. The Adaptive Learning Environments Model (ALEM), for example, includes a student Self-Schedule System (Wang, 1980). A major topic during pre-implementation training for the ALEM is the Self-Schedule System as a whole. The use of the self-scheduling board and self-schedule sheets is explained, and guidelines are provided for their construction. Examples developed by teachers at other sites are given, and participants are assisted in designing their own boards and sheets. Methods for teaching students to use the Self-Schedule System and for phasing it in during the first weeks of school are mentioned. Detailed discussion of this topic, however, is left for classroom implementation planning with individual teachers (see chap. 5, this volume, for a thorough discussion).

*Training for Specialist Teachers*   In schools implementing adaptive education programs, students with special needs can spend all or most of their time in regular classrooms. Classroom teachers and specialist teachers work together in planning and delivering instruction, and the specialist teacher becomes a member of the instructional team. Therefore, a major training topic for specialist teachers is specific ways of sharing with regular educators the responsibility for instructing students with special needs. Regular and specialist teachers need to discuss and renegotiate their roles and functions to develop cooperative and collaborative arrangements that use their combined expertise for effective teaching. In adaptive education programs, special educators are expected to spend a significant amount of time working in regular classrooms, and they need a good working knowledge of the adaptive education approach so that they can effectively function as team members. For example, they should know how to use the program's diagnostic–prescriptive process to coordinate supplemental assignments with assignments prescribed by regular teachers. They also need basic knowledge about the program's management system to work efficiently with the classroom teacher.

*Training for Implementation Support Staff*   Organizational and administrative support is a key ingredient in successful implementation of an adaptive education program. Pre-implementation training must include all relevant building- and district-level administrators and instructional leaders who are responsible for managing, evaluating, and refining the program and for training for program implementation. The implementation support staff at the building level generally includes the school principal or other designated administrators, as well as educators who are released from some instructional duties to coordinate and support implementation efforts. At the district level, implementation support staff include administrators such as superintendents, assistant superintendents for instruction, other supervisory and instructional support staff, school psychologists, and counselors. Each has a specific role in providing support for program implementation. All of these individuals need to have an overall sense of what the program aims to achieve.

Pre-implementation training should emphasize the role of support staff in assisting the teaching staff to achieve a high degree of program implementation as well as in providing staff development needed to improve program implementation. This aspect of the training focuses on procedures for formal and informal assessment of classroom implementation, including assessment instruments and feedback procedures to improve teacher implementation. When the program is operating, support staff can receive additional training in procedures for monitoring implementation. The school principal and program coordinator are largely responsible for working with teachers to improve program implementation and for providing ongoing staff development.

*Individualized Training* The last segment of pre-implementation training focuses on instruction tailored to the roles and needs of individual staff. Training is perhaps too formal a term, and a better term might be individualized pre-implementation support. This support is offered as teachers and staff are preparing their classrooms or workplaces for the start of school. This aspect of training is concerned with the same topics as those dealt with in group training sessions. Individualized training provides help with specific aspects of implementation that need to be strengthened based on observations and on requests from individuals. Some participants will need additional information and skills training (e.g., in the process of prescribing), while others only need confirmation that they are proceeding correctly.

If possible, participants should have the opportunity to indicate areas in which they want help, rather than have it imposed on them by the trainer. The following are suggested approaches:

> To a teacher who is busy arranging furniture or materials and seems confident of what he or she is doing: "You seem to be on top of the situation. Is there anything I can help you with? Do you have any questions about anything we covered in the last few days?"
>
> To a teacher who seems unsure about the best way to proceed: "How about trying it this way?"
>
> To a teacher or staff member whose behavior during group sessions indicated a misunderstanding or concern: "I noticed that you seemed a little doubtful about x. Would you like to talk about it?"

Whether or not participants ask for help, the trainer should work along with them while observing. For example, instead of just watching a teacher prepare a display on a bulletin board, the trainer can help assemble materials and glue or tack things up as directed. Not only will participants appreciate the help, but they will perceive the trainer as someone who is willing to pitch in, not just someone who gives advice. Questions can often be answered and problems resolved in this way.

Thus, individualized training provides an opportunity for program staff members to consolidate what they have learned, extend and apply their knowledge, and try out new things in a collegial, supportive environment. This stage of training is important in preparing for the start of school, and it can be the occasion for considerable growth in the abilities and confidence of staff members in implementing the new program.

***Development of Classroom Implementation Plans***   A final task of the participants of pre-implementation training is development of a classroom implementation plan for the first 2–3 weeks of school. The plan outlines how the instruction and management systems will be implemented. The plan is constructed to consider program requirements and teacher preferences, routines, and teaching style. The plan provides a well-defined document to guide the teacher's activities during the first few weeks. This plan should include specific activities to be carried out by the classroom teacher, the collaborating specialist teacher, and the students. A chart format, such as that shown in Figure 6.3., is recommended. A detailed plan should be prepared for the first 2 weeks of school, and the teacher and support personnel can continue the process after that time.

A good way to begin an implementation planning session is to ask the teacher, "What do you usually do on the first day of school?" It is usually possible to incorporate the teacher's accustomed way of beginning the school year in the adaptive education program. For example, if the teacher replies, "I like to get the kids started on their reading and math group work as early as possible," he or she may be encouraged to give placement tests in one or both subjects on the first day. If the teacher replies, "I like to spend the first day in group activities so we can get to know one another," the start of program implementation can be deferred until the second day. Even in these group activities, the teacher can begin to explain and teach students to follow classroom rules related to the adaptive education program.

When activities for the first day have been decided and entered in the implementation plan, teachers generally proceed with daily planning for all program components, or for one component for the entire 2-week period. Although the program coordinator or trainers may help with the plan by suggesting specific sequences of implementing program components, or the rate of implementation, teachers are responsible for developing the implementation plan. Because the finished plan will serve as the blueprint for implementation, it is critical that the plan is developed by the teachers responsible for implementation. The teacher is more likely to be motivated to follow his or her own plan than an imposed plan.

As an illustration, Figure 6.3. is a classroom implementation plan drawn up by Ms. Sullivan, a third grade teacher, for beginning an adaptive education program. Ms. Sullivan's school year began on the day after Labor Day so the first week includes only 4 days. Implementation was planned for the diagnostic–prescriptive process in reading and math and the instructional learning management system in using learning centers and the Self-Schedule System.

As the plan shows, Ms. Sullivan planned to conduct whole-group work in reading and math the first day, and to begin implementing the management system by explaining the classroom rules, describing and demonstrating learning center activities, and showing students how to use teacher call signals to request help. On Wednesday, September 7, Ms. Sullivan planned to implement the diagnostic–prescriptive process in reading with a placement test, and to continue whole-group activities in math. Also on Wednesday, Ms. Sullivan planned to have students use their teacher call signals consistently, and other means of seeking teacher attention would be ignored. On Friday, Ms. Sullivan would explain the self-scheduling board and its relation to the learning centers and students would move through the learning centers under teacher direction.

The figure shows that Ms. Sullivan, with help from the trainer, developed a plan that would teach the students to work within the program in a systematic, gradual, integrated manner. Students initially would sit in assigned seats and carry out activities only under teacher direction. By the end of the second week, it was anticipated that they would work in locations of their choice and perform some self-scheduling of tasks.

Of course, such a plan is subject to revision, and the trainer can suggest strategies for altering plans when they are not working well. It is also important to assure teachers that the deliberate efforts that went into devising their plans make it likely that the plans will work with only minor changes.

Teachers and other staff sometimes confess that they are uncomfortable with the new program and wonder if they can implement it effectively. The trainer needs to assure them that a feeling of not really knowing what they are doing is normal with any new education program, that their implementation of the program will become smoother and more assured with practice, and that help and support will be available when they need it.

At the end of implementation planning sessions, the trainer should arrange for copies of the plans to be made for him- or herself and for the education specialist or appropriate support staff. The trainer should also reserve time either before the end of pre-implementation training or very early in implementation to meet with the education specialist to review each teacher's classroom implementation plan. During this meeting, they can discuss ways that the implementation support person can help each teacher follow his or her plan and revise it if necessary. The implementation support person should also schedule a meeting with each teacher before the end of the second week of implementation to discuss the teacher's progress and to continue the classroom implementation plan for the next 1 or 2 weeks.

## Example of a Pre-implementation Training Program

This section describes pre-implementation training for the staff of a school preparing to implement the Adaptive Learning Environments Model (ALEM). Another school implementing the same education program would plan a different sequence of activities based on its particular needs, resources, and constraints. Nevertheless, this example may be helpful for program planners as they prepare to conduct pre-implementation training.

In the example, pre-implementation training took place on the first 3 days of the week before the start of school, and the staff participated in other inservice activities not related to the ALEM on the remaining 2 days. The schedule of pre-implementation training for teachers is shown in Figure 6.4. Similar schedules were drawn up for staff members with other program roles. In this particular site, the role of program coordinator (referred to as education specialist in the ALEM) was shared by two special education teachers.

Pre-implementation training was provided by specialists trained by the developers of the ALEM. Both trainers led the sessions for the entire school staff, and each trainer worked with a group when the staff was divided into subgroups for in-depth role training.

The first day, Monday, was devoted to awareness training and some in-depth

Grade __3__   Room __204__   Week __1__   Teacher __Ms. Sullivan__

| Day | Diagnostic-Prescriptive Process | | Instructional Learning Management System |
|---|---|---|---|
| | Reading | Math | |
| Mon. 9/5 | No | School | |
| Tues. 9/6 | Whole group | Whole group | Explain classroom rules and use of teacher call signals. Explain and demonstrate learning center activities |
| Wed. 9/7 | Placement test (Score tests and form 3 or 4 groups) | Whole group | Students must use teacher calls to get help from now on. Students rotate through learning centers under teacher direction. Each student completes one activity at each of 2-3 centers. Monitor closely and check all student work. |
| Thurs. 9/8 | Meet with each group. Distribute reading folders. Explain prescription sheets. Mark the same single assignment for all students in a group. | Placement test (Score tests and form 2-3 groups) | Students rotate through remaining learning centers under the same conditions as Wednesday. |
| Fri. 9/9 | Prescribe 2 tasks to each student. Allow students to choose order of completion within teacher-specified time. | Meet with each group. Distribute math folders. Explain prescription sheets. Prescribe 2 tasks to be completed in any order within teacher-specified time. | Explain and demonstrate self-scheduling board. At a teacher-specified time, each student selects one learning center, indicates his/her choice on the board, and completes one activity at the center. |

Note: Students sit in assigned seats for the first week.

**Figure 6.3.**  Classroom implementation plan.                              (continued)

training for all staff, and the entire school staff attended these sessions. The morning began with an overview of the ALEM, and since the staff had already received some information about the ALEM, this session was short.

Session 2 was devoted to a description of the ALEM diagnostic–prescriptive process in reading. The preparation of curriculum materials for individualized instruction was described, and sets of reading prescription sheets that had been

Grade __3__    Room __204__    Week __2__    Teacher __Mr. Sullivan__

| Day | Diagnostic-Prescriptive Process | | Instructional Learning Management System |
| --- | --- | --- | --- |
| | Reading | Math | |
| Mon. 9/12 | *Review use of prescription sheets. Same procedure as Friday, Sept. 9.* *Students continue to work in assigned seats.* | | *Review use of self-scheduling board. Distribute and explain self-scheduling sheets. Students select a learning center and mark choice on sheet. Check that they mark it correctly. Students do selected activity, after indicating center on board.* |
| Tues. 9/13 | *Prescribe 2 tasks in reading and 2 in math, to be done in any order and completed within specified time. Monitor closely!* | | *Same as Monday, but each student selects a different learning center than last time.* |
| Wed. 9/14 | *Same as Tuesday* | | *Each student selects two learning centers, marks them on self-scheduling sheet and, at a teacher-specified time, uses the board appropriately, and completes both activities in any order. Monitor use of sheets, board, & task completion!* |
| Thurs. 9/15 | *Prescribe 2 tasks in reading and 2 in math.* *First 1½ hr: Each student completes one reading, one math, and one learning center task in any order.* *Second 1½ hr: Each student completes remaining tasks in any order.* | | *Each student selects 2 learning centers and uses sheet and board.* |
| Fri. 9/16 | *Same kinds of teacher assignments and student selections. Students may complete their tasks at a location of their choice.* | | |

*Note: Meet with Education Specialist to plan next 2 weeks.*

**Figure 6.3.** (continued)

prepared during the summer were distributed and explained. Examples illustrated the use of prescription sheets, and participants practiced prescribing for a few hypothetical cases. Procedures for teaching students to use their prescription sheets were briefly mentioned, and detailed discussion of this was left for later sessions with individual teachers.

The third session, on the diagnostic–prescriptive process in mathematics,

| MONDAY | TUESDAY | WEDNESDAY |
|---|---|---|
| Session 1 (9:00 - 10:30)<br><br>Overview of Adaptive<br>Learning Environments Model | Session 5 (9:00 - 9:30)<br><br>Arranging Space and Facilities<br><br>Guidelines for Designing<br>Reading Area | Session 9 (9:00 - 9:30)<br><br>Guidelines for Designing<br>Math Area |
| Session 2 (10:30 - 11:30)<br><br>Diagnostic-Prescriptive<br>Process: Reading | Session 6 (9:30 - 11:30)<br><br>Arrange classroom furniture<br>according to ALEM requirements<br><br>Prepare reading area | Session 10 (9:30 - 11:30)<br><br>Prepare math area<br><br>Begin development of individual<br>classroom implementation plans |
| Session 3 (12:30 - 1:30)<br><br>Diagnostic-Prescriptive<br>Process: Math | Session 7 (12:30 - 1:00)<br><br>Guidelines for Designing<br>Exploratory Learning Centers | Session 11 (12:30 -1:00)<br><br>Procedures for Implementation<br>of Instructional Learning<br>Management System |
| Session 4 (1:30 - 3:00)<br><br>Exploratory Learning<br>Center Component<br><br>Instructional Learning<br>Management System | Session 8 (1:00 - 3:00)<br><br>Construct five Exploratory<br>Learning Centers | Session 12 (1:00 - 3:00)<br><br>Construct self-schedule sheet<br><br>Construct self-schedule board<br><br>Continue development of individual<br>classroom implementation plans |

**Figure 6.4.** Pre-implementation training for ALEM teachers.

was similar to the previous session. By this time, staff members were more comfortable with the subject matter and with the trainers, and lively discussion took place.

The second and third sessions primarily addressed the basic skills curricula. In Session 4, selection and development of extension and enrichment activities for learning centers in reading, mathematics, and other subjects were discussed. Examples of learning centers and the activities designed by teachers at other sites were described and illustrated by slides. The instructional learning management system, the Self-Schedule System, was described. The use of the self-scheduling board and self-schedule sheet were explained, slides were shown of boards developed at other sites, and sample self-schedule sheets from other sites were distributed. Methods for teaching students to use the self-scheduling system were briefly mentioned, and in-depth discussion was left for later training with individual teachers.

No particular session was scheduled for discussing cooperation among staff members, particularly regular and specialist teachers, to provide services to students with special needs. Instead, this topic was introduced in various sessions where it seemed appropriate. For example, in Sessions 2 and 3, teachers raised questions about the assignment of students with special needs to instructional groups, methods of preparing prescriptions for them, and ways of dealing with problems. The trainers described ways that regular and special education teachers cooperated in these tasks at other sites and suggested possibilities, but they dictated no specific procedures for this school, and teachers were urged to try various strategies that seemed appropriate to them. If pre-implementation training had been scheduled for 4 days instead of 3, a separate session to discuss these working arrangements would have been a useful addition.

Teacher assistants attended no sessions after the first day, and the principal prepared a master schedule for the school on the second and third days and engaged in other managerial activities. Tuesday's sessions were attended by classroom teachers and education specialists. The day's sessions consisted of a group session followed by work in individual classrooms. In Session 5, participants met briefly for a presentation about the ALEM requirements for arrangement of space and facilities, with particular emphasis on storage of curriculum materials in the reading area. Floor plans and designs developed at other sites were shown, and teachers drew preliminary sketches for their own classrooms. During the rest of the morning (Session 6), teachers arranged the classroom furniture and prepared the reading area according to their plans. The education specialists, who did not have classrooms of their own, rotated among the classrooms, helping where needed. The trainers also circulated among the rooms making suggestions, reinforcing the teacher's work, and providing additional individualized help.

In Session 7, the participants met again as a group to prepare for construction of learning centers. The trainers distributed and discussed guidelines, and the teachers exchanged ideas and began to design their own centers. During Session 8, each teacher was encouraged to construct five learning centers in his or her classroom using readily available materials. Some teachers were able to construct only two or three centers in the session. Teachers were assured that they could implement the program with fewer centers and continue to work on these later. Trainers discussed with individual teachers ways to keep learning centers current, change centers and materials, and select and construct additional materials. The program coordinator was urged to work closely with classroom teachers to help them select and create instructional materials on a continuing basis.

The sessions on Wednesday morning (Sessions 9 and 10) followed the same pattern as those of the previous day, and again participants included classroom teachers and education specialists. The group first met for discussion of guidelines to design mathematics areas. Then teachers, with the help of education specialists and trainers, prepared the mathematics areas in their own classrooms. If the task was completed before scheduled, teachers either continued to work on their exploratory learning centers or met individually with a trainer to develop their classroom implementation plans.

In Session 11, one trainer met with the classroom teachers to describe procedures for implementing the ALEM instructional learning management system, including the design and construction of self-scheduling boards and self-schedule sheets. Options in design and instruction were discussed by the group before the teachers returned to their classrooms to implement system components. The other trainer met with the school principal and the education specialist to discuss monitoring and supporting the teachers in their classroom implementation during the early weeks of school. Dates were scheduled in early October for training the principal and education specialist in the administration of the Implementation Assessment Battery, a formal process for collecting data on program implementation in classrooms.

Teachers constructed self-scheduling boards and self-schedule sheets and put the finishing touches on their classrooms during the rest of the afternoon. Sometime in the afternoon, teachers who had not met individually with a trainer to develop an implementation plan did so. When implementation plans were completed, copies were distributed to the education specialists, who met briefly with the trainers to review and discuss the plans.

As Figure 6.4. shows, pre-implementation training officially ended at 3:00 P.M. on Wednesday. Before leaving the school, however, the trainers promised their continued support to all staff members and explained their planned schedule for future visits. Teachers were assured that, although they were new to the ALEM, they were experienced educators and could depend on their teaching expertise and professional judgment to deal with most problems that might arise in implementation.

## SUMMARY

Effective implementation of an adaptive education program requires appropriate and well-organized staff training. Planning for pre-implementation training begins with an assessment of training needs and then development of a site-specific training design matched to these needs. Training prepares school staff to begin program implementation as effectively and with as much confidence as possible. Discussion in this chapter focuses on a model for data-based pre-implementation training that can serve as a guide for delivery of training. Pre-implementation training, carefully planned and well-conducted, helps administrators, teachers, and support staff begin developing expertise in the delivery of adaptive education.

## REFERENCES

Ellet, C.D., & Wang, M.C. (1987). Assessing administrative and leadership components of program implementation in an innovative ECE program. *Journal of Research in Childhood Education*, 2(1), 30–47.

Fullan, M. (1990). Staff development, innovation, and institutional development. In B. Joyce (Ed.), *Changing school culture through staff development*. Alexandria, VA: Association for Supervision and Curriculum Development.

Hall, G.E., Loucks, S.F., Rutherford, W.L., & Newlove, B. (1975). Levels of use of the innovation: A framework for analyzing innovation adoption. *Journal of Teacher Education*, 24, 52–56.

Joyce, B. (Ed.). (1990). *Changing school culture through staff development.* Alexandria, VA: Association for Supervision and Curriculum Development.

Little, J.W. (1981). *School success and staff development: The role of staff development in urban desegregated schools.* Boulder, CO: Center for Action Research.

Reynolds, M.C. (1989). Children with special needs. In M.C. Reynolds (Ed.), *Knowledge base for the beginning teacher* (pp. 129–142). Oxford: Pergamon.

Showers, B. (1990). Aiming for superior classroom instruction for all children: A comprehensive staff development model. *Remedial and Special Education, 11*(3), 35–39.

Stein, M.K., & Wang, M.C. (1988). Teacher development and school improvement: The process of teacher change. *Teaching and Teacher Education, 4*(2), 171–187.

Vaughan, E.D., Wang, M.C., & Dytman, J.A. (1987). Implementing an innovative program: Staff development and teacher classroom performance. *Journal of Teacher Education, 36,* 40–47.

Wang, M.C. (1980). Adaptive instruction: Building on diversity. *Theory into Practice, 19*(2), 122–127.

Wang, M.C., Haertel, G.D., & Walberg, H.J. (1990). What influences learning? A content analysis of review literature. *Journal of Educational Research, 84*(1), 30–43.

# Chapter 7

# Implementation Assessment and Staff Development

Consider the following scenario: An innovative school program has been adopted with great enthusiasm on the part of teachers, administrators, and parents. Armed with new materials and methods from intensive pre-implementation training, teachers are eager to practice their newly acquired expertise in their classes. After several months of program implementation, however, only traces of the new program can be seen. Although teachers worked very diligently to utilize the new materials and techniques, teachers and administrators are frustrated because they are not moving at the pace they had anticipated. The comprehensive program designed for the school is clearly not being implemented as planned. Fears arise that students may have regressed from where they were before the introduction of the new program, and teachers worry that the program is not as useful to them as they had originally perceived.

This scenario is not uncommon. What has happened? There are several possible explanations. The first is that the pre-implementation training was not sufficient. Another explanation is that local administrators have not provided an organizational structure to support program implementation. A stronger possibility is that the teachers and administrators did not understand implementation support needs of the staff and the need for continuing staff development to establish and maintain program implementation. Without such continued support, any new program, no matter how well designed, is likely to flounder even if initiated successfully.

This chapter discusses the importance of staff development and technical assistance to help teachers and administrators maintain a high degree of program implementation of the innovative programs. Largely through the impetus of the effective schools movement and the push for excellence in instruction and learning, most school districts now have school improvement programs in which staff development plays a major part. Although numerous models of staff development and delivery modes, ranging from university-based courses and workshops to teacher centers, have been widely implemented, there are few systematic ongoing staff development programs tied to daily operations of innovative programs. This chapter describes an approach to systematic staff development, Data-Based Staff Development (Wang & Gennari, 1983), and how this approach can be operationalized to support school-based implementation of innovative programs such as adaptive education.

The Data-Based Staff Development Program is an ongoing, year-round staff development process designed to promote program implementation and maintenance. It is based on the premise that teachers need staff development and technical support closely linked to their day-to-day implementation problems and concerns. All too often, this is not what they receive. If educators are asked to free-associate with the term staff development, they are likely to respond with terms such as "inservice day," "workshop," and "lecture." As these responses indicate, staff development activities in schools are usually separated both in time and space from teaching in classrooms, and they involve topics and modes of delivery divorced from teachers' daily concerns. This does not mean, of course, that such activities are useless. Indeed, teachers may leave a workshop on classroom management or teaching students to think, for example, with many useful ideas. Nevertheless, how they can actually apply the ideas is likely to remain unclear, and other more immediate implementation problems remain unresolved.

Instead of workshops, courses, lectures, and other staff development activities divorced from immediate concerns, the Data-Based Staff Development Program is designed to identify and resolve specific problems of implementation. The content and delivery of staff development activities are based on observation and assessment of classroom implementation needs, and they are tailored to meet the needs of individual teachers and the school as a whole.

The Data-Based Staff Development Program includes three levels of training: Basic (Awareness) Training, Individualized (In-Depth) Training, and Inservice (Ongoing) Training. Basic and individualized training are delivered before the start of program implementation and have been discussed in detail in Chapter 3 and Chapter 6. This chapter focuses on training and support to school staff throughout the year as they implement an innovative program. The first part of the chapter describes the human and administrative resources required to support program implementation and presents guidelines for supporting implementation during the early weeks of a new program. The remainder of the chapter deals with staff development as a repeated cycle of activities continuing throughout the year.

The material in this chapter is intended for school and district administrators, staff developers, university faculty, program developers, and others who are concerned with the implementation, maintenance, and continued improvement of the delivery of innovative programs in schools. It is hoped that such individuals will find the Data-Based Staff Development Program to be useful for conceptualizing the process of staff development in the context of the training needs of the schools of the readers, and that they will be able to adapt the approach to their own settings.

## SETTING THE STAGE FOR CONTINUING STAFF DEVELOPMENT

### Support by School Staff

In most schools, the principal is responsible for scheduling and planning staff development activities for teachers. Most school administrators, however, do not have time to handle all aspects of daily implementation of staff development.

Therefore, some responsibility for monitoring program implementation and for providing training and implementation support should be assigned to another staff member. Ideally, this person is an experienced and respected teacher, or someone whose role can be adapted to include coordinating implementation support needs of the classroom teacher. This person is generally referred to as the program coordinator or by some similar functional title.

Regular and specialist teachers play important roles in staff development too, not only as recipients of training but also as planners and trainers. The roles of the principal, the program coordinator, and teachers responsible for project implementation are described below.

***Role of the Principal*** Traditionally, principals have been administrators and managers who are concerned with management functions such as budgeting and scheduling, and with public relations functions. Research suggests, however, that principals of effective schools tend to focus their efforts on "instructional leadership" tasks (Wang, Englert, & Manning, 1989), or the role of learning facilitator (Leithwood, 1990; U.S. Department of Education Office of Educational Research and Improvement, 1991). They not only are responsible for scheduling and overseeing staff development activities but also actively participate in staff development, visit classrooms regularly, are available to teachers who seek help, and chair staff meetings that deal with program implementation concerns.

To implement effective staff development, principals must work hard to foster feelings of trust among the school staff. Teachers often perceive the principal as the person who evaluates them regarding tenure and promotion. Teacher evaluation is, of course, a necessary function of the school principal. When teacher evaluation, however, aims not to judge but to help teachers become more proficient in program implementation, it tends to be perceived as helpful rather than adverse. Thus, when a principal visits a classroom to observe program implementation, the visit is likely to be viewed by the teacher not as an evaluation of performance, but to provide program implementation support. Furthermore, when program implementation is the focus of dialogue between the principal and teaching staff, it signals recognition that the problems of implementation are not necessarily related to the teacher's competence or performance and that solving them may call for action by the principal or other staff.

***Role of the Program Coordinator*** As a member of the school's instructional staff, the program coordinator is in a particularly good position to understand teachers' implementation concerns and to recognize and appreciate their day-to-day implementation needs. In many ways, the program coordinator functions as a lead teacher (Lieberman, Saxl, & Miles, 1988). He or she is a consultant and facilitator who supports the work of the school staff and exhibits expertise in achieving a high degree of implementation of the program. Some functions of the program coordinator include:

> Works with the principal to identify areas for improvement
> Works with teachers to identify and develop solutions to implementation problems
> Collects formal and informal data on the degree of program implementation in classrooms to identify needed program refinement and staff development
> Ensures that improvement plans are implemented
> Works with the principal to plan, deliver, and manage staff development activities

Assists in evaluating the effects of training and provides feedback to teachers

Coordinates and documents the implementation and effects of all staff development activities

**Role of the Teacher**  Classroom teachers (regular and specialist) do not merely receive training but participate actively in planning staff development by identifying their program implementation needs and by working with the principal and the program coordinator to establish staff development priorities and methods. In addition, teachers are important resources for delivery of training. Teachers with specific expertise can help other teachers by providing suggestions and by demonstrating and modeling appropriate techniques. In addition, through group problem solving, teachers can address common or individual implementation concerns. By these actions, teachers furnish vital input, actively participate in their own staff development, and provide support that facilitates the work of their colleagues.

## Administrative Support

Administrative support for staff development involves providing time and resources for all activities of program implementation and support. The principal and program coordinator need to schedule frequent visits to classrooms to meet with teachers, to plan staff development, and to document these activities. Similarly, teachers need time to assess and plan implementation and to meet with the program coordinator, the principal, or other teachers to discuss assessments and other aspects of program implementation.

In addition, all teachers need to meet regularly as a group with the program support staff. It is advisable to allow a minimum of 1 hour per week for meetings of the entire program staff or other appropriate groups such as all the program staff in a grade, or regular teachers and specialists on the same team. The principal generally chairs staff meetings in an open and encouraging manner that promotes professionalization of the staff and input from all participants. At these meetings, staff are encouraged to:

Discuss the level of program implementation and methods for improvement

Relate problems of individual teachers or the group as a whole

Consider the progress of particular students, including solutions to their learning problems

Engage in group problem solving and decision making about program resources, implementation needs, and related matters

Plan staff development activities

Participate in staff development activities such as workshops or research seminars

It is important that staff development meetings do not become mere gripe sessions. Certainly, all staff members should have an opportunity to air problems or difficulties with program implementation, which are a common experience in the first weeks of implementation. If a group session threatens to become nothing more than a forum for complaints, the principal may need to step in and turn the discussion to solutions to the problems. Whenever possible, suggestions for dealing with problems should be elicited from staff rather than imposed on them. By working to solve their own implementation problems, teachers develop greater feelings of competence in program delivery and a heightened sense of program ownership.

## Supporting Implementation in the Early Weeks of School

The early weeks of school can be difficult for school staff even during normal circumstances. When staff members are also attempting to implement a new education program with unfamiliar materials and methods, the start of school can be very trying indeed. It is easy for teachers to become discouraged when things do not run as smoothly as they would like, which is almost inevitable considering the changes that comprehensive innovative programs require.

A high level of support is essential from the principal, from specialists, and possibly from experts outside the school such as experienced teachers of adaptive education programs. Such support helps teachers make changes in their teaching methods and fosters trust in their own abilities to institute an innovative program. Supportive collegial working relationships and shared responsibility for implementation are key ingredients in maintaining high degrees of program implementation throughout the year.

The program coordinator or other instructional support persons use classroom visits and discussion with each teacher to check if program implementation is proceeding according to the plan and to the satisfaction of the individual teacher. If this is the case, little may be needed other than a commendation or an encouraging remark. If difficulties arise, the teacher and the program coordinator can discuss alternative courses of action and revise the implementation plan as needed. The program coordinator's schedule should include time for working with each teacher, yet remain sufficiently flexible to allow extra time for any teachers who need more help—an adaptive approach to staff development.

A teacher's initial implementation plan generally covers the first 2 weeks of school. Before the end of the second week, the program coordinator meets with each teacher to jointly develop a plan for the following 2 weeks. A reasonable goal for the next 2-week implementation plan is to have all program features operational by the end of the fourth week. Although practical wisdom points to allowing sufficient time to make incremental steps leading to full program implementation, progressing too slowly is not an advisable strategy. Full implementation of other components or the entire program may be compromised by nonimplementation of program components.

Weekly staff meetings constitute a vital support structure during these early weeks. Providing extra staff development time (generally after school) during the initial implementation period of a program is probably the most important investment, and the only critical start-up cost, of school implementation of an adaptive education program. It is vital that the principal and the program coordinator be particularly supportive in these early staff meetings. They must provide assurance that the problems teachers are having are common and surmountable, that the teachers are getting better and better at what they are doing, and that they will become increasingly comfortable with the program and confident in their abilities to implement it in the next several weeks.

If the guidelines for implementation support outlined in this chapter are followed, a new program can be essentially in place and operational by the end of the first 4–5 weeks of school. Teachers and specialist staff are making the shift from mechanical to routine use of the innovation. Staff roles have been differentiated, and cooperative collegial relations established among the teachers and implementation support personnel. At this point, the school staff is probably ready for a formal, comprehensive assessment of classroom implementation to determine the extent to which critical program features are being implemented. The process of assessing degree of program implementation after 5–6 weeks is the first step in the Data-Based Staff Development Program.

Figure 7.1. shows the conceptual model for the Data-Based Staff Development Program. An underlying premise of this model is that staff development is a repeated cycle of activities. The cycle begins with assessment of classroom implementation based on data provided by teachers' reports, classroom observations, records of student learning progress, parent feedback, and possibly other sources as well. The assessment provides information for the diagnosis of training needs, by indicating the degree to which each critical feature is being implemented as planned. Teachers and instructional support staff can then plan training and support activities to improve implementation. Some activities may involve the entire program staff, while others are designed for individual teachers. Delivery of training follows. Data on classroom implementation are collected during and after training, and the cycle begins again. Thus, the model provides for continuous fine tuning of program delivery throughout the school year.

Readers who are familiar with the literature on clinical supervision may note a similarity between the Data-Based Staff Development Model shown in Figure 7.1. and the clinical supervision model developed by Goldhammer and his colleagues at Harvard University (Goldhammer, Anderson, & Krajewski, 1980). In clinical supervision, too, staff development is data-based and involves a cycle of activities that begins with a pre-observation conference between the supervisor and a teacher and proceeds through four additional steps. Both models stress the importance of monitoring and assessing classroom events as the bases for improving instruction.

At least three important differences exist between the Data-Based Staff De-

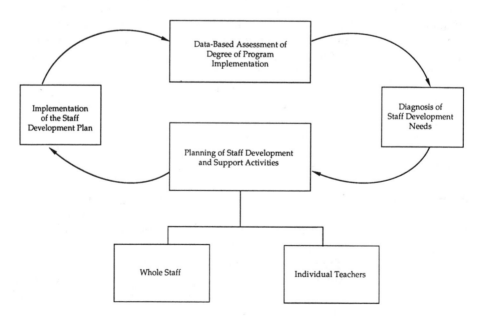

**Figure 7.1.**   Conceptual model of data-based staff development.

velopment Model and the model of clinical supervision, however. The clinical supervision model describes interactions between two persons with distinct roles: a supervisor who is typically a nonteaching administrator and a classroom teacher. Although staff development support activities in the Data-Based Staff Development Model are directed toward teachers, these activities are not delivered only by administrators or instructional supervisors, and the delivery system involves specialists as well as classroom teachers. The Data-Based Staff Development Model incorporates comprehensive, systematic, and standardized assessment of implementation classrooms and uses the resulting implementation data to develop staff development activities that are responsive to the needs of individual teachers. The present model includes the process of engaging teachers in the analysis of their own training and technical assistance needs in a tailored staff development plan.

A more apt analogy for data-based staff development is the model of the instructional cycle described in Chapter 4. The instructional cycle model includes provisions for assessment, diagnosis, planning (prescribing), and delivering instruction. The resemblance between the two models is not accidental. The purpose of both is growth—student growth in the case of the instructional cycle and teacher growth in the case of the staff development cycle. In both cases, growth depends on collection of relevant data, assessment of progress and diagnosis of learning needs, and the design and delivery of activities for promoting continued progress. And, in both cases, the iterative nature of the cycle makes it possible to adapt training and instruction to the changing needs of learners, whether they are students or teachers.

## DATA-BASED ASSESSMENT OF PROGRAM
## IMPLEMENTATION TO IDENTIFY STAFF DEVELOPMENT NEEDS

Data-based assessment of program implementation requires the collection of specific information concerning implementation of critical program components from many sources: teachers' self-reports, feedback from parents or students, classroom observations, and records of student learning progress. Informal collection of information about program implementation actually goes on all the time. Each teacher, monitoring his or her own behavior and that of students, notices what is working well and what is not. Based on their children's reports of school activities and the materials they bring home, parents make judgments about the school's instructional program. On informal visits to classrooms, principals and program coordinators observe classroom events and compare them with the events that are part of the program design. Such informally gathered information can provide a useful base for certain staff development and support activities. If, however, data collection rests on informal procedures alone, important problems and progress in program implementation may be overlooked. This may happen, for example, if a teacher is unaware of discrepancies between the program design and his or her activities. Similarly, a program coordinator may not notice certain deficiencies over several classroom visits because the opportunity to observe them does not arise. For example, if students misinterpret their prescription sheets, it may not be noticed unless they are asked to give their interpretations; or if a teacher does not explain new concepts clearly, this may be overlooked because he or she is not observed while giving explanations.

To determine the degree to which the school's instructional program as a whole is being implemented, program implementors need a comprehensive and systematic assessment procedure. Several procedures have been developed and field-tested. For example, Hall and his associates describe methods for designing an implementation configuration component checklist, which yields qualitative information about implementation of major components of an innovation (Heck, Stiegelbauer, Hall, & Loucks, 1981). Wang and associates designed the Implementation Assessment Battery for Adaptive Instruction (Wang, Catalano, & Gromoll, 1986), which yields quantitative indices of the degree of implementation of critical dimensions of adaptive education in individual classrooms and across the school or district (see appendix).

The critical dimensions of adaptive education incorporated in the battery include the following 12 scales:

Arranging space and facilities
Creating and maintaining instructional materials
Establishing, communicating, and refining rules and procedures
Coordinating and managing support services and extra personnel resources
Record keeping
Diagnostic testing
Prescribing
Monitoring and diagnosing
Interactive teaching
Instructing
Motivating
Developing student self-responsibility

Each critical dimension is measured by a scale with specific indicators, which are referred to as performance indicators. Each describes an observable teacher or student behavior or a feature of the classroom environment that should be present if the dimension is being implemented. The performance indicators are assembled into six data collection forms or instruments:

Checklist for physical design of the classroom
Checklist for classroom records
Teacher observation form
Student observation form
Student interview form
Teacher interview form

The battery yields a score for each classroom on each critical dimension. For example, if 7 of 10 performance indicators of a dimension are present in a classroom, the score on that dimension is 70%. By comparing scores to desired standards, principals, program coordinators, and teachers can decide the dimensions that need to be strengthened, and they can plan relevant staff development.

Program planners and implementors of adaptive education programs may be able to adapt the Implementation Assessment Battery for Adaptive Instruction for their own use. For planners who prefer to construct their own instrument, guidelines follow.

## Constructing an Implementation Assessment Instrument

There are seven steps in the process of developing instruments and procedures for comprehensive, formal assessment of program implementation.

1. Identification of the critical program dimensions
2. Identification of performance indicators for each critical dimension
3. Selection of methods for measuring performance indicators
4. Establishment of procedures for administration
5. Establishment of scoring criteria
6. Testing and revision
7. Empirical validation of the instrument

*Identification of the Critical Program Dimensions*  Program planners begin by listing and defining the major features of the adaptive education program, which was done in designing the program. The critical dimensions included in the Implementation Assessment Battery for Adaptive Instruction may be useful for developing specific indicators for adaptive education programs to be implemented at specific sites (see appendix). The specific indicators and program dimensions included in the battery may need to be modified and redefined for specific programs. After listing and describing the program's critical dimensions, planners review the dimensions carefully to ensure that they form a coherent and comprehensive picture of the program.

*Identification of Performance Indicators for Each Critical Dimension*  A good way to approach this task is to ask for each dimension, "How can one tell if this dimension is being implemented as planned? What would one look for, or listen for?" Listing the performance indicators for a dimension is equivalent to stating an operational definition of the dimension.

For a dimension such as Arranging Space and Facilities, performance indicators describe observable aspects of the classroom environment. For example, "Furniture is arranged in such a way that students and teachers can move about with ease," or "Student work spaces in specific activity areas are appropriate to the activity." Most performance indicators of a dimension such as instructing describe aspects of teacher behavior such as "The teacher demonstrates new procedures," or "The teacher groups students for instruction according to the subject matter and students' diagnosed needs."

The number of performance indicators need not be the same for all critical dimensions, nor do they need to be at the same level of detail. For example, in a program that requires teachers to provide students with guided practice of new skills but does not specify how this is to be done, the Instructing dimension may include only one performance indicator referring to guided practice such as "The teacher provides opportunities for guided practice of new skills." If the program requires the guided practice to be carried out in a particular sequence, there may be as many performance indicators as there are steps in the sequence.

*Selection of Methods for Measuring Performance Indicators*  Most performance indicators that describe classroom facilities, instructional materials, or teacher or student behavior are best measured by direct observation. Some teacher and student behaviors that occur infrequently or are difficult to observe directly may require other methods, such as interviews with teachers and students. For example, to measure a performance indicator such as "Students understand how to use their prescription sheets," it may be best to ask a sample of students to explain their reading and mathematics prescriptions to an interviewer. A performance indicator such as "The teacher conducts weekly mathematics maintenance drills" is best measured by determining if this is done. Examination of records may be appropriate for performance indicators such as "Records of student progress in reading and mathematics are accurate and up-to-date."

Despite the fact that performance indicators may number 100 or more, it is likely that three to six procedures will suffice to measure all of them. The Implementation Assessment Battery for Adaptive Instruction includes two observational checklists (one for classroom design and materials and the other for examination of classroom records), two forms for observing classroom events (one each for recording observations of students and teachers), and two interview forms (one each for questioning students and teachers).

**Establishment of Procedures for Administration**   The complexity of developing procedures and instruments to assess degree of program implementation vary according to the program and its critical features. For example, administering a checklist of classroom facilities or student records is straightforward and involves examining materials related to each indicator. Administering a student or teacher interview involves asking each question, recording responses, and probing for additional information. Instruments that involve observation of classroom events require much thoughtful deliberation and validation. Administering these instruments requires training to ensure the reliability of the information.

Perhaps the most difficult decision regarding classroom observation concerns the frequency and length of observation periods. Teacher and student behaviors vary from one occasion to another, depending on the subject matter being taught, specific lesson objectives, who is in the classroom, and even events external to the classroom. Therefore, teacher or student behavior during a single brief observation session may be unrepresentative of typical behavior. Relatively lengthy observations, carried out over a series of days or weeks, would be ideal. However, due to limited time and the need to observe many classrooms, some compromise is usually necessary. It is recommended that at least two sessions of 1 hour or more each be allotted for teacher and student observations in each classroom. If possible, the two sessions should be scheduled when different events are taking place, for example, one during which the teacher spends most of his or her time conducting small-group instruction and the other during which he or she spends more time traveling about the classroom and interacting with individual students. Assessment planners must also decide how many and which students to observe and interview in each class. Time usually does not permit all students to be observed and interviewed, but selection of only one or two students per classroom may not yield representative data. The best course is to observe and interview at least five or six randomly selected students. If it is important to obtain data from distinct subgroups within the class, regular education and mainstreamed students, a representative sample should be selected from each subgroup.

**Establishment of Scoring Criteria**   The range of possible scores for each performance indicator and criteria for assigning each score need to be determined for each implementation assessment instrument. The smallest possible range of scores for a given performance indicator is 2 points (0 and 1), depending on if the indicator is present at an acceptable level or not. However, a larger range may be selected. Although the 2-point scale may seem crude, it is the recommended choice. Scoring decisions, which must generally be made on the spot, become more difficult and less reliable as the number of scoring categories increases. Since the primary purpose of implementation assessment is to determine the presence or absence of critical dimensions, scores indicating presence (1) or absence (0) are more meaningful, particularly when the data are used for staff development planning. Furthermore, since the entire instrument includes a large number of indicators, a wide range of total scores for a dimension is possible even if the scoring range is only 2 points.

Clear and unambiguous criteria must be developed for assigning scores, regardless of the chosen range. In some cases this is easily done. Consider the performance indicator "There is a wall clock in the room." Either there is one (score = 1), or there is not (score = 0). Unfortunately, the decision is often not so clear-cut with indicators such as "Furniture is arranged so that students and teachers can move about with ease." What criterion determines ease of movement? In the case "The teacher gives students ample time to frame answers to questions," how much time is ample? There are no general rules for setting scoring criteria, and the criteria developed for each performance indicator depend on the nature of the indicator itself and on professional judgments concerning what is and what is not an acceptable level of performance. In any case, criteria must be stated explicitly, objectively, and unambiguously in written form. These written instructions for scoring are used in training people to administer the instrument and are available for reference during administration.

***Testing and Revision***    No matter how much care has gone into the design of an instrument, its effectiveness is determined by its usefulness. A test under realistic conditions is necessary to ensure that the instrument can be administered as designed and that it yields useful information. Difficulties can be remedied before the instrument is final.

Examples of difficulties that may surface during a tryout are: instructions for administration or scoring are unclear, insufficient time is allotted for classroom observation, and the method of measuring certain performance indicators seems inappropriate. The greater the effort and care that went into the design, the less likely it is that the tryout will reveal serious problems. Nevertheless, some minor changes are likely to be suggested by the tryout results, and making these changes will result in a better, more useful tool for assessing program implementation and identifying areas for program improvement.

***Empirical Validation of the Instrument***    Empirical validation of an implementation assessment instrument involves determining the degree to which the instrument yields consistent results (reliability or generalizability) and the degree to which it measures what it is supposed to measure (validity). The many possible ways of estimating the reliability and validity of instruments are beyond the scope of this chapter and only a few pertinent considerations are discussed here.

The scoring of many performance indicators depends on judgments made by the administrator while observing classroom events and the assurance of equivalent scoring by two or more observers at the same time (interobserver reliability) is especially important. Consistency over two or more observations within a relatively brief time (retest reliability) ensures that a classroom's scores during one assessment are representative of the classroom's level of implementation. These and other kinds of reliability can be established, both for the instrument as a whole and for individual critical dimensions, by calculating reliability (or generalizability) coefficients.

Validity studies of implementation assessment instruments generally address the following questions:

Are different degrees of implementation associated with different types of classroom processes, as predicted by the model of adaptive education (see chap. 1, this volume)?

Do levels of implementation measured by the instrument agree with those resulting from independent assessment by other means?

Do scores on given dimensions increase after training has been provided on those dimensions?

Validity questions such as these were addressed for the development of the Implementation Assessment Battery for Adaptive Instruction studies (Wang & Gennari, 1983; Wang, Nojan, Strom, & Walberg, 1984; Wang & Walberg, 1983a, 1983b).

Readers should not infer from this discussion that an instrument cannot be put to use until empirical validation of its reliability and validity is completed. On the contrary, such instruments are ready for use after a field test and revision. Although determining the validity and reliability of a measure is necessary for implementation evaluation purposes or to test the program design for achieving desired outcomes, empirical studies of psychometric validation of the instrument are not necessary to determine the extent of implementation and the need for training. To identify program implementation training needs, a general measure of the presence or absence of essential program features is needed. An expedient way to validate degree of implementation instruments is to carry out a systematic series of reliability and validity studies while using the experimental version of the instrument to assess staff development.

***Administration of the Assessment***   School staff are generally ready for their first formal assessment of implementation after 4–5 weeks of school, or mid-October. The results provide data for planning staff development activities over the next months. Additional formal assessments depend on school needs and time constraints. A minimum of two additional assessments, one in midwinter (February) and one near the end of the school year (May), are recommended. The midwinter assessment provides program administrators with information about the efficacy of staff development activities and a database for planning continued staff development. The spring assessment provides information for evaluating staff development, the overall implementability of the particular adaptive education program being implemented, and data for planning implementation support and staff development activities for the next school year.

Formal assessment of implementation three times per year does not necessarily mean that implementation is monitored only at those times. As indicated earlier, informal assessment occurs continuously based on classroom visits by the principal and program coordinator, feedback from students and parents, and teacher self-monitoring. Moreover, individual teachers can be encouraged to request additional formal assessments whenever they think results will be useful for their own implementation planning. By comparing the results with their self-assessments, teachers can become increasingly effective monitors and evaluators of their program implementation.

***Training to Administer the Assessment***   Adequate training for those responsible for collecting program implementation information, such as the principal, program coordinators, or teachers who will use the instrument for self-monitoring and assessment of their implementation and training needs, will ensure reliable and accurate measurement. This training may take place prior to program implementation if there is time, or during the early weeks of school, but in either case, it must be completed before the first scheduled administration of the instrument. Training is hands-on and interactive, and trainees use materials in simulated or real settings and receive feedback to improve their administration. The training program for the Implementation Assessment Battery for Adaptive Instruction, for example, consists of three 3-hour sessions in which trainees receive instruction and practice administration and scoring using videotapes of classroom events, simulated classroom records, and interviews. Training in the administration of an implementation assessment instrument is a useful strategy for learning essential program implementation requirements. Detailed instructions for conducting training are provided in the *Training Manual for the Implementation Assessment Battery for Adaptive Instruction* (Wang, Catalano, & Grommol, 1986).

## Scoring the Implementation Assessment

Individual performance indicators are generally scored during the administration of the implementation assessment instrument in each classroom. Next, the sum of a teacher's scores within each critical dimension is calculated to obtain the raw score for that dimension, and raw scores are converted to percentages so that dimensions can be compared. For example, if a teacher has received credit for 8 of 12 Instructing performance indicators and for 4 of 5 Monitoring and Diagnosing indicators, his or her scores on the two dimensions are 67% and 80%, respectively.

Program support staff need to develop standard forms for summarizing the performance of individual teachers. A sample form is shown in Figure 7.2. The form not only lists the teacher's scores in each critical dimension but also shows circles around the item numbers of performance indicators for which a score of 0 (not acceptable) was recorded. Forms such as these are useful for providing feedback to teachers concerning implementation and for identifying areas that need improvement.

Calculating scores within dimensions and converting to percentages can be done manually, but because the number of dimensions, the number of performance indicators per dimension, and the number of teachers and classrooms may be quite large, computerized scoring is recommended. A sample printout summarizing the results of the Implementation Assessment Battery for Adaptive Instruction for an individual teacher is shown in Figure 7.3., and a summary report for a school district is shown in Figure 7.4. Figure 7.3. shows features present in a teacher's implementation and areas that need further work for each degree of implementation assessment. Figure 7.4. lists percentage scores for each teacher, average scores for each school and for each grade across schools, and overall averages across the district.

## Using Assessment Results to Identify Training Needs

The information provided in Figure 7.3. and Figure 7.4. is used to determine staff development needs. Presenting implementation assessment results as percentage scores for each dimension (as shown in Figure 7.4.) for individual teachers and across classrooms enables staff developers to see the strengths and weaknesses in program implementation at a glance. For example, if a school's averages for Arranging Space and Facilities and Creating and Maintaining Instructional Materials are 95% and 40%, respectively, it is obvious that the teachers as a group need help and support with instructional materials, but not with arranging space and facilities. If most teachers average 90% or above on a particular critical dimension while one teacher scores 50%, that teacher apparently needs help on that dimension.

How low does a score need to be in order to indicate a need for training?

Teacher ___ 003 ___  Grade ___ 3 ___  School ___  A  District ___  X  Date ___ 3/2/90 ___  Observer ___ Jones ___

| Critical Dimension | Indicator Numbers | Total Number of Indicators | Number of Indicators Implemented | Percentage Score |
|---|---|---|---|---|
| Arranging Space & Facilities AS&F | 1 2 3 (4) 5 6 7 8 / 9 10 11 12 13 14 15 | 15 | 14 | 93 |
| Creating & Maintaining Instructional Materials CMIM | 16 17 18 (19) 20 21 22 23 / 24 (25) (26) 100 | 12 | 9 | 75 |
| Establishing, Communicating, & Refining Rules & Procedures ECRRP | 37 38 39 (66) 68 69 80 81 / 82 83 84 85 86 87 88 | 15 | 14 | 93 |
| Coordinating & Managing Support Services and Extra Personnel Resources CMSS | 103 104 105 | 3 | 3 | 100 |
| Record Keeping RK | 27 28 31 | 3 | 3 | 100 |
| Diagnostic Testing TEST | 95 96 97 98 | 4 | 4 | 100 |
| Prescribing PRES | 29 32 33 34 35 36 58 | 7 | 7 | 100 |
| Monitoring & Diagnosing M&D | 30 44 46 (50) 51 89 90 99 / 106 107 | 10 | 9 | 90 |
| Interactive Teaching IT | 41 42 (56) 59 60 61 | 6 | 5 | 83 |
| Instructing INST | 48 (49) 52 53 54 55 62 / 63 91 92 93 94 | 12 | 11 | 92 |
| Motivating MOTI | 43 45 47 (57) 64 | 5 | 4 | 80 |
| Developing Student Self-Responsibility DSSR | (67) (70) 71 72 (73) (74) 75 (76) / 77 78 79 101 102 | 13 | 8 | 62 |

**Figure 7.2.** Form for coding an individual teacher's implementation data. (The circled numbers are indicators that require further work.)

There is, of course, no absolute cutoff point between "good" and "poor" implementation. A score of 85% is generally used as the criterion for a high level of implementation, 50%–80% for an average level, and below 50% for a low level. Dimensions with high levels of implementation require continued monitoring but little direct help, while those in the average and low ranges are candidates for further training.

The level of implementation considered adequate may vary from one site to another and from early to later in the school year. Thus, program officials may regard a school average of 45% on a critical dimension in mid-October to be within an acceptable range, especially if there are indications of continued progress in that area. The same score in February or May would probably be an indication that further training is required and that the level and nature of implementation support need to change.

It is important to note that the degree of implementation scores represent a rough estimate of implementation levels, and that scores are not viewed as absolute measurements. Rather, they are used as a gauge for planning and for program refinement and, most of all, by teachers as a way to determine their implementation support needs and to monitor their own implementation.

The degree of program implementation from the first formal assessment of a new program is likely to be low for many staff members, yet training time and resources are limited. Therefore, the implementation support staff must decide where to direct their initial training efforts.

Research on effective schooling provides some guidelines for setting training priorities. For example, little meaningful instruction can take place in a disorderly classroom environment (Doyle, 1986); therefore, if scores on a dimension such as Establishing, Communicating, and Refining Rules and Procedures are low, it is well to direct intensive training efforts to this dimension before proceeding to others. In most cases, decisions about training priorities are based not only on good pedagogy but also on judgments of what is best for the school and the instructional program. Two schools with similar patterns of implementation scores might make different decisions: One school might first address activities related to implementing individualized instruction in basic skills (Prescribing, and Monitoring and Diagnosing), while the other might begin with Developing Student Self-Responsibility.

It is important to consider teachers' preferences when prioritizing staff development needs. For example, if two critical dimensions both require training, teachers should provide input on which to address first. Teachers become motivated participants in their own training when they are involved in planning staff development.

## PLANNING AND DELIVERY OF STAFF DEVELOPMENT

The topics for discussion in this section include preparation of comprehensive staff development plans for a school, planning staff development for individual teachers, and some issues in planning for staff development.

### Preparation of School Staff Development Plans

When training priorities have been established, implementation support staff, in consultation with teachers, prepare a comprehensive staff development plan for

# DEGREE OF IMPLEMENTATION
## School 007, Philadelphia

Teacher: 183
Grade: 3
Date: 5/5/90

### Dimension: Arranging Space and Facilities

| Item | | |
|------|---|---|
| 1. Furniture and learning centers are arranged properly | X |
| 2. There are signs that clearly label the separate learning areas | X |
| 3. There is a system controlling the number of students in activity areas | X |
| 4. There is a clock which students can use to keep track of time | X |
| 5. Sufficient teacher calls are available in the work areas | X |
| 6. There is a separate area for working with individual students | X |
| 7. An area for storage and display of learning materials is labeled | X |
| 8. The location of display areas encourages integration of materials | X |
| 9. Student work space in each storage area is located conveniently | X |
| 10. There is adequate work space for individual and group activities | X |
| 11. Each student has an individual place for personal belongings | X |
| 12. Student's completed work is on display | X |
| 13. Prescriptive materials are marked with an easily deciphered code | — |
| 14. Materials are categorized to facilitate selection and replacement | X |
| 15. Records, tapes, and similar items are labeled with pictures or words | X |
| **Degree of implementation score** | **93%** |

### Dimension: Creating and Maintaining Instructional Materials

| Item | | |
|------|---|---|
| 16. Alternative prescriptive learning materials are available in room | X |
| 17. In each exploratory center, there are at least two activities | X |
| 18. There are sufficient activities to accommodate student differences | — |
| 19. There is an up-to-date list of learning tasks for curricular objectives | — |
| 20. Equipment and materials are neat, durable, and in usable condition | X |
| 21. Materials are interesting and attractive to students | X |
| 22. Some activities are designed to encourage social interaction | X |
| 23. There is at least one learning task for each curricular objective | X |
| 24. Teacher-constructed learning tasks are related to curricular objectives | X |
| 25. Learning tasks are accompanied by list of materials and script | X |
| 26. Directions and questions on learning tasks relate to objectives | X |
| 100. Exploratory materials are changed at least once a month | X |
| **Degree of implementation score** | **67%** |

### Dimension: Establishing, Communicating, and Refining Rules and Procedures

| Item | | |
|------|---|---|
| 37. Self-schedule form shows teacher's expectation and work completed | X |
| 38. Students select 1-2 exploratories at least 4 days of the week | X |
| 39. Students complete prescribed activities within the specified time | X |
| 66. The number of students working in activity areas does not exceed limit | X |
| 68. Students obtain adult help by using designated call signals | X |
| 69. Students finish one task and ask the teacher to check work | X |
| 80. Students know when they must work on their prescriptions | X |
| 81. Students know when they may do exploratory work | X |
| 82. Students know how to signal for help when needed | X |
| 83. Students know when they may not do exploratory work | X |
| 84. Students know which materials may be used without teacher's help | X |
| 85. Students know the consequences for not finishing their work on time | X |
| 86. Students know what would happen if they finish work ahead of time | X |
| 87. Students help out in the classroom by doing odd jobs | X |
| 88. All students help out in the classroom by doing odd jobs | X |
| **Degree of implementation score** | **100%** |

### Dimension: Coordinating and Managing Support Services and Extra Personnel Resources

| Item | | |
|------|---|---|
| 103. There is an established time each day to exchange information | X |
| 104. Teacher assigns duties for the assistant during this time | X |
| 105. Teacher discusses the performance of students with the assistant | X |
| **Degree of implementation score** | **100%** |

### Dimension: Record Keeping

| Item | | |
|------|---|---|
| 27. All classroom records are neat, up-to-date, and accessible | X |
| 28. Student progress charts for the various activities are complete | — |
| 31. There is an up-to-date record of student's completed tasks | — |
| **Degree of implementation score** | **33%** |

**Dimension: Diagnostic Testing**

| | |
|---|---|
| 95. Placement tests are given when students enter a new curriculum | x |
| 96. Pretests are given at the beginning of each unit of instruction | x |
| 97. Pretests are given at the end of each unit of instruction | x |
| 98. Placement tests are given to determine level of transfer student | x |
| Degree of implementation score | 100% |

**Dimension: Prescribing**

| | |
|---|---|
| 29. Students are working in different units within each curriculum | — |
| 32. Different tasks are prescribed if a student is given more work | x |
| 33. Prescriptions are related to diagnostic test results | x |
| 34. Prescriptions include the tasks and pages to be completed | x |
| 35. Prescriptions follow the sequence recommended for each curr. area | x |
| 36. The teacher varies prescriptions to meet individual student needs | — |
| 58. When appropriate, the teacher restructures specific learning tasks | — |
| Degree of implementation score | 57% |

**Dimension: Monitoring and Diagnosing**

| | |
|---|---|
| 30. Most students pass at least 1 unit post-test in each curricular area | — |
| 44. The teacher checks work in students' presence | x |
| 46. The teacher determines individual students' sources of difficulty | x |
| 50. The teacher helps students complete work on time | x |
| 51. The teacher discusses with students their work plans and progress | x |
| 89. Teacher responses about students' levels agree with classroom records | x |
| 90. Teacher knows whether individual students have a curriculum preference | x |
| 99. Teacher sometimes changes prescriptions when checking students' work | — |
| 106. Teacher discusses the performance of students with their parents | — |
| 107. Teacher discusses the performance of students with other staff | x |
| Degree of implementation score | 70% |

**Dimension: Interactive Teaching**

| | |
|---|---|
| 41. The teacher spends short periods of time with each student | x |
| 42. The teacher responds to those students who signal properly | x |
| 56. The teacher travels through all areas where students are working | — |
| 59. The teacher looks around the room after each student contact | — |
| 60. The teacher notices and acknowledges each student who needs help | x |
| 61. The teacher encourages students to help each other with their work | x |
| Degree of implementation score | 67% |

**Dimension: Instructing**

| | |
|---|---|
| 48. The teacher helps students structure learning tasks | x |
| 49. The teacher communicates criteria for successful performance | x |
| 52. The teacher uses questioning | x |
| 53. The teacher uses explaining | x |
| 54. The teacher uses cueing or prompting | x |
| 55. The teacher uses demonstrating and/or modeling | x |
| 62. The teacher interacts with students concerning specific tasks | x |
| 63. The teacher's questioning techniques encourage student responses | x |
| 91. Small groups are used as part of prescribed activities | x |
| 92. Small groups are formed based on diagnosed needs | x |
| 93. Math maintenance drills are conducted at least twice a week | x |
| 94. Students are grouped for supplementary instruction | x |
| Degree of implementation score | 92% |

**Dimension: Motivating**

| | |
|---|---|
| 43. The teacher shows personal regard for each student | x |
| 45. The teacher gives praise when appropriate | x |
| 47. The teacher encourages self-management | x |
| 57. The teacher shows an interest in student work | x |
| 64. The teacher communicates that students are expected to succeed | x |
| Degree of implementation score | 100% |

**Dimension: Developing Student Self-Responsibility**

| | |
|---|---|
| 67. Students readily locate prescriptions | x |
| 70. When waiting for assistance, students are occupied with other tasks | — |
| 71. Students readily locate materials and equipment for all tasks | x |
| 72. Students use learning materials and equipment appropriately | x |
| 73. Students return materials and equipment to the correct places | x |
| 74. After work is checked, students put it in a designated place | x |
| 75. Each student knows how to use his or her prescription sheet | x |
| 76. Each student knows how to use his or her self-schedule form | x |
| 77. Students know how many assignments they have left to finish each day | x |
| 78. Students know which assignments they have left to finish | x |
| 79. Students know when they must finish the work on their prescription sheet | x |
| 101. Students are encouraged to self-schedule consistently | x |
| 102. Students are encouraged to self-schedule at a more advanced level | — |
| Degree of implementation score | 85% |

Figure 7.3. Computer printout of an individual teacher's implementation of program features. (X indicates that the performance indicator was observed to be present.)

205

**Critical Dimension Codes**

| | | |
|---|---|---|
| AS&F | Arranging Space & Facilities | TEST Diagnostic Testing |
| CMIM | Creating & Maintaining Instructional Materials | PRES Prescribing |
| ECRRP | Establishing, Communicating, & Refining Rules and Procedures | M&D Monitoring & Diagnosing |
| | | IT Interactive Teaching |
| CMSS | Coordinating & Managing Support Services & Extra Personnel Resources | INST Instructing |
| | | MOTI Motivating |
| RK | Record Keeping | DSSR Developing Student Self-Responsibility |

**District X, Fall 1989**

| School/Grade | | AS&F (15) | CMIM (12) | ECRRP (15) | CMSS (3) | RK (3) | TEST (4) | PRES (7) | M&D (10) | IT (6) | INST (12) | MOTI (5) | DSSR (13) |
|---|---|---|---|---|---|---|---|---|---|---|---|---|---|
| **School A** | | | | | | | | | | | | | |
| | Teacher A | 87 | 67 | 73 | 67 | 33 | 50 | 71 | 70 | 67 | 83 | 60 | 77 |
| Grade 1 | Teacher B | 93 | 83 | 87 | 67 | 100 | 25 | 57 | 90 | 50 | 75 | 60 | 69 |
| Grade 2 | Teacher C | 87 | 67 | 80 | 67 | 67 | 75 | 86 | 70 | 83 | 92 | 80 | 62 |
| Grade 3 / Kindergarten | Teacher D | 73 | 58 | 93 | 100 | 67 | 75 | 86 | 80 | 83 | 92 | 80 | 92 |
| Average for School | | 85 | 69 | 83 | 75 | 67 | 56 | 75 | 78 | 71 | 86 | 70 | 75 |
| **School B** | | | | | | | | | | | | | |
| Grade 1 | Teacher E | 67 | 75 | 73 | 67 | 67 | 75 | 71 | 80 | 50 | 83 | 40 | 54 |
| Grade 2 | Teacher F | 80 | 67 | 73 | 33 | 67 | 25 | 14 | 60 | 50 | 75 | 20 | 46 |
| Grade 3 | Teacher G | 87 | 83 | 87 | 67 | 100 | 75 | 86 | 90 | 67 | 92 | 80 | 85 |
| Kindergarten | Teacher H | 93 | 83 | 93 | 67 | 67 | 50 | 71 | 70 | 83 | 100 | 60 | 77 |
| Average for School | | 82 | 77 | 82 | 59 | 75 | 56 | 61 | 75 | 63 | 88 | 50 | 66 |
| **Average for Site** | | | | | | | | | | | | | |
| Grade 1 | | 77 | 71 | 73 | 67 | 50 | 63 | 71 | 75 | 59 | 83 | 50 | 66 |
| Grade 2 | | 87 | 75 | 80 | 50 | 84 | 25 | 36 | 75 | 50 | 75 | 40 | 58 |
| Grade 3 | | 87 | 75 | 84 | 67 | 84 | 75 | 86 | 80 | 75 | 92 | 80 | 74 |
| Kindergarten | | 83 | 71 | 93 | 84 | 67 | 63 | 79 | 75 | 83 | 96 | 70 | 85 |
| **Overall Average** | | 84 | 73 | 83 | 67 | 71 | 56 | 68 | 76 | 67 | 87 | 60 | 71 |

**Figure 7.4.** Computer printout of a summary of degree of implementation data for a school district. [Numbers in parentheses indicate number of performance indicators included in the Implementation Assessment Battery for Adaptive Instruction [Wang, Catalano, & Gromoll, (1986.)]

the school. This written plan includes specific areas to be addressed by training, the training methods to be used for each area, the schedule for delivery, and persons responsible for training activities. The plan is effective until the next formal assessment.

It is probably best to prepare staff development plans using a format such as that shown in Figure 7.5. The figure presents an excerpt from a staff development plan that followed a midwinter assessment of implementation and included staff development activities for the months of March and April. The excerpt shows activities related to two critical dimensions, Creating and Maintaining Instructional Materials and Student Planning. Four specific tasks are listed under each dimension, and columns list for each activity the date(s) of the training, person(s) responsible, the type of activity, the expected outcome(s), and the evidence (data) gathered to evaluate the effectiveness of the training.

A school staff development plan must take the strengths and limitations of the school into account; for example, it would be unreasonable to schedule a 3-hour workshop for teachers on a school day, or require program coordinators to train two activities at the same time. A carefully developed plan ensures that the school's implementation needs are addressed appropriately without overtaxing human or material resources. Sharing the plan with teachers in a staff meeting provides them with staff development goals and the teachers' roles in meeting them and helps to elicit their cooperation in planned activities.

In the course of staff development, support staff and teachers sometimes find it necessary to deviate from the planned schedule or change the nature of activities. If this happens, the plan is revised and updated as needed.

Teachers, like students, differ in their learning needs and require different kinds of help, and staff development needs to be tailored to meet the training needs of each teacher. Good staff development, like good teaching, is a carefully orchestrated mix of group-based and individual instruction.

As soon as possible after the implementation assessment has been scored, the program coordinator meets with each teacher to review the assessment results and to plan staff development activities for the individual teachers or a group of teachers with the same implementation problems. The planning process should provide ample opportunities for teacher input and suggestions, and the staff development plans that emerge are a joint product of the teachers and program coordinator. Plans for staff development include the program dimensions that will be the focus of training, the schedule, and the expected outcomes. Basic questions to consider include the kinds of changes that teachers need to make, and the resources required to help the teachers make these changes. The program coordinator elicits teacher input in determining staff development needs and leads the planning, when appropriate, based on his or her teaching expertise and knowledge of the adaptive education program. Planning decisions are recorded on a document such as that illustrated in Figure 7.6., and this plan includes information about strategies to be employed, expected outcomes, and provisions for follow-up.

Planning staff development support for an individual teacher should incorporate the individualized training with the school's staff development activities whenever possible. For example, all program teachers are scheduled in March for a workshop about construction of instructional materials. If a teacher has particular problems with this dimension, the program coordinator should

| Task (Training Objective) | Date(s) | Person(s) Responsible | Type of Activity | Expected Outcome(s) | Evidence of Effective Service |
|---|---|---|---|---|---|
| **1. Creating and Maintaining Instructional Materials** | | | | | |
| 1.1 Conduct inservice workshop on criteria for creating exploratory activities. | March 18 | A Specialist Consultant on Learning Centers Program Coordinator Principal | Workshop | Increased awareness of criteria used in constructing exploratory activities. | Teachers use criteria in designing and evaluating exploratory activities. |
| 1.2 Teachers evaluate materials according to criteria. | March 23-27 | Classroom Teachers | Evaluation | Teachers examine exploratory materials. | Materials which meet criteria are used in exploratory activities. |
| 1.3 Teachers categorize self-constructed materials according to curricular area. | March 23-27 | Classroom Teachers | | Materials are categorized and ready for classroom use. | Exploratory materials are labeled according to curricular area. |
| 1.4 Teachers list useful materials (as per criteria). | Ongoing | Classroom Teachers | Consultation | Teachers list materials already constructed and add new materials as they are constructed. | Update of list. |
| **2. Student Planning** | | | | | |
| 2.1 Review performance indicators included in the degree of implementation measures related to student planning in weekly staff meeting. | March 11 | Program Coordinator School Principal | Staff meeting | Teachers understand the rationale and need for developing supports for student planning and for developing strategies to help students plan. | Teachers are able to help students gain increased responsibility for planning. |
| 2.2 Classroom rules and procedures are re-established and written down. | March 16 | Classroom Teachers Program Coordinator | Discussion and development of list | Rules and procedures are listed. | Listing of classroom rules and procedures. |
| 2.3 Teachers review planning procedures and rules with students. | March 18 | Classroom Teachers | Discussion with students | Teachers and students establish rules. | Students are able to verbalize rules. |
| 2.4 Students are observed and interviewed by teachers and education specialist during self-scheduling. | April 14 | Classroom Teachers Program Coordinator | Observation | Description of each student's functioning under the Self-Schedule System. | Students communicate rules and procedures to observers verbally and nonverbally. |

**Figure 7.5.** Excerpt from school-wide staff development plan.

**Staff Development Plan**

School: _____J. J._____   District: _____A_____   Grade: ____2____

Teacher: _____Smith_____   Date: __November 9, 1990__

Program Coordinator: _____Hughes_____

| Observed Behavior | Strategy Suggested | Expected Outcome |
|---|---|---|
| Math skills introduced without use of concrete aids. | Use concrete aids to introduce new skills. | Concepts are introduced with manipulatives. Less time is spent teaching a skill. |
| Students marked self-scheduling folder on their own. | Only classroom assistant or teacher marks self-scheduling sheet. | Students ask teacher (or classroom assistant) to check their self-scheduling sheet when work has been completed. |
| Paper/pencil tasks used in math exploration. | Include math activities — math bingo. | More hands-on tasks are included. |

Follow-up: An observation of Smith's class has been scheduled for December 5.

**Figure 7.6.** Monthly training plan for an individual teacher.

schedule the staff development activity for the teacher in March as well so that the teacher can participate in the school-wide staff development activities while receiving individual assistance from the program coordinator. In this way, a teacher's training is coordinated not only with his or her individual implementation needs but also with simultaneous school-wide instructional and training activities.

## Some Issues in Planning for Staff Development

In planning for staff development, two issues may emerge. They are "minimal competency versus expertise" and "theory versus practice." These are discussed below.

*Minimal Competency versus Expertise*   A person learning a complex skill goes through a sequence of stages, ranging from lack of skill through minimal competency to expert performance. The acquisition of teaching skills often follows this pattern. If program-related skills are initially at a low level, as may be the case when an innovative program is first implemented, should each skill be trained to a near-expert level before moving onto the next, or should all skills first be brought to a minimal competency? Although the answer may vary from one dimension to another, the latter course of action is generally recommended. Fine tuning of individual skills can be achieved when all program-related skills have been brought to minimal competency.

An example may help to clarify the situation. An October implementation assessment has revealed that Mr. Smith, a third grade teacher, is having difficulty with diagnosing and prescribing. The performance of students in each of his reading and mathematics groups varied widely on the last unit pre-test although all students in each group were given the same basic skill and enrichment assignments. Mr. Smith checks students' work as they carry out assignments, but he makes no revisions in their prescriptions, although some students apparently need additional work and others find the assignments too easy. Should the program coordinator first work with Mr. Smith to help him become an expert diagnostician and then help him write individual prescriptions based on diagnoses? Should the program coordinator help Mr. Smith make relatively simple diagnoses, then help him match prescriptions to diagnoses, and then work with him to develop a higher level of skill in both areas? The latter is a better course of action for two reasons. First, Mr. Smith will more quickly see the relationship between his diagnoses and his prescriptions. Second, when he sees the positive effect of the diagnostic–prescriptive process on his student learning, he will be more motivated to develop both skills to a higher level.

The program coordinator, principal, and teachers should not be disappointed if their level of skill in certain aspects of adaptive education remains relatively low after several months, as long as progress is being made. Given the newness and complexity of many of these skills, and the organizational and administrative supports required for program implementation, a high degree of implementation may require a longer period of time. One or more years may be required for solutions to evolve from the cycle of assessment, feedback, and training through program refinement and development (Vaughan, Wang, & Dytman, 1987).

*Theory versus Practice*   A basic premise in the development and implementation of innovative programs is that research and theory-based knowledge should be applied to improve practice. Innovative programs generally are grounded in complex psychological theories about learning and instruction. For example, techniques for teaching cognitive knowledge and skills are based on information processing theories that include many components, concepts, and interrelations.

An issue for staff development is if teachers should first learn the theory behind a particular teaching technique, or first learn the technique, or learn both simultaneously. Although a brief rationale for a new technique is generally considered the first step, it is best to teach applications of techniques before relevant theories are presented in detail. Teachers are practice oriented and tend to focus on solving daily practical problems before trying to acquire a thorough knowledge of why certain innovative practices work. In addition, teachers tend to disbelieve or discount a theory if they encounter it first in theory without seeing it applied. If, however, they find that a technique does enhance their performance or student learning, they have a better framework for addressing "Why does this work?" Thus, practical experience points to a brief overview of theories and the research base, followed by systematic training on application of the theories and research findings, followed by an extended explanation of the theory underlying the practice. Technical skills, however, are not all that are needed for effective implementation. Teachers are best able to refine their teaching techniques when they possess a concept of what is happening and why so that they can continue the process of implementation and refinement that furthers their professional development.

As an example, consider the use of reinforcers to motivate students. Most teachers have learned a smattering of reinforcement theory and know that positive reinforcement strengthens behavior. All teachers at some point, however, encounter students for whom this rule does not seem to apply, students who when praised show no improvement in performance. If this is a problem, the program coordinator or school psychologist might suggest alternative motivational techniques. If these are effective and arouse teachers' curiosity about why they worked, then sessions explaining new approaches to motivation and reinforcement (e.g., attribution theory) can be planned. The new concept may then enable teachers to design still more effective motivational systems for their students.

## Implementation of Staff Development Plans: Modes of Delivery

The method selected for delivering staff development depends on the knowledge or skill to be taught and sometimes on participant preference or available time and resources. Four modes are described in the approximate order of participant involvement: seminars, demonstration and modeling, workshops, and coaching.

*Seminars* Seminars that combine lecture and discussion, supplemented with reading, are particularly well suited to presenting theoretical information or teaching methods before methods are demonstrated. Discussion is also a good way for teachers to exchange ideas and engage in group problem solving. Staff development seminars can usually be held during regular staff meetings. Seminars about a teaching method may enable teachers to apply a method that they have already learned. Seminars alone are not appropriate for teaching new techniques or behaviors.

*Demonstration and Modeling* Demonstration and modeling are useful techniques that show how a particular behavior or skill is applied. Demonstrations may be presented with video- or audiotapes, or participants may observe the program coordinator, for example, modeling a new technique. The effectiveness of both live and taped demonstrations is increased when important features of the observed behaviors are discussed in conjunction with these sessions. A particularly effective way to use modeling as a training technique is by having teachers observe one another. By observing a demonstration, teachers form a conceptualization or cognitive model of the desired behavior.

Demonstration and modeling alone may be sufficient to help teachers acquire relatively simple skills. For more complex skills, techniques involving more active participation by trainees are generally necessary.

*Workshops*  Workshops are particularly well-suited to the development of skills that create or use instructional materials. For example, if program classrooms lack innovative, teacher-made instructional materials, a workshop can give teachers ideas and guidelines and the opportunity to construct materials. A school starting to use new curriculum materials or adjuncts such as new prescription sheets would benefit from a workshop, which gives participants an opportunity to practice with the new materials. Mini-workshops on single topics that do not require extensive time can be held during regular staff meetings, and workshops that require more than 1 hour can be scheduled after school or during inservice days.

*Coaching*  The term coaching applied to teaching has the same meaning as in athletics, and it involves intensive skill training with feedback. Coaching is particularly suited to the acquisition of complex skills and uses a combination of techniques already discussed. Participants first learn theory through seminars, discussion, or reading, and then observe demonstration and modeling. Participants practice the skill, first in limited or simulated settings (microteaching), then in their own classrooms. After practice, they receive feedback from trainers and incorporate this information in their next practice attempts. Practice and feedback continue until a certain skill level is reached or for a specified time. Coaching is a highly labor-intensive and time-consuming method of training. Program coordinators who plan to include coaching in staff development activities must be able to commit the time and resources. Readers who wish to learn more about coaching and its effects can refer to Joyce and Showers (1980) and Showers (1985).

## Documentation and Evaluation of Staff Development Activities

The program coordinator and principal need to accurately record all group and individual training activities. Records document that training has been delivered according to plan, provide the information base for program refinement and revisions in staff development plans, provide evidence of continuing school improvement efforts or accountability, and provide data for validation studies of implementation assessment procedures and for studies of training effectiveness.

A daily log of training topics, modes of delivery, and names of participants provides a database on staff development and outcomes. If outcome measures are collected, they too are recorded. A format for recording staff development activities is illustrated by Figure 7.7. This form is well-suited to recording training activities of individual teachers on critical dimensions. When a teacher re-

Program
Coordinator _____

Critical Dimensions

| Teacher's Name | Date | Arranging Space and Facilities | Creating and Maintaining Instructional Materials | Establishing, Communicating, and Refining Rules and Procedures | Managing Services and Personnel | Diagnostic Testing | Record Keeping | Monitoring and Diagnosing | Prescribing | Interactive Teaching | Instructing | Motivating | Developing Student Self-Responsibility |
|---|---|---|---|---|---|---|---|---|---|---|---|---|---|
| | | | | | | | | | | | | | |
| | | | | | | | | | | | | | |
| | | | | | | | | | | | | | |
| | | | | | | | | | | | | | |
| | | | | | | | | | | | | | |
| | | | | | | | | | | | | | |
| | | | | | | | | | | | | | |
| | | | | | | | | | | | | | |
| | | | | | | | | | | | | | |
| | | | | | | | | | | | | | |
| | | | | | | | | | | | | | |
| | | | | | | | | | | | | | |
| | | | | | | | | | | | | | |
| | | | | | | | | | | | | | |
| | | | | | | | | | | | | | |

**Figure 7.7.** Form for recording staff development activities.

ceives training, his or her name and the date are recorded, and the amount of time spent is entered in the appropriate cell.

Staff development activities are expected to produce certain outcomes. Staff development plans, such as those in Figure 7.5. and Figure 7.6., describe the expected outcome or evidence of effective service for each activity. Outcome data and comparison with expectations provide the information for evaluating training results. Many outcome data can be collected informally, on a daily basis. For example, the program coordinator's visits to a classroom where the teacher received training on questioning techniques can confirm the extent to which the teacher is using more appropriate questioning techniques. More formal and comprehensive assessment of outcomes is provided by the results of the next implementation assessment. If teachers' scores improve in areas or dimensions in which they have received training, then the training can be judged to have been effective. Just as good classroom teaching is expected to result in student learning, carefully planned and well-conducted staff development will almost certainly result in improved program implementation. Improved implementation, in turn, is expected to result in improved classroom processes and positive effects on student achievement and attitudes.

Each formal assessment provides data not only for evaluating staff development efforts, but also for diagnosing new training and technical assistance needs. Thus, the cycle of continuing staff development begins anew.

## EXTENDING THE CYCLE OF STAFF DEVELOPMENT

The staff development described in this chapter continues throughout the life of the program. Although staff development during the first year of a new program is emphasized, the process is expected to extend beyond the first year and be extended to other school staff as well.

By the end of the first year of a new program, teachers are usually relatively comfortable with the program and are implementing it routinely. This does not mean, of course, that there is no room for improvement.

The spring implementation assessment sets the stage for training at the start of the following year. Second-year training usually involves review of acquired skills and fine tuning of skills used at a more rudimentary level.

Although training needs in the second year and beyond may be different from those of the first year, they are no less intense, and resources allocated to staff development should not be reduced. Research has shown that provision of appropriate training can result in continued improvement in program implementation even after many years. In a study conducted at four sites that had been implementing a particular adaptive education program for 12 years, a new data-based staff development program led to improved implementation during the next year (Vaughan, Wang, & Dytman, 1987).

Other members of the instructional staff can probably benefit from the same kinds of training that classroom teachers receive, especially special educators participating in programs providing coordinated programming and delivery of individualized instructional and service supports in regular classroom settings. Members of the implementation support staff with noninstructional roles need training that increases their abilities to carry out their program responsibilities. Although principals and program coordinators typically have primary responsibility for the design and delivery of staff development, they require training that strengthens their abilities to provide program support. School principals profit from staff development that increases their effectiveness as instructional leaders. Similarly, program coordinators need training to increase their abilities to monitor program implementation in classrooms, to help teachers improve their implementation, and to provide material and training support.

Although specific training needs and methods for individuals with other program roles have not been discussed, the cycle of data-based staff development applies to them also. For example, a staff development program for principals requires collection of data to assess the implementation of program features by principals, analysis of the results to identify training needs, followed by plans for staff development, implementation of the staff development plan, and assessment of implementation. Thus, appropriate data-based staff development programs for training principals, program coordinators, and other school staff responsible for program implementation can be generalized from the procedures described in this chapter.

## SUMMARY

This chapter describes a data-based staff development approach to support the implementation of innovative school programs by teachers and provides a step-by-step discussion of how ongoing staff development can be carried out to improve teachers' classroom implementation. It describes the roles of the school staff and the resources needed for effective staff development. Procedures for supporting implementation during the early months of a new program are discussed. A specific approach to staff development, the Data-Based Staff Development Program, characterizes effective staff development as an iterative cycle with four successive and interrelated components: assessment of program implementation, diagnosis of training needs based on results of assessment, planning of training and support activities to improve implementation, and delivery of training. Procedures for implementing the successive components of the staff development cycle are detailed, including various modes of training delivery. Procedures described in this chapter are generic, that is, they can be easily adapted to specific settings to meet the staff development needs of the principal, the program coordinator, and other school staff.

## REFERENCES

Doyle, W. (1986). Classroom organization and management. In M.C. Wittrock (Ed.), *Handbook of research on teaching* (pp. 392–431). New York: Macmillan.

Goldhammer, R., Anderson, R.H., & Krajewski, R.J. (1980). *Clinical supervision* (2nd ed.). New York: Holt, Rinehart & Winston.

Heck, S., Stiegelbauer, S.M., Hall, G.E., & Loucks, S.F. (1981). *Measuring innovation configurations: Procedures and applications.* Austin, TX: Research and Development Center for Teacher Education, University of Texas at Austin.

Joyce, B., & Showers, B. (1980). Improving inservice training: The message of research. *Educational Leadership, 37,* 379.

Leithwood, K.A. (1990). The principal's role in teacher development. In B. Joyce (Ed.), *Changing school culture through staff development.* Alexandria, VA: Association for Supervision and Curriculum Development.

Lieberman, A., Saxl, E.R., & Miles, M.B. (1988). Teacher leadership: Ideology and practice. In A. Lieberman (Ed.), *Building a professional culture in schools*. New York: Teachers College Press.

Showers, B. (1985). Teachers coaching teachers. *Educational Leadership, 42*(7), 43.

U.S. Department of Education Office of Educational Research and Improvement. (1991). *Developing leadership for restructuring schools: New habits of mind and heart*. Washington, DC: Author.

Vaughan, E.D., Wang, M.C., & Dytman, J.A. (1987). Implementing an innovative program: Staff development and teacher classroom performance. *Journal of Teacher Education, 36*, 40–47.

Wang, M.C., Catalano, R., & Gromoll, E. (1986). *Implementation Assessment Battery for Adaptive Education*: Philadelphia, PA: Temple University Center for Research in Human Development and Education.

Wang, M.C., Catalano, R., & Gromoll, E. (1986). *Training manual for the Implementation Assesssment Battery for Adaptive Instruction* (Vols. 1 & 2). Philadelphia, PA: Temple University Center for Research in Human Development and Education.

Wang, M.C., Englert, R.M., & Manning, J.B. (1989). Educational leadership development and the implementation of innovative schooling practices. *Educational Considerations, 16*(2), 39–44.

Wang, M.C., & Gennari, P. (1983). Analysis of the design, implementation, and effects of a data-based staff development program. *Teacher Education and Special Education, 6*(4), 211–226.

Wang, M.C., Nojan, M., Strom, C.D., & Walberg, H.J. (1984). The utility of degree of implementation measures in program implementation and evaluation research. *Curriculum Inquiry, 14*(3), 249–286.

Wang, M.C., & Walberg, H.J. (1983a). Adaptive instruction and classroom time. *American Educational Research Journal, 20*, 601–626.

Wang, M.C., & Walberg, H.J. (1983b). Evaluating educational programs: An integrative, causal-modeling approach. *Educational Evaluation and Policy Analysis, 5*(3), 347–366.

*Appendix*

# Implementation Assessment Battery for Adaptive Instruction

The battery consists of six forms: Checklist for Physical Design of the Classroom, Checklist for Classroom Records, Teacher Observation Form, Student Observation Form, Student Interview Form, and Teacher Interview Form.

*General instructions:* This battery is intended to serve as a model, not as a universally applicable instrument for implementation assessment. It is strongly recommended that the reader modify and redefine the specific indicators and program dimensions included in this battery to reflect local conditions before applying it in a particular school setting.

*Time required to administer:* Administration of the battery takes approximately 3 hours and should be completed in 1 day. Each form describes its specific time requirements.

*When to administer:* The Checklists for Physical Design of the Classroom and Classroom Records can be completed before, during, or after class time. The Teacher and Student Observation Forms and the Student Interview Form must be administered during class time. (Check with the teacher for the most convenient time to administer the Student Interview Form.) The Teacher Interview Form is administered at the teacher's convenience.

Before starting to administer the Battery, please fill in the data below.

Teacher _____ Grade _____ School _____ District _____

Number of Students _____ Observer _____ Date _____

---

FOR CRHDE USE ONLY

MO _____      YR _____      RND _____

SN _____      SCN _____      TN _____      GR _____      TNS _____

NAD _____      TAD _____      AA _____      OB _____      TR _____      CC _____

CW _____      COT _____      CFT _____

SL _____

NI _____

N L _____

---

## CHECKLIST FOR PHYSICAL DESIGN OF THE CLASSROOM

This checklist is designed to assess the presence or absence of specific
sets of performance indicators related to the arrangement of classroom
space and facilities, quality and maintenance of prescriptive and exploratory learning materials, and the quality and maintenance of teacher-
constructed learning materials.

When to                                   Time Required
Administer: Before, during, or after class time     to Administer: 30 - 40 minutes

Directions: Read the descriptor for each performance indicator and circle Y (Yes) if it is present and N (No) if it is not
present. Some items require close examination of learning materials. Where appropriate, specific directions for
individual performance indicators have been provided.

| Item Number | Item | Response Y = Yes | N = No |
|---|---|:---:|:---:|
| 1. | Furniture and learning centers are arranged in such a way that students and teachers can move about with ease. | Y | N |
| 2. | There are signs that clearly label the separate learning areas (e.g., reading, math, art, construction, library). | Y | N |
| 3. | There is a system (e.g., Self-Schedule Board) controlling the number of students in, and movement among, activity areas. | Y | N |
| 4. | There is a clock or other method students can use to keep track of the time. | Y | N |
| 5. | Sufficient teacher call signals are available in work areas for prescriptive and exploratory learning activities. | Y | N |
| 6. | There is a separate area for the teacher to work with individual students (e.g., tutoring, testing). | Y | N |
| 7. | An area for storage and display of learning materials for each component of the curriculum is clearly labeled, demarcated, and accessible to students. | Y | N |
| 8. | The location of storage and display areas encourages appropriate integration of materials within a curricular area. | Y | N |
| 9. | To the extent possible, student work space in each storage and display area is located conveniently according to activity type. | Y | N |
| 10. | There is adequate work space for individual and group activities and independent work. | Y | N |
| 11. | Each student has an individual place for his or her personal belongings. | Y | N |
| 12. | Students' completed work is on display. | Y | N |
| 13. | Prescriptive learning materials are arranged in sequential order and marked with an easily deciphered identification code. | Y | N |

Checklist for Physical Design of the Classroom, continued

| Item Number | Item | Response Y = Yes   N = No | |
|---|---|---|---|
| 14. | Materials are categorized to facilitate selection and replacement by students (e.g., workbooks separated from read-alones, blocks separated by shape, tapes housed in storage racks). | Y | N |
| 15. | Records, tapes, and similar items are labeled with pictures and/or words that are intelligible to students with limited reading ability. | Y | N |
| 16. | Alternative prescriptive learning materials are available in the room. | Y | N |
| 17. | In each exploratory learning center, there are at least two or three activities that vary in content, level of difficulty, and format. | Y | N |
| 18. | There is a sufficient variety of activities to accommodate student differences and allow students a choice. | Y | N |
| 19. | There is an up-to-date list of learning tasks for each curriculum objective. | Y | N |

Special Instructions, Items 20 - 23: Examine three prescriptive and three exploratory learning materials. Use the criterion of five out of six to score a Yes response.

| | | | |
|---|---|---|---|
| 20. | Equipment and materials are neat, durable, and in usable condition and sufficient supply for carrying out activities. | Y | N |
| 21. | Materials are interesting and attractive to students (e.g., are often used by students, sustain students' attention). | Y | N |
| 22. | Some activities are designed to encourage social interaction. | Y | N |
| 23. | There is at least one learning task for each curriculum objective. | Y | N |

Special Instructions, Items 24 - 26: Examine three teacher-constructed prescriptive and three teacher-constructed exploratory learning tasks. Use the criterion of five out of six to score a Yes response.

| | | | |
|---|---|---|---|
| 24. | Teacher-constructed learning tasks are related to specific curriculum objectives. | Y | N |
| 25. | Teacher-constructed learning tasks are accompanied by a list of materials and a script suggesting teacher statements and questions. | Y | N |
| 26. | Directions, statements, and questions on scripts for teacher-constructed learning tasks relate to, and are consistent with, curriculum objectives and they are understandable to students. | Y | N |

## CHECKLIST FOR CLASSROOM RECORDS

This checklist is designed to assess whether classroom records are kept accurately and are up-to-date. Classroom record categories include student progress charts, records of prescriptive tasks, and self-schedule forms.

When to
Administer: Before, during, or after class time

Time Required
to Administer: 30 minutes

Directions: Read the descriptor for each performance indicator within each classroom record category and circle Y (Yes) if it is present and N (No) if it is not present. Where appropriate, specific directions for individual performance indicators have been provided.

| Item Number | Item | Response Y = Yes N = No |
|---|---|---|
| 27. All classroom records are neat, up-to-date, and accessible. | | Y  N |

Student Progress Charts
Special Instructions: Before responding to items 28 - 30, randomly select three students and record their names and reading and math curricular levels on items 89 and 91 of the Teacher Interview Form. This information will be used to verify the teacher's response to item 90.

| | | |
|---|---|---|
| 28. Student progress charts for the various curricular activities are complete. | | Y  N |
| 29. Students are working in different units within each prescriptive curriculum. | | Y  N |

Special Instructions, Item 30: Randomly select five student progress charts. Use the criterion of four out of five to score a Yes response.

| | | |
|---|---|---|
| 30. Most students pass at least one unit posttest in each curricular area every one to two months. | | Y  N |

Prescription Sheets
Special Instructions, Items 31 - 36: Randomly select five student current prescriptions. Use the criterion of four out of five to score a Yes response. (See additional instructions for Item 33.)

| | | |
|---|---|---|
| 31. There is an up-to-date record of the prescriptive tasks completed by each student in each curricular area. | | Y  N |
| 32. If a student is given additional work for a curriculum objective, different tasks or pages, rather than the same tasks, are prescribed. | | Y  N |

Special Instructions, Item 33: Compare five prescriptions with curricular location indicated on diagnostic tests.

| | | |
|---|---|---|
| 33. Prescriptions are related to diagnostic test results. | | Y  N |
| 34. Prescriptions include the number of tasks and/or workbook pages to be completed. | | Y  N |
| 35. Prescriptions follow the sequence recommended for each curricular area. | | Y  N |
| 36. The teacher varies prescriptions (tasks and amount of work) to meet the needs of individual students. | | Y  N |

Self-Schedule Forms
Special Instructions, Items 37 - 39: Randomly select five students' self-schedule forms for the last full week. Use the criterion of four out of five to score a Yes response.

| | | |
|---|---|---|
| 37. The self-schedule form shows the teacher's expectations and the amount of work completed for a given day and for the week. | | Y  N |
| 38. Students select one to two exploratories at least four days of the week. | | Y  N |
| 39. Students complete prescribed activities within the specified time periods. | | Y  N |

## TEACHER OBSERVATION FORM

This form is designed to be used in assessing the teacher's traveling and
instructing behaviors as he/she interacts with students. It is used in conjunction and alternately with the Student Observation Form.

When to                                    Time Required
Administer: During class time              to Administer: One hour for both observation forms

Directions: Observations of the teacher (using this form) are alternated with observations of the student
(using the Student Observation Form). There are six observation intervals (three on each form) and each
interval lasts five minutes. Record the start and stop time of each interval.

At the end of Interval 1, complete the response column for that interval on the Teacher Observation Form
by reading the descriptor and circling Y (Yes) if it occurred and N (No) if it did not occur. Repeat the procedure
for Interval 2 on the Student Observation Form. Continue to alternate between the two forms until six intervals
have been completed. Where appropriate, specific directions and/or instructions for scoring have been provided.

| Item Number        Item | Interval 1 | Interval 3 | Interval 5 | Response Y - Yes   N =No |
|---|---|---|---|---|
| Record the start and stop time of each interval. | ____to____ | ____to____ | ____ to____ | |

Special Instructions, Item 40: Tally each student contact in each observation interval. A student contact is
defined as any acknowledgment of an individual student. It is not restricted to verbal contact, and can include a nod
across the room or a hand on the shoulder. Enter the average of the three intervals in the response column.

| 40. Number of student contacts. | _____ | _____ | _____ | _____ |
|---|---|---|---|---|

Special Instructions, Items 41 - 56: At the end of each interval, read the descriptor and circle Y (Yes) if it
occurred and N (No) if it did not occur. Use the criterion of two out of three for the response column.

| | Interval 1 | Interval 3 | Interval 5 | Response |
|---|---|---|---|---|
| 41. The teacher spends short per-iods of time with each student. | Y    N | Y    N | Y    N | Y    N |
| 42. The teacher responds to those students who signal properly. | Y    N | Y    N | Y    N | Y    N |
| 43. The teacher shows person-al regard for each student. | Y    N | Y    N | Y    N | Y    N |
| 44. The teacher checks work in students' presence and interacts with students about the work. | Y    N | Y    N | Y    N | Y    N |
| 45. The teacher gives praise when appropriate. | Y    N | Y    N | Y    N | Y    N |
| 46. The teacher determines individual students' sources of difficulty in the completion of their tasks. | Y    N | Y    N | Y    N | Y    N |

| Item Number | Item | Interval 1 | Interval 3 | Interval 5 | Response Y = Yes N = No |
|---|---|---|---|---|---|
| 47. | The teacher encourages self-management. | Y  N | Y  N | Y  N | Y      N |
| 48. | The teacher helps students structure learning tasks and communicates the procedures required for performing the tasks. | Y  N | Y  N | Y  N | Y      N |
| 49. | The teacher communicates to students the criteria for successful performance. | Y  N | Y  N | Y  N | Y      N |
| 50. | The teacher helps students complete work on time. | Y  N | Y  N | Y  N | Y      N |
| 51. | The teacher discusses with students their work plans and/or their progress toward completion of their work. | Y  N | Y  N | Y  N | Y      N |
| 52. | The teacher uses questioning. | Y  N | Y  N | Y  N | Y      N |
| 53. | The teacher uses explaining. | Y  N | Y  N | Y  N | Y      N |
| 54. | The teacher uses cueing or prompting. | Y  N | Y  N | Y  N | Y      N |
| 55. | The teacher uses demonstrating and/or modeling. | Y  N | Y  N | Y  N | Y      N |

Special Instructions, Items 56 - 64: At the end of Interval 5, read the descriptor, enter Y (Yes) if it occurred and N (No) if it did not occur.

| Item | Response |
|---|---|
| 56. The teacher's traveling route, an established pattern, includes all areas in which students are working. | Y      N |
| 57. In contacts with students working on exploratory activities, the teacher shows an interest in student work. | Y      N |
| 58. When appropriate, the teacher restructures specific learning tasks for students. | Y      N |
| 59. The teacher looks around the room (scans) after each student contact. | Y      N |
| 60. The teacher notices and acknowledges each student who requests/needs help. | Y      N |
| 61. The teacher encourages students to help each other with their work (peer tutoring). | Y      N |
| 62. The teacher interacts with students concerning the content of specific tasks/ assignments. | Y      N |

Teacher Observation Form, continued

| Item Number    Item | Response Y = Yes  N = No |
|---|---|
| 63. The teacher's questioning techniques encourage extended student responses. | Y        N |
| 64. The teacher's words and behavior communicate that students are expected to succeed. | Y        N |

Please provide the data below by filling in the blank or circling the appropriate number(s) in the response column.

A.  Number of other adults in the classroom.                                    _____

B.  Titles of other adults in the classroom.

   (1)  Aide                                                                1
   (2)  Paraprofessional                                                    2
   (3)  Student teacher                                                     3
   (4)  Chapter 1 teacher                                                   4
   (5)  Parent volunteer                                                    5
   (6)  Other (specify) _____                                     6

C.  Activities of other adults.

   (1)  Traveling                                                           1
   (2)  Testing                                                             2
   (3)  Tutoring                                                            3
   (4)  Clerical work                                                       4
   (5)  Small-group instruction                                             5
   (6)  Materials construction                                              6
   (7)  Other (specify) _____                                     7

D.  These observation intervals were conducted:

   (1)  Beginning of the school day                                         1
   (2)  Middle of the school day                                            2
   (3)  End of the school day                                               3

E.  The person(s) who regularly engages in traveling and interactive teaching is (are):

   (1)  Teacher                                                             1
   (2)  Aide                                                                2
   (3)  Both                                                                3
   (4)  Other (specify) _____                                     4

F.  During the observation the teacher was primarily involved in:

   (1)  Interactive teaching                                                1
   (2)  Small group instruction                                             2
   (3)  Testing                                                             3
   (4)  Tutoring                                                            4
   (5)  Other (specify) _____                                     5

## STUDENT OBSERVATION FORM

This form is designed to be used in assessing students' behaviors while working within an adaptive learning environment. It is used in conjunction and alternately with the Teacher Observation Form.

When to
Administer: During class time

Time Required
to Administer: One hour for both observation forms

Directions: Observations of the students (using this form) are alternated with observations of the teacher (using the Teacher Observation Form). The first observation interval is of the teacher. Please see the Teacher Observation Form for directions on how to proceed.

Remember, you are observing the total group of students, not a few individuals.

| Item Number    Item | Interval 2 | Interval 4 | Interval 6 | Response Y = Yes    N = No |
|---|---|---|---|---|
| Record the start and stop time of each interval. | ___ to___ | ___ to___ | ___ to___ | |

Special Instructions, Item 65: At the conclusion of each observation interval, count the numbers of students waiting, on-task, and off-task. Record the numbers in the designated spaces under the appropriate interval. At the conclusion of Interval 6, enter the average of the three intervals in the Response column.

| 65. Number of students waiting (W), on-task (T), and off-task (O). | W ____ T ____ O ____ | W ____ T ____ O ____ | W____ T____ O____ | W ____ T ____ O ____ |
|---|---|---|---|---|

Special Instructions, Items 66 - 76: At the end of each interval, read the descriptor and circle Y (Yes) if it occurred and N (No) if it did not occur. Use the criterion of two out of three for the response column.

| | Interval 2 | Interval 4 | Interval 6 | Response |
|---|---|---|---|---|
| 66. At any given time, the number of students working in each activity area does not exceed the specified limit. (Refer to the self-scheduling system.) | Y    N | Y    N | Y    N | Y    N |
| 67. Students readily locate prescriptions. | Y    N | Y    N | Y    N | Y    N |
| 68. Students obtain adult help by using designated call signals rather than by raising their hands. | Y    N | Y    N | Y    N | Y    N |
| 69. Students finish one task and ask the teacher to check work before starting another, except when waiting for teacher assistance. | Y    N | Y    N | Y    N | Y    N |
| 70. When waiting for teacher assistance, students are occupied with other curricula-related tasks or constructive interactions with other students. | Y    N | Y    N | Y    N | Y    N |

Student Observation Form, continued

| Item Number    Item | Interval 2 | Interval 4 | Interval 6 | Response Y = Yes  N = No |
|---|---|---|---|---|
| 71. Students readily locate materials and equipment for all tasks. | Y    N | Y    N | Y    N | Y    N |
| 72. Students use learning materials and equipment appropriately. | Y    N | Y    N | Y    N | Y    N |
| 73. Students return materials and equipment to the correct places and clean up their work places when tasks are completed. | Y    N | Y    N | Y    N | Y    N |
| 74. After their completed work is checked, students put it in a designated place. | Y    N | Y    N | Y    N | Y    N |
| 75. Each student knows how to use his or her prescription. | Y    N | Y    N | Y    N | Y    N |
| 76. Each student knows how to use his or her self-schedule form. | Y    N | Y    N | Y    N | Y    N |

STUDENT INTERVIEW FORM

These questions are designed to probe students' understanding and knowledge of work requirements, classroom procedures, and rules for scheduling activities.

When to
Administer:  Check with classroom teacher

Time Required
to Administer:  Ten minutes
per Interview
(30 minutes)

Directions: Randomly select three students to interview from the class roster or the student progress charts. Enter each student's name in the appropriate place on the form. Find a quiet place to conduct the individual interviews.

Read the introductory statement and begin asking the questions. Allow approximately 10 seconds of wait time. If the student does not respond or the response indicates that the student has not understood the question, the question may be repeated or the prompt may be used. Repetitions and prompts should be used only when the student does not understand a question. They should never be used for encouraging the student to guess.

There are no right or wrong answers. For each question, circle Y (Yes) in the appropriate interview column if the student answers with sound knowledge of how to function in the classroom; circle N (No) if the student indicates he/she does not know the answer or gives an inappropriate response. Use the criterion of two out of three for the response column.

| Item Number          Item | Interview 1 | Interview 2 | Interview 3 | Response Y = Yes  N = No |
|---|---|---|---|---|
| Enter the student's name | _____ | _____ | _____ | |

Read the following statement: What I'm going to do, (student's name), is ask you some questions about your classroom. I'm going to ask you about how things are organized, what the rules are, and how you do your work. These questions are a little different from your math questions because there are no right or wrong answers. I just want you to tell me what you know about the classroom. O.K., (student's name), the first question is . . .

| | Interview 1 | Interview 2 | Interview 3 | Response |
|---|---|---|---|---|
| 77. How many assignments do you have to finish today? (Prompt: Name the things you have to do today.) | Y     N | Y     N | Y     N | Y     N |
| 78. How many assignments do you have left to do today? (Prompt: Name the things you still have to do today. ) | Y     N | Y     N | Y     N | Y     N |
| 79. When must they be completed? (Prompt: By what time do you have to have all the work you just named completed?) | Y     N | Y     N | Y     N | Y     N |
| 80. When are you allowed to do the work on your prescription sheets? (Prompt: Is there a particular time of day that you must do your reading prescription and your math prescription?) | Y     N | Y     N | Y     N | Y     N |

Student Interview Form, continued

| Item Number　Item | Interview 1 | Interview 2 | Interview 3 | Response Y = Yes　N = No |
|---|---|---|---|---|
| 81. When are you allowed to do your exploratory work? | Y　　N | Y　　N | Y　　N | Y　　N |
| 82. What do you do when you need help with your work? (Prompt: How do you get help in class when you need it?) | Y　　N | Y　　N | Y　　N | Y　　N |
| 83. Is there any time during the day that you are not allowed to use the exploratory areas? (Prompt: Can you use construction or make-believe any time you want?) | Y　　N | Y　　N | Y　　N | Y　　N |
| 84. Are there things in the exploratory areas that you are not allowed to use without your teacher's help? (Prompt: Can you use anything you want in the exploratory areas if your teacher isn't there?) | Y　　N | Y　　N | Y　　N | Y　　N |
| 85. What would happen if you did not finish your work? (Prompt: What happens when you don't finish all the things on your prescription sheets?) | Y　　N | Y　　N | Y　　N | Y　　N |
| 86. What would happen if you finished your work ahead of schedule? (Prompt: What happens when you get all the work on your prescription sheets done early?) | Y　　N | Y　　N | Y　　N | Y　　N |
| 87. Do you ever help out by doing jobs like erasing the blackboard and putting back the chairs? (Prompt: Do you ever clean the paintbrushes or water the plants?) | Y　　N | Y　　N | Y　　N | Y　　N |
| 88. Do other kids help with these jobs? | Y　　N | Y　　N | Y　　N | Y　　N |

## TEACHER INTERVIEW FORM

These questions are designed to probe the teacher's knowledge of individual students' placement within the curricula and to discover the procedures the teacher uses with instructional groups, diagnosis and placement of students, and planning.

**When to Administer:** At the teacher's convenience

**Time Required to Administer:** Ten minutes

**Directions:** Randomly select three students from the student progress charts and enter their names and math and reading curricular levels in the spaces provided under Items 89 and 90.

Read the introductory statement and ask the questions. Do not deviate from or rephrase the questions.

| Item Number          Item | Response Y = Yes   N = No |
| --- | --- |

Read the following statement: I am going to ask you some questions about specific students and about the procedures you use in the classroom. This interview is one of six instruments used to gather information on the degree of program implementation

Special Instructions, Item 89: Compare the teacher's response to the information from classroom records. Circle Y (Yes) if the response agrees with the records two out of three times.

89. Tell me about (student's name). At what level is he/she working?          Y          N

| Student | Information from Classroom Records Reading     Math | Teacher's Response Reading     Math |
| --- | --- | --- |
| _____ | ____ ____ | ____ ____ |
| _____ | ____ ____ | ____ ____ |
| _____ | ____ ____ | ____ ____ |

Special Instructions, Item 90: Use the students that were used for Item 89. Circle Y (Yes) next to the student's name if the teacher indicates that the student has a preference. This information does not need to be verified. Circle Y (Yes) in the response column if the teacher names a preference for two out of three students.

90. Is there a specific curriculum that (student's name) prefers?          Y          N

Student
_____          Y          N
_____          Y          N
_____          Y          N

Special Instructions, Item 91 -107: Read each question and circle Y (Yes) or N (No) as the teacher responds. Where appropriate, specific directions or criteria have been provided. When an extended response is given, please summarize.

91. Do you use small groups as part of prescribed activities?          Y          N

92. On what basis do you form small groups of students for group work? _____
_____ (Circle Y [Yes] if the teacher indicates grouping is based on diagnosed need. Circle N [No] if the teacher indicates grouping is based on age or general ability level.)          Y          N

Teacher Interview Form, continued

| Item Number | Item | Response Y = Yes N = No | |
|---|---|---|---|
| 93. | How often do you conduct math maintenance drills? _____<br>(Circle Y [Yes ] if drills are conducted at least twice a week.) | Y | N |
| 94. | Do you group students for supplementary instruction? | Y | N |
| 95. | Do you give placement tests? When? _____<br>(Circle Y [Yes] if the teacher responds that placement tests are given when students enter a new curricular area or when the teacher feels a reevaluation is necessary. Circle N [No] if the teacher indicates that placement tests are only given at the beginning of the year.) | Y | N |
| 96. | Do you give pretests at the beginning of each unit of instruction? | Y | N |
| 97. | Do you give posttests at the end of each unit of instruction? | Y | N |
| 98 | When determining instructional levels for transfer students, do you give placement tests? | Y | N |
| 99. | Do you ever change (or write new) prescriptions as you travel and check students' work? | Y | N |
| 100. | How often and on what basis do you change exploratory materials? _____<br><br>_____<br>(Circle Y [Yes] if the response includes at least once a month, when a new unit of instruction is introduced, or when students no longer need or use materials.) | Y | N |
| 101. | At what self-scheduling objective* are 50% or more of your students functioning? (Read definitions of self-scheduling objectives if necessary.)<br><br>(a) Objective A<br>(b) Objective B<br>(c) Objective C<br>(d) Objective D<br>(e) Objective E<br>(f) Objective F<br>(g) They are not self-scheduling | Y<br><br><br>a<br>b<br>c<br>d<br>e<br>f<br>g | N |
| 102. | What is the percentage of students in your class who can consistently manage self-scheduling at Objective D or E? (Circle Y [Yes] if answer is 80% or more.) | Y | N |

### *DEFINITIONS OF SELF-SCHEDULING OBJECTIVES

Objective A   Given two (or more) prescriptive tasks within one subject area, the students choose which take to complete first.

Objective B   Given two (or more) exploratory activities, the students choose which activity to complete first.

Objective C   Given two (or more) exploratory and prescriptive activities within one subject area, the students choose which activity to complete first.

Objective D   Given the exploratory and prescriptive activities for all subjects included in the program and one-half of the school day, students choose the order in which to complete all tasks.

Objective E   Given the range of exploratory and prescriptive activities in the program and one school day, students choose the order in which to complete all tasks.

Objective F   Given the range of exploratory and prescriptive activities in the program and five school days, students choose the order in which to complete all tasks.

Special Instructions, Items 103 -105: Aide includes any paid or volunteer adult in the classroom

| | | | |
|---|---|---|---|
| 103. | Is there an established time each day when you and your aide(s) exchange information? | Y | N |
| 104. | Do you assign duties for the aide(s) during this time? | Y | N |
| 105. | Do you and your aide(s) discuss the performance of individual students during this time? | Y | N |
| 106. | Do you discuss the performance of students with their parents? | Y | N |
| 107. | Do you discuss the performance of students with other relevant instructional staff? | Y | N |

## Chapter 8

# Evaluation of Program Effects

Schools and districts adopt innovative educational programs with the expectation that such programs will facilitate attainment of important educational goals, such as student achievement of basic skills, development of achievement motivation, self-responsibility, and higher order problem-solving skills; improved teaching and management practices; and teacher and parent satisfaction. It is vital to determine if and to what extent the goals of a new program are achieved. For this evaluation, data are collected to determine if the program is producing the desired effects, to what degree is each expected outcome occurring, to what degree are important program features implemented, what aspects of the program are working well, and which need to be strengthened. The answers to questions such as these provide school and program officials with information to make decisions about improving program delivery and provide policymakers with information to make decisions about program continuation.

The evaluation process of a comprehensive education program such as the adaptive education approach is necessarily complex. Evaluation involves activities that begin well before classroom implementation and continue throughout the program. It is essential that these activities be guided by a systematic evaluation plan that specifies:

1. Program design and implementation requirements
2. Expected program outcomes to be assessed
3. Measurement procedures to be used and means for obtaining and constructing them
4. Schedules and data collection procedures
5. Procedures for coding, scoring, and analyzing the data

Data are collected and analyzed throughout the year according to the plan, and the results are disseminated. School and district administrators and policymakers use these reports to decide about program continuation, extension, and improvement.

This chapter is designed to provide school administrators and others with guidelines for managing and coordinating all activities of documenting and evaluating school implementation of adaptive education programs, including evaluation planning, data collection and analysis, and use of the results. First, a conceptual model for evaluation of adaptive education programs is presented.

Second, the evaluation planning process is discussed. The final section provides a brief discussion of procedures for data collection, analysis, interpretation, and reports of evaluation findings. This discussion is intended to provide a general guideline to enable program planners and decision makers to develop their site-specific evaluation plan.

## A CONCEPTUAL MODEL OF SCHOOL LEARNING

Figure 8.1. provides a schematic representation of a conceptual model of school learning that has been identified as a useful framework for guiding documentation and evaluation of adaptive education programs (Wang & Walberg, 1983). The theoretical research base of the model and its application for program evaluation are briefly discussed in this section.

Research has identified a large number of variables related to school learning (cf. Pollack & Bempechat, 1991; Wang, Haertel, & Walberg, 1990). There is a substantial research base on what makes learning productive. Educational researchers, policymakers, and practitioners interested in improving teaching and learning in schools have been perplexed about the relative importance of distinct and interactive influences on student learning. A pressing concern is the delineation of variables most likely to maximize school learning.

Several notable theoretical developments have attempted to synthesize and explicate the interactive effects of variables related to learning. The 1960s and 1970s were marked by the introduction of several important models of learning, including those of Bennett (1978), Bloom (1966), Bruner (1966), Carroll (1963), Glaser (1976), and Harnischfeger and Wiley (1976). All of these models recognized the primary importance of the learning characteristics of the individual student, including constructs such as aptitude, prior knowledge, and other learning and personal characteristics. Most models also addressed the importance of motivation with such constructs as perseverance, self-concept of the learner, and attitude toward school subject matter. This acknowledgment of individual variables among learners stood in contrast to more narrow psychological studies of influences on learning, which generally treated individual differences as a source of error and focused on instructional treatment variables (Hilgard, 1964).

Although these models brought some refinement to definitions of individual and instructional variables and the ways in which they were related, more recent models have extended the range of variables. Findings from a study by Haertel, Walberg, and Weinstein (1983), for example, showed that previous models of school learning neglected extramural and social–psychological influences. Models of school learning were further advanced with the introduction of models of adaptive instruction (Wang, 1989; Wang & Lindvall, 1984; Wang & Walberg, 1985). These models pay particular attention to new variables associated with instructional delivery systems, program design, and implementation.

Another contribution to models of school learning came from sociologists concerned with the identification of effective schools. R. Edmonds (1979) is most strongly associated with identification of variables associated with exceptionally effective schools, especially for the urban poor. Significant contributions to effective schools models were also made by Brookover (1979), Brookover and Lezotte (1977), and Rutter, Maughan, Mortimore, and Ouston (1979). The vari-

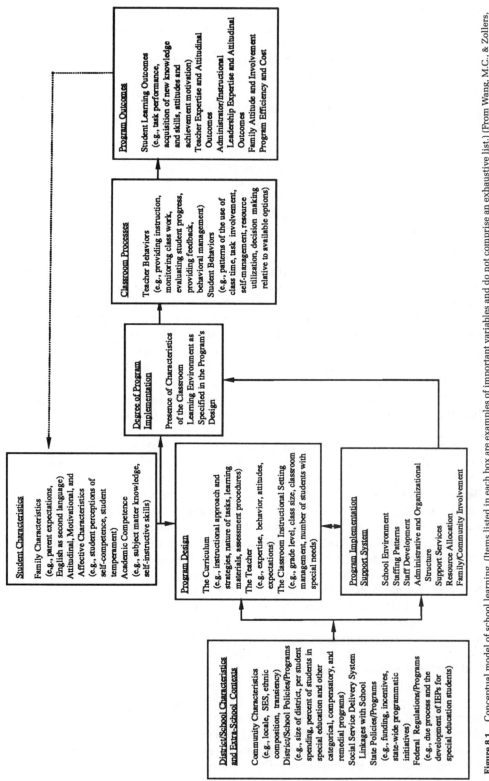

**Figure 8.1.** Conceptual model of school learning. (Items listed in each box are examples of important variables and do not comprise an exhaustive list.) (From Wang, M.C., & Zollers, N.J. [1990]. An alternative service delivery approach. *Remedial and Special Education, 11*[1], 7–21. Copyright 1990 by PRO-ED, Inc.; reprinted by permission.)

ables that characterize effective schools include degree of curriculum articula-
tion and organization, school-wide staff development, parental involvement and
support, school-wide recognition of academic success, maximized learning
time, district support, clear goals and high expectations, orderly and disciplined
school environment, and leadership of the principal characterized by attention
to quality of instruction (Purkey & Smith, 1983). These models of school learning
played an important role in the development of the conceptual model of school
learning shown in Figure 8.1. Seven categories of variables provide the framework:

> Student characteristics
> District and school characteristics and extra-school contexts
> Program design
> Program implementation support system
> Degree of program implementation
> Classroom processes
> Program outcomes

The rationale for including a multiplicity of factors in the model of school learning is well-documented in the research literature on learning and instruction (cf.
Glaser & Takanishi, 1986; Resnick, 1987; Wang & Lindvall, 1984) and is supported by findings in literature on social–cognitive psychological research and
on effective teaching research. In their explication of essential elements in the
acquisition of information and in the process of accessing and using knowledge, Brown and her associates (Brown, Bransford, Ferrara, & Campione, 1983)
pointed to the "readiness" of the field for moving from learning models that address learner knowledge, the learning process, and learning tasks in isolation toward a model that addresses the more complex, interactive processes of
learning.

Similarly, distinct patterns of interaction among elements of program design
features, student and teacher behaviors, and student outcomes have been noted
in studies of the differential effects among instructional approaches (e.g.,
Berliner, 1983; Hedges, Giaconia, & Gage, 1981; Walberg & Wang, 1987; Webb,
1982). Findings from a study of program implementation and effects by Wang
and Walberg (1986) suggest, for example, that programs that feature student
choice, task flexibility, teacher monitoring, peer tutoring, student-initiated requests for teacher help, a variety of curriculum materials, and task-specific instructions are associated with student self-management, personal interactions
between students and teachers, student work in small groups, and substantive
interactions between teachers and students. Furthermore, these patterns of
classroom processes were found to be positively associated with instructional
approaches that recognize an active role for students in mediating their own
learning and negatively associated with program features such as whole-class
and teacher-directed instruction.

The validity of using the person–environment–process–product paradigm
is further supported by developments in research concerned with social–
psychological processes and attitudes (Bossert, 1979; Gordon, 1983; Marshall &
Weinstein, 1984; McCombs, 1991; Wang & Peverly, 1986). Classroom events
(teacher behaviors, peer interactions) tend to have different meanings for different students, and these meanings influence student behavior and learning outcomes. Social comparison information, for example, can be either detrimental or

positive. In his review of research in this area, Levine (1983) notes that social comparison is likely to produce feelings of inferiority, low aspirations, a lack of motivation, and interpersonal hostility and competitiveness in low achievers. Under other circumstances, however, comparisons with classmates have not been found to have negative effects. Information about one's own performance in relation to that of one's peers may provide a clue as to student competence. Rather than being the cause of social comparison, this information could be construed as a "resource" (Marshall, Weinstein, Sharp, & Brattesani, 1982; Thurston & Lotto, 1990).

Research also suggests that students' perceptions and interpretations of particular aspects of the classroom affect their learning processes and outcomes. For example, student perceptions of classroom environments consistently have been found to account for variation in learning outcomes beyond the variation that can be attributed to ability (Haertel, Walberg, & Haertel, 1979; Wang, Reynolds, & Schwartz, 1988; Zimmerman, 1986). Classroom characteristics also affect student behavior. Weinstein (1983) found that the evaluative cues used by students vary as a function of the structure and climate of the classroom. Similarly, in a study designed to investigate differences in the learning processes of high- and low-achieving students, DeStefano, Wang, and Gordon (1984) found that students' personal characteristics, such as temperament, knowledge, and motivation, interacted with learning conditions, such as the physical and organizational structure of the classroom, to elicit certain learning behaviors, such as time on task, energy deployment, task involvement, autonomy, decision making, and resource utilization.

Thus, the need to examine the interactions among individual characteristics of students, the school learning environment, the classroom instructional and learning processes, and learning outcomes is underscored by findings from psychological and educational research. A major assumption underlying the conceptual framework shown in Figure 8.1. is that failure to recognize the relevance of certain extra-school and classroom factors can hamper both research and innovative program efforts to improve school success of individual students. Both quantitative and qualitative methodologies are required to collect information on the categories included in the model. Table 8.1. provides a sample list of variables with candidate measures and data sources. A first planning activity for program evaluation is to define the specific set of data to be collected to determine if the adaptive education program is achieving the specific improvement goals of the school.

## PLANNING THE EVALUATION OF PROGRAM OUTCOMES

Steps in evaluation planning include:

1. Identifying the evaluation questions to be addressed
2. Identifying expected program outcomes
3. Selecting and constructing suitable measurement instruments
4. Planning data collection

### Evaluation Questions

The following are sample questions to be addressed from the data to be generated based on the conceptual model of school learning.

**Table 8.1.** A sample list of variables and candidate measures and data sources

| Variables | Candidate measures and data sources |
| --- | --- |
| 1. Student Characteristics | |
| Demographic and family characteristics | School record |
| Motivation and attitudinal characteristics | My Class Inventory (Fraser, Anderson, & Walberg, 1982) |
| Subject matter knowledge | Curriculum-based assessment |
| History of educational placements | School records |
| Social and behavioral | Walker-McConnell Scale of Social Competence & |
| Cognitive and meta-cognitive process | School Adjustment (Walker & McConnell, 1987) |
| Relationship with peers | Interviews and sociometric measures |
| Perceptions of self-competence | Perceived Competence Scale (Harter, 1982) |
| 2. Program Design | |
| Curriculum (instructional approach and strategies, nature of tasks, learning materials, testing program) | Curriculum guides and classroom material<br>Teacher Roles Observation Schedule (Waxman, Wang, Lindvall, & Anderson, 1983d) |
| Teacher (expertise, subject matter knowledge, instructional strategies, behavior, attitudes, expectations) | Teacher Attitudes and Assessment Survey (Waxman, Wang, Lindvall, & Anderson, 1983c) |
| Classroom environment (class size, classroom management system, number of students with special needs, number of adults) | The Teachable Pupil Survey (Keogh, Pullis, & Cadwell, 1982)<br>School records |
| 3. Program Implementation Support System | |
| School environment (e.g., academic and social characteristics: stability of test scores, disciplinary referrals, attendance, extracurricular participation, drop-out rates, student attitude) | School records and interviews with school personnel |
| Staffing patterns (e.g., demographics, attendance, turnover rate) | School records and interviews with school personnel |
| Staff development | School records and interviews with school personnel |
| Organizational structure | School records and interviews with school personnel |
| Resource allocation | School records and interviews with school personnel |
| Family involvement | School records and interviews with school personnel |
| Community involvement | School records and interviews with school personnel |
| District-level support | School records and interviews with school personnel |
| 4. Degree of Program Implementation | |
| Classroom implementation support | Observation and interviews with school personnel |
| Implementation of program features | Observation Rating Scale for Features of Adaptive Instruction (Waxman, Wang, Lindvall, & Anderson, 1983b) |
| 5. Classroom Processes | |
| Teacher behaviors | Teacher Roles Observation Schedule (Waxman, Wang, Lindvall, & Anderson, 1983d) |
| Student behaviors | Student Behavior Observation Schedule (Wang, 1976) |
| Instructional grouping patterns, feedback mechanisms | Classroom Observation Scale (Waxman, Wang, Lindvall, & Anderson, 1983a) |
| Teacher–student interactions | Classroom Observation Scale (Waxman, Wang, Lindvall, & Anderson, 1983a) |
| 6. District/School Characteristics and Extra-School Contexts | |
| Community characteristics | School documents and interviews with school staff |
| Demographic characteristics: district/school | School records |
| Per pupil expenditure for all students/students in at-risk circumstances | School records |

*(continued)*

**Table 8.1.** *(continued)*

| Variables | Candidate measures and data sources |
| --- | --- |
| Size of district/school | School records |
| Teacher/pupil ratio across districts and within the school | School records |
| District-wide organizational and resource support structure | School records |
| Percent of students in special education programs across district and within the school (those served in self-contained special education vs. those in main-streamed settings) | School records |
| Percent of students served in Chapter 1, bilingual, and other categorical compensatory and remedial programs (across district/school, those served in self-contained special education vs. those in mainstreamed settings) | School records |
| Characteristics of students in top 20% vs. bottom 20% of the achievement distribution across district/school | School records |
| Peer group characteristics | School records |
| Social service delivery system linkages with school | School records and interviews with school and social service delivery staff |
| Student use of out-of-school time | Interviews |
| 7. Program Outcomes | |
| Student learning | School records, classroom observations |
| Teacher expertise and attitude toward students/program, collegial collaboration | Teacher Self-Assessment Interview (Freilino, 1984) |
| Administrator/instructional leader expertise and attitude toward students/program | Interviews |
| Family attitudes toward students/program | Parent Survey (Wang, 1982) |
| Program cost | School records and interviews with the principal and district staff |
| Classroom climate | The Instructional Environment Scale (Ysseldyke & Christenson, 1987)<br>Comprehensive Assessment of School Environment (NASSP, 1987)<br>Scales for the Assessment of the Accommodation of Differences among Pupils by Teachers (Reynolds, 1989) |

What are the unique demographic characteristics, relevant resources, and organizational and operating policies of the schools and school districts implementing the program? What is the nature and extent of family and community involvement? Are there external factors operating in the community and school that are facilitative or disruptive to program implementation? Are there school climate characteristics (i.e., school environment or the culture of the school) that differentiate the program school from other schools in the district?

Are there specific district, state, and federal policies that support (or interfere with) implementation of the adaptive education program? How do they affect implementation? What are the strategies schools use to offset the external influences that may negatively affect implementation and the teaching and learning process?

Who are the students attending the program school? Who are the students ranked at the top and bottom 20% in academic achievement in the school and class (scores from standardized district-or state-wide achievement tests) and how do they compare to the district, state, and national norms? Are there characteristics unique to the sample schools/classes/group of students (attitudes about schooling and academic achievement; attitudes toward the school, teachers, classmates, school subjects; perception of self-competence and how they are viewed by teachers and peers; expectations from families about schooling success and other student variables)?

Who are the teachers in the program schools? Are there differences between the program school and other schools in the district? Are there teacher differences among program schools in attitudes and expectations about the students, program, or collaboration with colleagues compared with nonprogram schools? Do teachers in the program schools differ from teachers in nonprogram schools in their training or other characteristics such as sex, age, or number of years spent teaching in the particular school?

What are specific features of the program being implemented? What are the implementation requirements? What are the cost requirements for implementing the program? Is there a high degree of program implementation? What is the principal's role in program implementation? What are the roles of the classroom teacher, support personnel, and parents? Do schools in the study sample differ in these variables?

What is the nature of the school day for students in the program? Are there differences in the curriculum, instructors, or how students spend their school time between those in the bottom and those in the top 20% of the class and school? Are there major differences in these variables across the program schools included in the study?

How is student progress monitored? What evaluation data on student progress are being collected by the school? How are these data being used by the school staff? What student learning outcome data are being collected by the school, district, and state? Do achievement scores differ across classes within the program school, between sample schools and other schools in the district, and across the study sample?

What is the pattern of progress in academic achievement of students in the program school during the past 3 years? How does this compare to the progress made prior to program implementation and to other schools in the district?

What are some of the consistent patterns of relationship between program outcomes and the categories of variables that have been hypothesized to be important to achieving program outcomes?

## Identification of Expected Outcomes

A vital step in planning program evaluation is defining the effects that the program is expected to produce. This step is necessary in order to avoid two pitfalls of poorly conducted evaluations. The first pitfall is overlooking one or more important outcomes. For example, studies comparing innovative with traditional programs often utilize standardized achievement tests as the sole criterion of program effectiveness, despite the fact that innovative programs almost always include additional important goals. For example, one such goal is student ability to think creatively, interpret information, and apply this in problem solving. This and other similar outcomes are referred to as "authentic academic achievement" (Newmann, 1991). The second pitfall is measuring outcomes that are unrelated or only tangentially related to program goals. Not only does this place an unwarranted strain on school resources, but important outcomes may be overlooked in a profusion of unnecessary data.

Since specific educational goals vary among programs and from one setting to another, it is not possible to provide a list of all the important outcomes of adaptive instruction. Nevertheless, it is possible to list a set of categories and subcategories, or a taxonomy into which most outcomes are likely to fall. Table 8.2. provides a taxonomy of expected program outcomes that were derived from a survey study (Wang, Haertel, & Walberg, 1990; Wang, Reynolds, Walberg, & Rosenfield, 1990).

As the table shows, program outcomes may be divided into process outcomes and product outcomes. Process outcomes refer to teacher and student behaviors and interactions and their use of time and other resources in the classroom. Product outcomes refer to changes in the abilities, dispositions, and attitudes of students, teachers, and others, which presumably result from the processes of program operation. Although product outcomes are what most people mean when they refer to program effects, process outcomes are also important, both as mediators of product outcomes and as desirable outcomes in their own right.

Process and product outcomes can be divided into two or more subcategories, as shown in Table 8.2. Two useful subcategories of process outcomes are those that refer to teacher behaviors and instructional processes and those that refer to student behaviors and interactions. Product outcomes can be distinguished by population and by domain—cognitive, social, or affective. Outcomes in the cognitive domain are related to achievement and learning. Social outcomes include social interactions and friendship and social acceptance patterns. Affective outcomes refer to dispositions and attitudes of program participants (e.g., self-perceptions, attitudes toward school). Because cognitive, social, and affective outcomes are often expected in students, all three are listed as subcategories under "Expected effects on students." Expected effects on other program participants most often occur in the affective domain.

**Table 8.2.** A taxonomy of expected outcomes

---

 I. Process Outcomes
    A. Expected effects on teacher behaviors and instructional processes
    B. Expected effects on student behaviors and interactions
 II. Product Outcomes
    A. Expected effects on students
        1. Cognitive (learning)
        2. Social
        3. Affective (emotional, attitudinal)
    B. Expected effects on teachers
    C. Expected effects on parents and/or the community
    D. Expected effects on other defined groups

---

The taxonomy of program outcomes presented here may be used by program planners to ask what process outcomes they expect from teacher behaviors and instructional processes and from student behaviors and interactions. Then program planners can identify expected product outcomes. A sample outline of outcomes for adaptive education programs is provided in Table 8.3.

The taxonomy presented in Table 8.2. does not include level of program implementation as a program effect. In the model of adaptive instruction presented in Chapter 1, program implementation is seen as the means to bring about desired process and product outcomes. Nevertheless, in an important sense, a high degree of program implementation is itself a valued program outcome because it indicates that the program can work in the setting. Furthermore, since process and product outcomes are assumed to result from the program design features, assessing the relationship between the degree to which design features have been implemented and the process and product outcomes attained is a major aspect of program evaluation. Therefore, periodic assessment of the level of program implementation is essential to comprehensive program evaluation.

## Procedures for Measuring Outcomes

Before beginning this section, a brief note on the use of the word "test" is in order. Some writers prefer to restrict the term to instruments that assess achievement, proficiency, or aptitude. This usage excludes many psychoeducational instruments, such as those that measure attitudes, preferences, behavioral interactions, and dispositions. The term test, however, has come to refer to a much broader range of instruments. Therefore, this chapter generally uses test in its broader sense to refer to any psychoeducational measurement technique, including assessment procedures such as authentic assessment (Wiggins, 1989) and curriculum-based assessment (Cohen & Spruill, 1990; Deno, 1985).

*Measuring Process Outcomes*    Process outcomes refer to teacher and student behaviors and interactions and to their use of instructional time and resources during instruction and learning. Therefore, process outcomes are most accurately assessed through direct observation of the processes as they occur. In a typical classroom observation session, one or more trained observers record events as they occur that are relevant to specific behavior categories that are selected on the basis of their relation to expected process outcomes. Observations may be focused on the whole class or on individual students and teachers. Videotaping or other recording techniques are sometimes used, but typically the observers enter results of observations on a standard printed form.

The sample may be determined by observation of a specified number of individuals and events or by a time period. When data collection has been completed in all classrooms, results are summarized and analyzed to yield information about the frequency or level of process outcomes in each classroom.

*Measuring Cognitive Outcomes*    The most common method for measuring attainment of cognitive outcomes is the basic achievement or proficiency test, although performance tests are useful for certain outcomes (e.g., ability to use a microscope). Schools typically employ a variety of tests, including standardized achievement tests, tests embedded within the school curricula, and tests constructed by teachers. Student work samples may also provide useful information about student learning.

**Table 8.3.** A list of expected outcomes of adaptive education programs

I. Process Outcomes
   A. Expected effects on teacher behaviors and instructional processes
      1. More teacher–student interactions for instructional purposes
      2. Fewer teacher–student interactions for management purposes
      3. Increased interactions between classroom teachers and specialized professionals for planning and instructional purposes
   B. Expected effects on student behaviors and interactions
      1. More time on task
      2. Less distracted behavior
      3. Decreased time spent waiting for teacher assistance
      4. Fewer disruptive behaviors
      5. More constructive interactions among students
II. Product Outcomes
   A. Expected effects on students
      1. Cognitive
         a. Achievement in basic skills (as assessed by standardized achievement tests)
         b. Mastery of curriculum objectives
         c. High rate of task completion
      2. Social
         a. Evidence of friendship/acceptance between regular students and students with special needs
      3. Affective
         a. Positive perceptions of academic and social competence and general self-esteem
         b. Perceptions of personal control over learning outcomes
         c. Positive perceptions of the classroom climate
   B. Expected effects on teachers
      1. Satisfaction with teaching in the program
      2. Perceptions of program efficacy in promoting student competence in academic learning and in social and self-management skills
      3. Perceptions of program efficacy in integrating special services into regular classrooms
   C. Expected effects on parents
      1. Satisfaction with student learning and progress
      2. Satisfaction with school goals, policies, and practices
      3. Expressed desire to have their children continue in the adaptive instruction program
   D. Expected effects on support staff and administrators
      1. Perceptions of program efficacy in meeting school and district goals
      2. Willingness to support program continuation and extension

Many school districts routinely administer standardized achievement tests every year as measures of student learning. These tests are generally the result of systematic test development procedures and are of high quality. Standardized test scores are particularly useful for evaluating student, school, and program performance because they enable comparison of student and class performance with nationwide norm groups. Gains from one year to the next can be assessed if the same test is administered every year. Standardized tests have certain limitations, because they are based on common instructional objectives nationwide so that their match with local curriculum objectives is often short of perfect. They tend to tap a limited range of learning outcomes that do not reflect outcomes recently advanced in cognitive psychology and research in effective instruction and learning. Moreover, standardized tests rarely provide the detailed information about student mastery of specific objectives that is needed for instructional planning.

More useful for instructional purposes are criterion-referenced tests, authentic assessment or curriculum-based assessments such as unit pre- and post-tests, other tests embedded in school curricula, and teacher-constructed tests.

Such tests are particularly important in adaptive instruction programs. Performance on curriculum-based tests that focus on authentic academic achievement yields information directly tied to instructing and improving student outcomes.

Some cognitive outcomes are best measured by student work samples, not tests. For example, if completion of tasks is an expected program outcome, both quantitative and qualitative assessments of student performance are appropriate measures of these outcomes. The combination of several cognitive outcome measures—performance on standardized and other tests, number of objectives mastered, and task completion—yields more comprehensive information about the attainment of cognitive outcomes than any single measure.

*Measuring Social Outcomes*   Various social outcomes have been cited as goals by designers of adaptive instruction programs. For example, the integration of regular and special education services in regular classrooms may be expected to result in positive interactions between students with special needs and other students, increased social acceptance of the students with special needs by their peers, and changes in friendship patterns between and in the two groups.

Certain types of social outcomes, in particular social behaviors and interactions in the classroom, are best measured by direct observation. However, peer acceptance and friendship patterns are more usually assessed by means of peer nominating or sociographic techniques (Moreno, 1960). These techniques have each student in the class name (nominate) one or more preferred partners for work assignments or other joint enterprises (e.g., "Name three students you would like to work with on a class project."). Analysis of student response reveals the students most frequently selected by their peers for each activity, which members of the class tend to select one another, and the extent that selection occurs between members of existing subgroups. The results may be displayed as diagrams called sociograms. If the activities for which students are asked to nominate peers are matched to expected outcomes, nominating techniques can yield valuable information about outcomes related to students' social preferences and friendship patterns.

*Measuring Affective Outcomes*   Affective outcomes include personal growth of students and, sometimes, teachers (e.g., self-competence, self-responsibility, self-efficacy, self-acceptance) and attitudes of students, teachers, parents, and others toward the program and classroom environment. Procedures for measuring affective outcomes typically require respondents to answer questions about themselves and their environment. Methods commonly used in educational contexts for measuring self-perceptions and attitudes toward the environment are described below.

A common method of assessing perceptions of self (e.g., self-esteem, self-efficacy, attribution of responsibility for one's own success and failure) is to have respondents complete a self-report inventory. Self-report inventories generally consist of sets of questions or statements that have two or more response alternatives. Each question or statement is read by or to the respondents, and respondents select the answer that describes them best. For example, a question in an inventory to measure students' perceptions of their academic competence might describe two children and ask the student to indicate the one most like him or her.

Valid responses to questions in self-report inventories require that respondents comprehend the questions and have sufficient insight to make self-appraisals, so the use of such inventories is not recommended with children below third grade. A popular alternative for young children is teacher assessment through the use of rating scales. Teachers are asked to rate each student on the degree to which he or she displays certain characteristics or behaviors (e.g., apparent degree of confidence in approaching school tasks or willingness to complete assigned work). The results are usually interpreted in much the same way as those obtained through self-report inventories.

A common method of measuring attitudes toward the program and the classroom environment is the attitude survey. For ease in administration and scoring, attitude surveys used in educational settings usually consist primarily of closed-response questions. For example, a survey may provide statements about the program and ask respondents to indicate their degree of agreement or disagreement by selecting one of several response alternatives (e.g., strongly agree, agree, disagree, strongly disagree) or by indicating statements with which they agree.

Attitudes toward educational innovations are often complex and difficult to measure from responses to closed-response or response-alternative questions only. Therefore, open-ended questions that allow respondents to answer questions in depth and to elaborate and extend their responses are often used in attitude surveys. For example, parents or teachers may be asked to mention aspects of the program that they particularly like and dislike. Attitude surveys, like self-report inventories, require a certain level of comprehension and insight on the part of respondents, and their use with very young children is not advisable.

## Identifying and Selecting Existing Tests

A major part of evaluation planning involves the selection and design of tests to measure outcomes identified as expected program effects. A variety of psycho-educational tests have been developed. Therefore, for many expected effects, particularly those related to student cognitive outcomes and to self-perceptions, appropriate instruments probably exist. Existing published and unpublished tests have appeared in sources such as books, journal articles, and informal papers. In the following sections, ways to locate existing tests and criteria for evaluating and selecting them are briefly discussed.

It is recommended that the potential user seeking tests to measure expected program outcomes begin by looking for published tests, since these are usually the easiest to find. The chief source of information for published psychological and educational tests is the series of *Mental Measurements Yearbooks* (Mitchell, 1985) that provide critical reviews of published tests, as well as practical information about the grade and age levels for which they are suitable, the time required for administration, the cost, and the publisher. *Tests in Print* (Mitchell, 1983) is a helpful companion to the yearbook, and it lists all in-print tests and indicates the yearbook in which each test was reviewed. In addition, recent publications on authentic assessment (e.g., Archbald & Newmann, 1988), curriculum-based assessment (e.g., Cohen & Spruill, 1990), and other syntheses on testing (e.g., Willson, 1989) are good reference sources.

Catalogues from test publishers are another source of information. Caution should be exercised with catalogue descriptions because they are generally less objective than the *Mental Measurements Yearbook* reviews. If a test appears promising, a specimen set may be ordered at a relatively low cost. A set typically includes a copy of the instrument, manuals for administration and scoring, and additional interpretive information.

Many tests developed primarily for research or for measuring variables in circumscribed settings have not been published. Sources of information about existing but unpublished tests include books, monographs, and anthologies; journal articles and other research reports; education program documents; and program developers.

Tests developed for research related to particular psychological or educational variables are sometimes included, or at least referenced, in scholarly monographs about the variables studied. For example, tests for measuring self-esteem may be found or mentioned in a book, monograph, or book chapter that deals with self-esteem. Discussions of particular instruments in such sources may be brief, but references are generally provided for further information.

The increased research on classroom teaching has resulted in the development of classroom observation instruments. Although most of these instruments are unpublished, a number of them have been compiled in anthologies by Borich and Madden (1977) and Simon and Boyer (1974). Recent publications include Freiberg (1990) and McGrail, Wilson, Buttram, and Rossman (1987).

Descriptions and reviews of new tests can be found in articles in journals devoted to measurement, such as the *Journal of Educational Measurement*, or those devoted to particular topics, such as the *Journal of Personality*, *Journal of Reading*, and *Journal of Classroom Interaction*. The most efficient method for finding relevant articles and other printed materials is to use indexing and abstracting services such as those maintained by the Educational Resources Information Center (ERIC). Most university libraries and some general libraries subscribe to one or more of these services, and libraries will often provide consultant services to help users plan and conduct searches.

A literature search may reveal major contributors of research in a given area and these persons are potential sources of information about measures of variables in those areas. For example, a researcher working in the area of ego development may be able to provide information about tests designed to measure ego development. Similarly, researchers who study teacher and student classroom behavior are often knowledgeable about instruments for measuring classroom processes. If a researcher's name appears regularly in writings about a particular educational or psychological research area, and if the reader is seeking to measure variables in that area, he or she would do well to contact that researcher.

Other sources are documents about innovative programs. Designers of the most widely used innovative programs have developed special instruments to measure the program's major expected outcomes. Copies of tests developed for particular programs and instructions for their use can often be obtained from program developers or from program documents.

## Factors to Consider in Selecting Existing Tests

The first and most important question to answer in assessing the usefulness of any test is if the test is a valid measure of the program outcome to be assessed. Assessment of test validity requires a close look at the content of the test and accompanying information in the test manual or printed materials to determine precisely the variables measured by the test. Achievement tests, for example, should include explanations of the process of test construction, lists of objectives, and specifications for item construction. To assess the validity of measures of affective outcomes such as aspects of personality, descriptions of the personality theory that guided test construction and evidence relating test performance to theoretical predictions should be carefully examined. For process (behavioral) measures, examine how well the behaviors in the instrument correspond with the behaviors expected as process outcomes.

For all types of tests, empirical analyses of test performance, such as factor analyses or correlations of test scores with external criteria, provide valuable evidence regarding the correlations of test scores with external criteria and the variables measured. Information about the generalizability and reliability of test scores should be examined to determine if the instrument yields results that are consistent over parallel forms, raters, and occasions. Some of the factors concerning test validity are technical, and program planners who are not highly knowledgeable about educational and psychological measurement should consult experts who can help them assess the validity of tests under consideration.

The second factor to consider in assessing tests is if the measure is practical in the context and setting in which it is to be used. The test should be appropriate to the ages and students to be tested. Time and expertise required for administration are other practical considerations. Very long tests, tests that must be individually administered, or tests that require special training to administer are usually difficult to justify in school settings. If there are two reasonably valid instruments to measure an outcome, and one is easier to fit into the school schedule or to administer, it may be advisable to select that one, even if the other may appear somewhat more valid.

Another practical consideration is, of course, cost. Most paper and pencil tests are relatively inexpensive to buy (or copy, in the case of unpublished tests) and to administer. Some tests may be quite expensive, especially those that require special materials. Ease of scoring the test is also a practical consideration. If an instrument yields multiple scores, as do achievement and interest batteries and classroom observation forms, hand scoring may be prohibitively time consuming. If hand scoring is not feasible, and a scoring service is too expensive or not available, there is no point in using the test.

The third factor in assessing tests is how well test scores can be interpreted in relation to expected program outcomes. Some expected outcomes imply norm-referenced interpretations, for example, "The average reading achievement of program students will equal or exceed that of the national norm." In this case, the test that measures the outcome must provide appropriate norms. Other outcomes imply criterion-referenced interpretations, such as "Students will demonstrate mastery of objectives X, Y, and Z." An achievement test is useful in this case only if it includes items that measure each objective, as well as criterion levels that indicate mastery.

Most widely used published tests, whether measures of achievement or other outcomes, provide information useful for norm-referenced interpretations. Some achievement tests and most curriculum-embedded tests permit criterion-referenced interpretations. Some published instruments and most unpublished ones provide inadequate or inappropriate information for interpreting performance in norm-referenced or criterion-referenced terms. In such cases, program evaluators may need to find other tests, develop their own norms or criteria, or develop alternative methods for interpreting performance.

## Constructing Instruments to Measure Program Outcomes

A search may fail to yield any potentially useful tests for measuring program outcomes, or those that have been located may fail to meet program needs. In particular, instruments for measuring outcomes specific to the program or setting are not likely to have been developed elsewhere. Therefore, those responsible for designing and conducting program evaluations often must construct their own instruments to assess program outcomes.

Detailed procedures for constructing valid and reliable measuring instruments are beyond the scope of this book, but an overview of the major steps involved in test construction is presented instead. Although the specific methods used in test construction differ somewhat from one type of instrument to another, the test constructor must in all cases proceed through a particular sequence of steps. These steps are:

1. Developing a detailed test plan
2. Deciding on test format, length, administration, and scoring
3. Constructing and assembling the test
4. Conducting a field test
5. Analyzing the results and revising the test

Each step is discussed briefly, and Table 8.4. lists activities involved with each step in the construction of five measurement instruments: classroom observation techniques, classroom achievement tests, nominating techniques, attitude surveys, and rating scales.

A test plan, sometimes called a test blueprint or set of test specifications, consists of detailed specification of the content of the test. The test plan ensures that the instrument will yield information concerning the specific objectives or behaviors to be assessed. Without a plan, the instrument may omit some important pieces of information while overemphasizing others. For example, a classroom achievement test developed without a comprehensive plan might contain many questions related to objectives that are easy to measure, but include few questions related to equally important but less readily measurable objectives. As Table 8.4. shows, a test plan generally consists of a detailed list or outline of the precise content of the instrument. If appropriate, the plan also indicates the relative importance or weight to be assigned to each part of the test.

The second step in test development concerns the structure, administration, and scoring of the instrument. The test designer specifies the format of individual questions or items and of the test as a whole, assignment of points or other scores to test items and subparts, length or time of test, and conditions and procedures for administration. This last step requires a technical knowledge of formats and procedures for administration.

The two previous steps provide the framework for actual construction of test items or questions and for assembling them in a usable form. Writing questions and assembling the test are time consuming and often tedious tasks that must be conscientiously performed. Evaluation planners should allow time and resources to ensure that the test specifications are followed and that the questions or items are of high quality. Answer sheets and recording forms must also be developed at this stage.

An important step in developing a measure or instrument for assessing program outcomes is conducting a field test. A field test determines if the content of

**Table 8.4.** Constructing measurement instruments

| | | | Measurement instrument | | |
|---|---|---|---|---|---|
| Step | Classroom observation techniques | Classroom achievement tests | Nominating techniques | Attitude surveys | Rating scales |
| 1. Developing a detailed test plan. | List and explicitly define specific behaviors to be observed. | Prepare a list outline or table of curriculum objectives to be tested and the relative weights accorded to each. | Specify activities for which students are to select (nominate) peers. | List aspects of the program to be assessed and observable outcomes associated with each. | List the particular behaviors and/or disposition to be rated. |
| 2. Deciding on format, length, administration, and scoring. | Decide on format (e.g., checklist vs. behavior tally). Design procedures for administration (e.g., observation of all students vs. continuous recording). Decide on number of observations per student and total length of the observation session. Develop instructions for observers, including criteria for presence or absence of each behavior. | Decide on format (e.g., performance vs. oral vs. pencil and paper, essay vs. objective, types of objective items). Decide on number of points for each item. Prepare instructions for students. | Decide on the wording or format for presenting task to students. Decide on number of peers to be nominated for each activity. Select oral or written administration. Prepare instructions to be presented to students. Decide how answers will be recorded and tallied. | Decide on the number and type of open-ended and closed-response questions. For the latter, decide on the number of response options (e.g., yes, no; strongly agree, agree, disagree, strongly disagree). Decide how responses will be scored. Prepare cover letter and instructions. | Decide on rating scale to be used (e.g., graphic, behaviorally anchored, checklist). Design response options for rated behaviors. Decide how ratings will be scored. Prepare instructions for raters. |
| 3. Constructing and assembling the test. | Prepare forms for observers to record classroom processes. Forms should permit entry of relevant data quickly, efficiently, and accurately. | Construct questions or items. Order the items and assemble the test. Prepare student answer sheets (if applicable). | Finalize questions to be asked. Prepare student answer forms. | Write attitude statements, questions. (Make sure that an equal number are worded positively and negatively.) Assemble in appropriate order and subgroups. | Prepare items in scale and assemble in easily usable form. |

*(continued)*

**Table 8.4.** (continued)

| | Measurement instrument | | | | |
|---|---|---|---|---|---|
| Step | Classroom observation techniques | Classroom achievement tests | Nominating techniques | Attitude surveys | Rating scales |
| 4. Conducting a field test. | Train observer(s). Administer under realistic classroom conditions. | If possible, try out the test on students (a comparable class or a small sample). Ask teachers to react to the test and provide feedback about particular items. | If possible, try out in a comparable classroom. Ask teachers to provide suggestions and comments. | Administer to a pilot sample comparable to the population to be tested, and ask them for comments and suggestions. | Have teachers in comparable classrooms use the scale to rate a sample of their students and ask them for comments and suggestions. |
| 5. Analyzing the results and revising the test. | Identify problems in use and their source (e.g., ambiguity of definitions of behaviors, difficulty in using forms). Make revisions. | Score the test and examine score distribution. Conduct item analysis. Eliminate or revise items as needed. | Analyze the data (e.g., prepare sociogram). Identify any problems in use, and reword or change questions and change nominating procedures, if needed. | Score and examine distribution of responses to each question. Analyze responses to open-ended questions to determine if they provide needed information. Eliminate or reword ambiguous questions that do not provide needed information, or yield no variability of response. | Score and examine the distribution of ratings for each item. Identify possible rater biases and change instructions if needed. Eliminate or reword items that are ambiguous or yield no variability in ratings. |

the test and conditions of administration are suitable, if the test yields the desired information, and the revisions, if any, that are needed prior to actual use. Ideally, the instrument should be field tested on a representative sample of the population for which it has been designed, under conditions identical to those of its planned use. In the real world of schools, however, program needs and organizational constraints often preclude realization of the ideal. In such cases, compromises that approximate ideal conditions should be arranged. Table 8.4. suggests sample populations and conditions that may be appropriate for several instruments.

In addition to field testing, the test should also be submitted to knowledgeable persons such as program designers and teachers for review. Their criticisms and suggestions should be considered in test analysis and revision.

Problems in administration (e.g., inadequate instructions, insufficient time) may be revealed during the field test. Subsequent analyses of test performance and comments by reviewers may reveal problems with scoring or with test content. The test designer may need to revise content and procedures for administration. Procedures for identifying some of these problems are listed in Table 8.4.

The work required in the final step, analyzing results and revising the test, depends to a great extent on previous steps. The more carefully the first three steps in test construction have been carried out, the less likely that serious problems with test content or administration will occur. If the test was well-planned and the content developed in accordance with the plan, needed revisions are likely to be minor.

## Data Collection

Collection of valid outcome data depends on the availability of a variety of school resources and the cooperation of many people. Schedules for collecting outcome data should be prepared before the start of program implementation. First, pre-program (baseline) measures will probably be needed for some outcomes. Second, teachers whose classes will be tested need to know the schedule for data collection so that they can plan compatible activities and inform students. Third, it may be necessary to order or prepare special materials such as test booklets and answer sheets, and planning ensures that materials will be available.

The frequency and schedule of data collection vary with the program outcomes. For some program outcomes, a single data collection near the end of the school year is sufficient. For others, repeated or continuous measurements are necessary. For example, the student achievement outcome "steady progress through the curriculum" implies continuous data collection throughout the year. Classroom process outcomes such as "decrease in managerial interactions between students and teachers" require repeated, though not continuous, assessments. For outcomes such as "positive attitudes of teachers toward individualized instruction," a single measurement, probably in the spring, may suffice.

The intended use of the data is also a consideration in scheduling collection. A single, year-end measurement is appropriate for data that are to be used primarily to summarize progress over the year and to elicit policymaker support for program continuation. On the other hand, if program planners intend to use data to improve delivery, then one or more measurements earlier in the school year are necessary.

Given the limitations of school resources, it is often necessary to compromise between what is desirable and what is possible in data collection. For example, although baseline measurements of all outcomes may be desirable, the demands on teachers and students during the early weeks of school generally make collection of comprehensive baseline data impossible. Similarly, although classroom process trends over the school year would certainly be more clearly revealed by monthly rather than by less frequent measurements, it is unlikely that monthly measurements can be scheduled.

Experience with adaptive instruction suggests that, except for student curriculum progress data that must be collected on an ongoing basis, three rounds of data collections per year are sufficient for assessment of program implementation measures and classroom processes. Year-end data collection is satisfactory for most other measures. A sample schedule for data collection that incorporates these suggestions is shown in Table 8.5.

Ideally, student outcomes are obtained for all students in the program, teacher outcomes for all teachers, and parent outcomes for all parents. In practice, however, this is sometimes not possible. This situation arises, for example, when tests must be individually administered, as may be the case in measuring affective outcomes in young children, or when direct observation is used to describe student classroom behaviors. In order to keep the time for testing or for conducting classroom observations manageable, yet obtain reliable data on program impact, it is advisable to employ a sample of the students rather than all of them. Depending on the purpose of the particular evaluation, appropriate sampling designs will ensure adequate representation, validity, and reliability of data. If the purpose is to assess program impact on a number of outcomes, rather than the learning outcomes of a specific student, then it is appropriate to obtain data based on a representative sample. Data must be collected from a sample that is representative of the entire group or class, however.

Random sampling techniques should be used whenever possible to increase the probability of selecting a representative sample. Random samples can be drawn from the entire group, or a stratified random sampling design can be used if the program includes two or more distinct subgroups (e.g., regular education

**Table 8.5.**   Sample schedule for data collection

| Data | Pre-implementation | Fall (October) | Winter (January/February) | Spring (April/May) |
|---|---|---|---|---|
| Program implementation | | X | X | X |
| Classroom processes | | X | X | X |
| Student learning | | | | |
|   Progress through the curriculum | | Ongoing | | |
|   Standardized achievement tests | X[a] | | | X |
| Student social and affective | | | | |
|   outcomes | | X | | X |
| Teacher attitudes | X | | | X |
| Administrator attitudes | X | | | X |
| Parent attitudes | | | | X |

[a]In most cases, standardized achievement test scores from the previous spring can be used as baseline (pre-implementation) data.

and students with special needs). If it is important to obtain data from each sub-group, each classroom sample might include a predetermined number of students randomly selected from each.

## Data Interpretation

Raw scores from psychological and educational measurements are rarely meaningful in and of themselves. A reference or comparison is needed to interpret such data. Four types of comparison are described:

1. Comparison with a standard or criterion
2. Comparison with a norm
3. Comparison with previous performance
4. Comparison with performance of nonprogram (control) groups.

*Comparison with a Standard or Criterion* Comparison with a standard or criterion is appropriate for some program outcomes. For example, if students are expected to achieve certain curriculum objectives, performance on tests to measure these objectives is interpreted in terms of if they mastered the objectives.

*Comparison with a Norm* Norm-referenced interpretations are appropriate for many outcome measures. For example, knowing that program students scored at the 60th percentile in reading when compared with students nationwide gives a reference for the students' performance. Obviously, these interpretations depend on norms based on an appropriate comparison group.

*Comparison with Previous Performance* Comparison with previous performance by the same individual before program implementation, or at an early stage of implementation, can provide meaningful information about program effects. This is particularly true for expected outcomes which refer to increases or decreases relative to previous levels. If comparisons to previous performance levels are important for assessing outcomes, evaluation planners need to ensure that baseline and/or multiple measurements are scheduled.

*Comparison with Performance of Nonprogram Groups* Perhaps the most significant measure of program effects on participants is obtained by comparing their performance with that of individuals not in the program (control groups). Comparisons with control groups, although often desirable, are difficult to arrange because of a lack of resources, time, or comparable groups. The importance of initial equivalence, or comparability, between program participants and control groups cannot be overemphasized.

Two groups may be considered comparable if initially they were alike, on the average, in all relevant respects except for participation or nonparticipation in the program. The best way to ensure comparability of program and nonprogram groups is by random assignment of individuals to program and nonprogram groups prior to program implementation. If the school plans both program and nonprogram classes at the same grade levels, random assignment of students to classes should be considered.

Sometimes, however, random assignment of students to program and nonprogram classes at the same grade levels is precluded by school policy, parent preference, or participation of all classes of the grade in the program. Furthermore, random assignment of program participants other than students (e.g., teachers) is rarely possible or desirable. In cases where random assignment is impossible, existing groups can be used as controls if they can be demonstrated to be comparable. For example, nonprogram students in the same or other schools who are in the same grades, have similar achievement records, and come from similar home backgrounds and communities can serve as controls for program students. Similarly, nonprogram teachers of the same grade levels, in the same or other schools, can serve as controls for program teachers, provided that their training and teaching experience have been similar.

Sometimes evaluation planners, unable to locate comparable groups, settle for groups that are known to differ in particular ways from program participants (e.g., past achievement or type of community). The problem with this strategy is that straightforward interpretation of results becomes impossible. For example, if program and nonprogram groups are found to differ with respect to a particular outcome, is this due to the program or to preexisting differences between the groups? Although statistical "corrections" are sometimes invoked to "equate" the groups (e.g., analysis of covariance), such procedures are controversial and problematic at best. The only way to ensure comparable data is to begin with comparable groups. If comparable groups cannot be found, it is better to do without comparisons between program and nonprogram participants than to compare noncomparable groups. Finally, if comparisons of program and nonprogram participants are planned, and if random assignment is not possible, evaluation planners should begin to locate comparable nonprogram groups as soon as possible.

## Administration of Outcome Measurement Tests

A few additional activities need to be completed before actual data collection:

1.  Obtain parents' permission for testing their children, if necessary.
2.  If special training is needed to administer tests, select and train the administrators, observers, or raters.
3.  Send reminders to teachers, parents, and others 1–2 weeks before scheduled testing dates.
4.  For tests administered to students outside the classroom (e.g., individually administered tests), make sure that space for testing is available and that teachers know which students will be tested and at what times.
5.  Assemble and inventory all needed materials.
6.  Make arrangements for scoring and analyzing the data.

Special care must be taken in collecting data from individuals involved with the program who are not students or staff—in particular, parents. Parents are not "captive audiences" in the sense that their children are. Students are tested at a time and a place determined by the school, but parents are generally asked to complete and return surveys by a certain date. Experience has shown that the initial return rate is often very low, and a return rate greater than 70% is required to make valid inferences about a group as a whole (Gay, 1981). To ensure a respectable return rate, program officials should take the following steps:

1.  Set a return date for surveys that is at least 2 weeks before the actual final date.
2.  Mail or hand-deliver surveys to parents well in advance of the return date.
3.  Include a cover letter explaining the purpose of the survey to parents and the importance of their responses.

4.  Include clear instructions for returning the survey, including the return date. If the survey is to be mailed, enclose a self-addressed, stamped return envelope.
5.  Send reminders and provide duplicate surveys to parents who have not responded by the return date.

If the activities listed above are undertaken in a timely and conscientious manner, the actual administration of the instruments in accordance with specified procedures is generally routine. Readers who desire more information about general procedures for test administration can refer to textbooks on educational measurement, such as those by Anastasi (1982), Linn (1989), and Nitko (1983).

## DATA ANALYSIS AND PROGRAM EVALUATION

The immediate results of tests, observation instruments, surveys, or other instruments are a mass of data consisting of tally marks on observation forms, pencil marks on answer sheets, and circles around numbers on rating scales. The data must be coded, organized, reduced, summarized, and analyzed before program effects can be evaluated. Procedures for dealing with the data are discussed briefly and relatively nontechnically in this section. Readers who want more detailed information are advised to consult textbooks on statistics and program evaluation or to seek help from persons with expertise in these areas.

Data analysis can be divided into three stages. In the first stage, raw data are coded, scored, and recorded or transcribed in a form that lends itself to analysis. In the second stage, data reduction procedures reveal important characteristics of score distributions in the tested groups, such as the range and average of achievement scores. The third stage involves examination of relations between outcomes, or between outcomes and other variables, for example, the relation between level of implementation and classroom processes, or differences in responsibility between program and nonprogram students.

## Coding, Scoring, and Recording Data

In the first stage of data analysis, tally marks and circles on answer sheets are converted to numerical scores by coding and counting procedures, and the scores are transcribed to record forms. For example, the set of pencil marks on an achievement test answer sheet is converted to a score for the student, and the scores of all students are transferred to classroom record forms. In another case, tally marks on an observation form are coded, counted, and combined to yield a score on each process outcome for each class, and the scores of all program classes are recorded or printed out.

Coding and scoring procedures for many tests are straightforward and relatively simple. For example, answers to individual items on achievement tests typically are coded as either correct or incorrect, and correct answers for all items in the test, or in each part, are added to yield a score. For some instruments, however, coding and scoring are more complex. On attitude and rating scales, for example, responses to each item typically must be converted to numbers. On sociographic instruments, coding and scoring involve manipulations that convert student nominations to graphic displays of choices in a class. Coding and scoring responses to open-ended questions are often complex and vary with the nature of the questions. Whatever the method of coding and scoring, however, program evaluators can take specific steps to reduce the possibility of error and ensure that important information is not lost.

Coding, scoring, and recording with or without a computer are boring, tedious, and unchallenging tasks. It is very easy to become careless and make errors when converting qualitative responses to numbers, transferring numbers from one place to another, or entering numbers with a keyboard. Errors at this stage tend to become magnified in later stages of analysis, and should be prevented and detected.

Three suggestions can help avoid errors in coding, scoring, and recording. First, the coding process should be as simple as possible. Coders should not have to add numbers in order to convert a pencil mark on an answer sheet to a numerical value. Second, another person should check (or at least spot check) the original coding, scoring, and transcribing of all data sets. Third, after data have been recorded, record sheets or computer printouts should be scanned for obvious inconsistencies such as abnormally large or small numbers, and any errors should be corrected.

In the process of coding and scoring, information is transferred, for example, from student answer sheets to coding sheets and class record forms or computer files. All relevant identifying information should be attached to or coded with each piece of data or each score at each step so that at a later time scores can be readily identified as those of particular students (or classes) in particular subgroups, grades, or education programs. For example, in a school with both program and nonprogram classes and with regular education, special education, and Chapter 1 students, each student entry should be coded with the student's name or number, but also according to grade level, class, subgroup membership, and status as a program or nonprogram student.

Individual scores are sometimes converted into norm-referenced forms (e.g., percentile ranks) or criterion-referenced forms (e.g., mastery vs. nonmastery of objectives). Further analyses can often, though not always, be performed on either original or transformed scores.

## Summarizing Data for Descriptive Purposes

Data reduction techniques can provide information about characteristics of the distributions of program outcomes in various groups (e.g., the distribution of reading achievement test scores in the program students with special needs). The characteristics of a distribution most likely to be of interest are shape (symmetrical vs. skewed or frequencies or percentages in various categories), average or central values (mean, median, mode), and variability or dispersion (range of scores and standard deviation). Discussion of the computation and meaning of such statistics is beyond the scope of this chapter. It is important to note, however, that any statistic, such as the mean, can be computed at various levels. For example, mean reading achievement may be computed for each classroom, for each of several subgroups of students within each classroom or school, for each grade, or for the entire school. Different levels of analysis are appropriate for different purposes. If data are to help individual teachers improve their instruction, classroom-level statistics are needed; if comparisons are to be made between student subgroups, relevant statistics must be computed in each of the subgroups; and if program students are to be compared with nonprogram students aggre-

**Table 8.6.** Mean TELLS scores of third grade students: School A (1989)

| Group | N | Mean score | Students above cut in %[a] |
|---|---|---|---|
| Math | | | |
| Pilot classes | 19 | 40 | 53 |
| Comparison classes | 25 | 34 | 44 |
| Reading | | | |
| Pilot classes | 19 | 36 | 42 |
| Comparison classes | 25 | 27 | 12 |

[a]Percent of students above the score that indicates remediation is required.

gated across classes, school-level statistics must be computed within each education program.

After descriptive statistics have been computed, it is often useful to display them in tabular or graphic form because characteristics of distributions are vividly revealed in such displays. Examples of summary tables of achievement data collected in one school are shown in Table 8.6. and Table 8.7. The format of these tables enables evaluators to compare scores between years and between pilot classes and comparison classes. Table 8.8. is an example of achievement data that examines NCE scores of special education students in pilot classes and comparison classes.

Descriptive statistics alone rarely are sufficient for program evaluation. Additional analyses of differences and relationships are often necessary to determine if expected program effects occurred as hypothesized. For example, if an expected program outcome is an achievement level for each grade at least equal to the level prior to program implementation, an analysis of the difference between pre-program and program means is necessary. Similarly, the expectation that higher levels of implementation will result in certain changes in classroom processes must be tested by analyzing the relationships between degree of program implementation and occurrence or level of the specific classroom processes.

Specific expected outcomes and analyses will differ from one program and setting to another. For illustrative purposes, examples are given in Table 8.9., and analyses such as these generally involve statistical tests, such as t-tests, analyses of variance, or correlational analysis. Discussion of specific procedures, conditions for their use, and interpretations of results is beyond the scope of this chapter.

**Table 8.7.** Comparison of citywide test results: NCE frequency distribution

| | Pilot classes (%) | | | Comparison classes (%) | | |
|---|---|---|---|---|---|---|
| NCE Scores | 1988 | 1989 | Difference | 1988 | 1989 | Difference |
| Math | | | | | | |
| 1–25 | 14 | 2 | − 12 | 17 | 7 | − 10 |
| 26–50 | 25 | 31 | + 6 | 33 | 55 | + 22 |
| 51–99 | 61 | 66 | + 5 | 50 | 38 | − 12 |
| Reading | | | | | | |
| 1–25 | 15 | 6 | − 9 | 29 | 12 | − 17 |
| 26–50 | 48 | 52 | + 4 | 36 | 62 | + 26 |
| 51–99 | 38 | 42 | + 4 | 36 | 25 | − 11 |

**Table 8.8.** Comparison of student NCEs between special education students from pilot classes and comparison classes: School A (Spring, 1989)

| ID | Room (Grade level) | Exceptionality | Chronologic age | Reading | | | Math | | |
|---|---|---|---|---|---|---|---|---|---|
| | | | | (Grade level of test administered)[a] | NCE | At or above district average[c] | (Grade level of test administered) | NCE | At or above district average |
| **Pilot classes** | | | | | | | | | |
| 0344248 | 102 (1) | EMR | 7 | (1) | 46 | | (1) | 52 | X |
| 0330819 | 104 (1) | SED | 7 | (1) | 51 | X | (1) | 98 | X |
| 0276386 | 105 (1) | LD | 7 | (1) | 46 | | (1) | 66 | X |
| 0276409 | 105 (1) | EMR | 7 | (1) | 51 | X | (1) | 46 | |
| 9984330 | 206 (2) | LD | 8 | (2) | 46 | | (2) | — | |
| 0221064 | 206 (2) | LD/MG | 8 | (2) | —[b] | | (2) | — | |
| 0852095 | 204 (3) | LD | 10 | (3) | 57 | X | (3) | 21 | |
| 9153931 | 204 (3) | LD | 10 | (3) | 40 | | (3) | 70 | X |
| 8941012 | 204 (3) | LD | 11 | (3) | 19 | | (3) | 36 | |
| **Mean** | | | | | 44.5 | | | 55.6 | |
| **Comparison classes** | | | | | | | | | |
| 0441543 | 304 | EMR | 7 | (K) | 8 | | (K) | 62 | |
| 0203311 | 304 | LD | 7 | (2) | 18 | | (2) | 58 | |
| 9311965 | 304 | LD | 8 | (2) | 30 | | (2) | 25 | |
| 0156053 | 304 | EMR | 9 | (1) | 33 | | (1) | 42 | |
| 9656230 | 304 | LD | 9 | (1) | 24 | | (1) | 54 | |
| 9291048 | 304 | LD | 10 | — | — | | (1) | 14 | |
| 9266104 | 304 | LD | 10 | (1) | 42 | | (2) | 58 | |
| 9629734 | 304 | EMR | 10 | (1) | 51 | | (1) | 54 | |
| 9159929 | 304 | EMR | 10 | (1) | 9 | | (1) | 65 | |
| 9291056 | 304 | EMR | 10 | (K) | 30 | | (K) | — | |
| **Mean** | | | | | 27.2 | | | 48.0 | |

[a]Scores in the table represent special education students for whom NCE scores were available. Students in pilot classes were tested at the grade level of the class they were mainstreamed into. Comparison students were generally tested out of their grade level, based on teacher judgment.

[b] = Scores not available.

[c]Only pilot classes are noted. Because the majority of comparison group students took the test out of grade level, this comparison is not meaningful.

**Table 8.9.** Examples of expected program outcomes and analyses required for testing them

| Expected outcome | Analysis |
|---|---|
| Level of implementation of critical program dimensions will increase over the course of the year | Comparison of mean level of implementation of each critical dimension in fall, winter, and spring |
| Student-initiated, relative to teacher-initiated, activities will increase from fall to winter | Comparison of percent of activities that are student-initiated in fall and winter |
| Higher levels of certain classroom processes (e.g., teacher–student interactions for instructional purposes) will be associated with higher levels of achievement | Assessment of relationships (correlations) between measures of specified classroom processes and levels of achievement |
| Students in the program will be more willing to accept responsibility for learning outcomes than comparable nonprogram students | Comparison of average levels of self-responsibility, as measured by an appropriate instrument, between program and nonprogram students |
| Teacher interactions with students with special needs will not differ from interactions with other students | Comparison of occurrence of various types of teacher–student interactions between students with special needs and other students |

## Preparation of Reports

Information about program effects is of value to almost everyone involved in an adaptive education program. Teachers and school staff use the information to evaluate their performances and to plan program revisions and improvements. Parents want to know how the program has affected their children. Information about program effects provides a database for decisions about the future of the program for administrators and policymakers. This information is best presented in written reports.

Reports of program effects should be tailored to the particular audience. Reports to parents should be brief, nontechnical, and emphasize effects on their children's cognitive, social, and affective growth. Reports for instructional staff should be more detailed, though relatively nontechnical, and include effects on classroom processes and teacher and student outcomes. Recommendations for program improvement suggested by outcome data are particularly helpful to instructional staff. For administrators and policymakers, discussions of product outcomes and their relation to program costs are particularly useful.

Brief oral presentations of report highlights at PTA or school board meetings are useful as supplements to written reports to help audiences focus on the main points. Written and oral reports should begin with a brief description of the program and the history of its implementation in the school. Expected and obtained effects should be described appropriately to the interests and background knowledge of the audience. If possible, tables, charts, and figures should be included to help the audience better understand the results. After reporting outcome data, the author or presenter can discuss the relation between obtained and expected outcomes and propose recommendations based on the results.

## Using Outcome Data for Program Evaluation and Improvement

Reports of program effects provide program staff and policymakers with a database related to program improvement (formative evaluation) and decisions concerning continued support for the program (summative evaluation). In this section, both types of decision making are discussed.

*Using Outcome Data for Program Improvement: Formative Evaluation*  In formative evaluation, data on program effects are used to identify aspects of program delivery that need to be changed or strengthened and to design strategies for change. The sequence of activities is presented in Figure 8.2. As the figure shows, the first step in formative evaluation is the collection and analysis of outcome data. The results are then examined to determine their agreement with expectations. If results do not meet expectations, the cause of the discrepancy between expected and obtained results must be determined or diagnosed. A strategy is designed to reduce the discrepancy based on the diagnosis. The strategy is then implemented, and data about the expected outcome are again collected and analyzed. Thus, the set of activities may be viewed as a continuing cycle of assessment–feedback–correction–assessment to improve program delivery. The first step, measurement and analysis of expected outcomes, has been discussed at length, and the remaining steps are described below.

Comparison of results with expectations appears straightforward, but the process is often quite complex. Professional judgment is usually required to decide if the results are sufficiently in accord with expectations. Results may be in accord with expectations at one site but not at another, and results in accord at an early stage in program implementation may not be in accord at a later stage. A discrepancy between expectations and results may be judged to be relatively unimportant if other aspects of the program need immediate attention, and a discrepancy may be judged important if other aspects of the program are functioning well.

To decide if results are in accord with expectations, site personnel must consider their own standards, the amount of discrepancy from expectations, the priorities and needs of the site, and the status of other program components. If evaluators decide that results are sufficiently in accord with expectations, then no specific action is needed, and evaluators can turn their attention to other outcomes. If results are not sufficiently in accord with expectations, reasons for the discrepancy are explored.

*Cause of the Discrepancy*   Diagnosis is essential to corrective action because specific actions to correct a problem depend on knowing the cause of the problem. For example, a comparison of achievement results with expectations shows that students have not been progressing through the curriculum at a satisfactory rate. Actions to resolve this discrepancy will be different if the problem lies in the curriculum (e.g., improperly sequenced objectives) or if it lies in teaching methods (e.g., inadequate instructional explanations).

Diagnosis involves in-depth analysis to determine what accounts for the discrepancy between obtained and expected effects. In many cases, additional data must be collected by examining materials, discussions with teachers, and focused classroom observations. A cause for the discrepancy is hypothesized based on the analysis of relevant data, and this hypothesized cause guides the design and selection of a strategy to reduce the discrepancy.

*Designing a Strategy to Reduce the Discrepancy*   Program planners, evaluators, or those responsible for monitoring implementation select or devise a strategy to reduce the discrepancy between expected and measured outcomes. There is no simple rule governing this procedure, and the selected strategy depends not only on the problem, but also on factors such as students, the curriculum, and other aspects of program delivery. The process may, however, be clarified by means of several hypothetical examples.

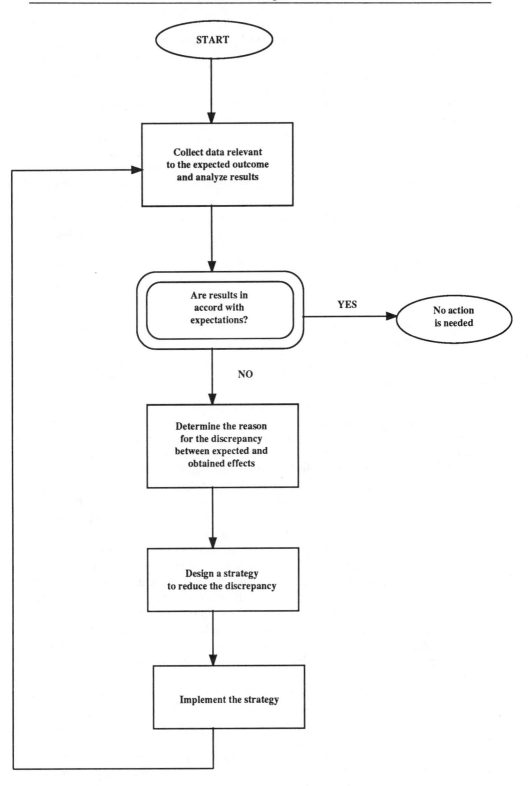

**Figure 8.2.** Cycle of activities of formative evaluation.

The first example continues the case of student failure to progress through the curriculum at the expected rate. Two possible sources of the discrepancy were suggested (though there may be others): deficiencies in the curriculum and inadequate teaching methods. Each diagnosis is considered with an examination of the corrective strategy that might be devised in each case.

One diagnosis, based on examination of classroom materials and student worksheets, indicates that the problem lies in improperly sequenced curriculum objectives. An appropriate strategy to correct this problem would involve re-sequencing objectives and the associated curriculum materials and activities. If the diagnosis suggests that the source of the problem is the inadequate explanations of concepts and procedures by the teachers, an appropriate strategy would involve working with the teachers to help them develop better skills.

For another example, students in a particular class are not working together and helping one another to the degree expected by program planners. Classroom observations, examination of materials and activities, and interviews with teachers and students are conducted to determine the reason for the discrepancy. Three possible diagnoses are presented along with strategies that might be chosen to correct the problem.

For the first diagnosis, an interview with the teacher reveals that he or she does not believe it is good teaching practice to encourage students to work together or help one another. In this case, a strategy must be devised to change the teacher's concept of good practice. The teacher could be presented with research evidence of the efficacy of peer tutoring, or encouraged to observe teachers who do implement peer tutoring and interaction successfully. These and actions such as coaching would have to be systematically developed to bring about a change.

A second possible diagnosis for lack of peer interaction is that the classroom lacks materials and activities to encourage students to work together. An appropriate strategy would be to work with the teacher to find and construct additional activities that promote student interaction and peer tutoring.

A third possible diagnosis for a low level of peer interaction and tutoring may be that the arrangement of student work spaces makes it difficult for students to communicate or interact. If this is the case, the problem may be resolved simply by rearranging student desks in clusters.

These examples demonstrate that no simple rules can be given for arriving at diagnoses and devising strategies. Evaluators must use their research and practical experience of factors that affect teaching and learning as well as their abilities to analyze complex learning situations. A high level of professional judgment is needed to identify causes for discrepancies between expected program effects and actual outcomes and to devise means for rectifying them.

A strategy must be carefully monitored to ensure that it is applied systematically and consistently. If the diagnosis and resulting strategy were correct, the next round of data collection and analysis should reveal results significantly in agreement with expected outcomes. If the situation remains unsatisfactory, however, the cycle of assessment should continue. It may be necessary to change or modify the diagnosis and design an alternate strategy to increase the accord between program expectations and program effects.

***Using Outcome Data to Make Decisions about Program Continuation: Summative Evaluation***   Local schools are accountable to the public that they serve. The school board has the responsibility of making decisions about the future of the program—whether it will be continued as is, expanded, cut back, or discontinued. Information about how well the program has met its goals, about improvements, and calculations of program costs provides a vital base for decisions. This section discusses program effects and costs as factors in summative program evaluation, and the implications of evaluation decisions for program planning.

In summative evaluation, as in formative evaluation, after collection and analysis of data, outcomes obtained are compared with expected outcomes. In summative evaluation, however, results are used to decide the degree to which the program was successful and the level of support for program continuation. As in formative evaluation, such decisions require professional judgment. First, data on program effects often present a complex pattern. Second, important long-term effects may differ from measured short-term effects. Third, measured effects must be weighed against less tangible benefits of program implementation.

Most comprehensive innovative programs have many varied goals and rarely is a program successful in meeting all its goals equally, especially in its first year. For example, students in a new program may show impressive achievement gains in math, while lagging behind their traditional education peers in reading; parents may be enthusiastic about the program, while teachers have serious reservations (or vice versa); or program students may demonstrate increased responsibility, but decreased time on task. Therefore, evaluators are required to make judgments about the relative worth of various outcomes. If certain important outcomes are disappointing, evaluators must estimate the possibility of patterns of effects changing during the following years, based on progress over the year and program improvement plans of school staff.

Program effects are likely to vary also with students. One program may be particularly effective with students who move quickly through the curriculum, another with students who move less quickly. One program may work best for assertive, confident students, another for students who are less self-assured. Program evaluators need to consider such attribute treatment interactions when making decisions about program continuation. If a program seems particularly effective with certain students, it may be wise to continue the program with those students, while revising program delivery to serve other students better.

*Short-Term versus Long-Term Effects* During the first years of an innovative program, staff spend considerable time and effort in resolving start-up problems. In addition, all program participants must learn new behaviors and ways of interacting with one another. As a result, program outcomes in the first year may differ from those to be expected in later years. For example, teacher adjustment to a new curriculum may temporarily lower student achievement test scores. For this reason, it is difficult to compare outcomes of a new program with those of an established one, or to predict likely long-term outcomes.

Moreover, educational and social programs sometimes have long-term effects that cannot be measured until several years after program implementation. For example, although adaptive instruction and conventional instruction students in a school may not appear to differ in their acceptance of responsibility for learning in primary or intermediate grades, a difference may emerge when students enter the less controlled environment of the middle school or junior

high. Until data measuring long-term goals become available, program evaluators must resort to their best judgments concerning probable, but not yet measured, effects.

Sometimes programs have unanticipated side effects that may be either beneficial or harmful. For example, parents may become more involved in their children's education in a new program, even though this was not a planned program
outcome. Conversely, a new program may lead to increased dissension among
program staff or between program and nonprogram staff. If such unanticipated
effects are noted, program officials and policymakers should acquire as much
information about them as possible, weigh their importance relative to other
program effects, and consider them in decisions about the program's future.
Judgments must be made about how serious the harmful side effects are, whether
they can be reduced, and what effects they are likely to have on future operation
of the program. In the case of beneficial side effects, ways of capitalizing on them
should be considered.

The benefits of an education program cannot be weighed on the basis of program effects alone. Many innovative education programs incorporate features
that produce few measurable effects, yet are worthwhile in their own right. For
example, teaching students to take increased responsibility for their learning
may be considered a worthy goal in itself, even if it does not result in higher
achievement test or self-report inventory scores. Similarly, programs that integrate students with special needs into regular classrooms may be considered inherently valuable, whatever their effects on achievement and other outcomes,
because they are more consistent with democratic ideals than programs that provide special services in segregated settings.

*Fiscal Considerations*   Due to their public fiscal accountability, policymakers
must consider program costs as well as effects in making decisions about continuation. Therefore, program evaluators should include precise cost data in reports for policymakers, and they should be prepared to compare costs of the
adaptive education program with those of the district's conventional program.

In considering program costs, it is important to distinguish between initial
start-up costs and ongoing costs. Any new educational program incurs certain
expenses that are necessary to start the program. Ongoing costs are those anticipated to continue throughout the life of the program. These include staff salaries,
administrative expenses, and costs for maintenance and replacement of materials and equipment. It is the ongoing costs of adaptive instruction, relative to
conventional instruction, that must be considered in decisions about the future
of the program.

Experience with implementation of adaptive instruction in elementary
schools has shown that, over the long run, the costs of operating an adaptive
education program are comparable to those of other programs. Although staffing
needs may appear to be greater than those of conventional programs, extra staffing expenses can usually be avoided by the creative reassignment of personnel
and by using volunteers as classroom aides. Other extra costs relative to those of
conventional instruction (e.g., for materials such as prescription sheets) tend to
be minimal.

Under some circumstances, implementation of adaptive education programs may result in savings rather than extra costs relative to conventional programs. For example, adaptive instruction allows collaboration among regular

teachers and specialists to provide all services to students with special needs in their own classrooms, reducing or eliminating the cost of maintaining special facilities. Clearly, program costs vary as a function of characteristics distinct to each site. Policymakers must consider site-specific factors as well as program needs in evaluating program effectiveness relative to cost.

After considering information about program effects and costs and the other factors discussed above, policymakers may make one of four decisions concerning the future of the program:

1. Continue the program at the current level
2. Expand the program to additional classes, schools, or students
3. Reduce the program
4. Discontinue the program

Considering that a new program usually needs to consolidate gains and improve delivery in the second year, a decision to continue the program at the current level may be a wise one. It is important to realize, however, that program planning and administrative and training support for staff must be maintained at a level at least as high as in the first year. Without a continued high level of support, implementation of innovative programs is likely to founder (Stein & Wang, 1988; Wang, Vaughan, & Dytman, 1985).

Although the support needs remain the same, the type of support needed in the second year is likely to differ. With the program operating, planners can direct more effort to integrating program components and to fine tuning program delivery to meet teacher, student, and school needs. Implementation and outcome data and staff input can help to identify areas that need improvement and to suggest ways for effecting changes.

A decision to extend the program beyond its current level represents a vote of confidence in the program and its staff. Although expansion is generally desirable, it must be carefully planned to ensure continued success. Growth is a good thing only if it can be managed without overtaxing available resources. Program planners must anticipate training new staff while maintaining a high level of support of existing staff. It is essential that neither group be neglected at the expense of the other. If expansion of the program includes changes in program components or the addition of new participants (e.g., inclusion of bilingual classes), the delivery system must be adapted and modified to accommodate the changes. To ensure that no aspects of planning are overlooked in preparing for expansion, it is recommended that program planners proceed systematically through all the steps of implementation planning discussed in Chapter 2.

Because of costs or other reasons, program officials may decide to reduce the size of the program. Although such a decision may be disappointing to program staff and others, it represents an opportunity to concentrate on the continued classes to consolidate gains from the previous year and to systematically eliminate problems that may have contributed to the decision for program reduction. Becoming smaller may provide the resources needed to become better, and becoming better, in turn, may lead to support for program expansion in the future.

The least desirable option is a decision by policymakers to withdraw support and discontinue the program. Such a decision may be based on evidence that the program has not succeeded in reaching its goals, but programs may be (and have been) discontinued for reasons that have little to do with program effectiveness. A case in point occurred in the New York City schools. A demonstrably effective adaptive instruction program was discontinued because the schools involved were threatened with loss of special education funding to support the program's mainstreaming provisions (Wang & Reynolds, 1985).

If a program is officially discontinued, program staff may nonetheless wish to continue implementing certain features that they consider worthwhile. For example, teachers may decide to continue using program materials and methods, perhaps in modified form, to individualize instruction or to encourage student responsibility. Thus, although the specific program is discontinued, the school's instructional program may remain more adaptive than it was before the program was implemented. If school officials and teachers truly believe that adaptive instruction benefits students, they can work together to plan, support, and maintain aspects of the program that they judge to be particularly valuable and compatible with the rest of the school's education program.

## Programs as Evolving Entities

It is easy to view program evaluation, particularly summative evaluation, as the end of a series of activities that began with pre-implementation activities, such as curriculum preparation, teacher training, and evaluation design, and continued with the implementation of the program in classrooms and monitoring and support activities. Program evaluation is better viewed as a stage in a continuing cycle. Although evaluation does indeed follow pre-implementation and implementation activities, it also sets the stage for a renewed set of pre-implementation and implementation activities in the years to come. A successful education program is an evolving entity. Effective education programs develop, grow, and change just as their students do.

Perhaps the best way to view evaluation is as a mechanism for systematically guiding the process of program change to enhance desirable effects, reduce undesirable ones, and meet the changing needs of students, teachers, and other participants. Basic program goals, such as the integration of students with special needs into regular classes, and major components, such as individualized student instructional plans, are likely to remain the same over many years. Ways of achieving these goals and utilizing these components, however, may change markedly. After several years of thorough evaluations and revisions based on evaluation results, the program may be quite different from the one originally designed and implemented. This is appropriate and desirable.

## SUMMARY

Collection of information about program implementation and effects provides a database for improvement of program delivery (formative evaluation) and for making decisions about program continuation (summative evaluation). The evaluation process includes identification of outcomes to be assessed, selecting and constructing tests to measure the outcomes, planning for data collection, collection of data, analysis of results, and use of the results for formative and summative purposes. By using guidelines and procedures, with technical assistance from experts in educational measurement and statistics, program planners and evaluators can design and carry out evaluation activities that meet site and program needs, availability criteria, and provide a comprehensive and accurate basis for determining program effectiveness and for future program planning.

## REFERENCES

Anastasi, A. (1982). *Psychological testing* (5th ed.). New York: Macmillan.

Archbald, D.A., & Newmann, F.M. (1988). *Beyond standardized testing: Assessing authentic academic achievement in the secondary school*. Reston, VA: National Association of Secondary School Principals.

Bennett, S.N. (1978). Recent research on teaching: A dream, a belief and a model. *British Journal of Educational Psychology, 48*, 127–147.

Berliner, D.C. (1983). Developing conceptions of classroom environments: Some light on the T in classroom studies of ATI. *Educational Psychologist, 18*, 1–13.

Bloom, B.S. (1966). Twenty-five years of educational research. *American Educational Research Journal, 3*, 211–221.

Borich, G.D., & Madden, S.K. (1977). *Evaluating classroom instruction: A sourcebook of instruments*. Reading, MA: Addison-Wesley.

Bossert, S.T. (1979). *Tasks and social relationships in classrooms*. New York: Cambridge University Press.

Brookover, W.B. (Ed.). (1979). *School social systems and student achievement: Schools can make a difference*. New York: Praeger.

Brookover, W.B., & Lezotte, L.W. (1977). *Changes in school characteristics coincident with changes in student achievement*. East Lansing: Michigan State University College of Urban Development.

Brown, A.L., Bransford, J.D., Ferrara, R., & Campione, J. (1983). Learning, remembering, and understanding. In J.H. Flavell & E. Markman (Eds.), *Mussen handbook of child psychology: Vol. 3. Cognitive development* (4th ed., pp. 77–166). New York: John Wiley & Sons.

Bruner, J.S. (1966). *Toward a theory of instruction*. New York: W. W. Norton.

Carroll, J.B. (1963). A model for school learning. *Teachers College Record, 63*, 722–732.

Cohen, L.G., & Spruill, J.A. (1990). *Practical guide to curriculum-based assessment for special educators*. Springfield, IL: Charles C Thomas.

Deno, S.L. (1985). Curriculum-based measurement: The emerging alternative. *Exceptional Children, 52*(3), 219–232.

DeStefano, L., Wang, M.C., & Gordon, E.M. (1984, April). *Differences in student temperament characteristics and their effects on classroom processes and outcomes*. Symposium at the annual meeting of the American Educational Research Association, New Orleans.

Edmonds, R.R. (1979). Effective schools for the urban poor. *Educational Leadership. 37*, 15–27.

Fraser, B.J., Anderson, G.J., & Walberg, H.J. (1982). *Assessment of learning environments: Manual for Learning Environment Inventory (LIE) and My Class Inventory (MCI)*. S. Bentley, Australia: Western Australia Institute of Technology.

Freiberg, H.J. (Ed.). (1990). Silver anniversay edition: 1965–1990 [Special issue]. *Journal of Classroom Interaction, 25*(1–2).

Freilino, M.K. (1984). *Teacher self-assessment interview:* Pittsburgh, PA: University of Pittsburgh, Learning Research and Development Center.

Gay, L.R. (1981). *Educational research: Competencies for analysis and application* (2nd ed.). Columbus, OH: Merrill.

Glaser, R. (1976). Components of a psychology of instruction: Toward a science of design. *Review of Educational Research, 46*, 1–24.

Glaser, R., & Takanishi, R. (Eds.). (1986). Psychological science and education [Special issue]. *American Psychologist, 41*(10).

Gordon, E.W. (Ed.). (1983). *Human diversity and pedagogy*. Westport, CT: Mediax.

Haertel, G.D., Walberg, H.J., & Haertel, E.H. (1979, April). *Socio-psychological environments and learning: A quantitative synthesis*. Paper presented at the annual meeting of the American Educational Research Association, San Francisco.

Haertel, G.D., Walberg, H.J., & Weinstein, T. (1983). Psychological models of educational performance: A theoretical synthesis of constructs. *Review of Educational Research, 53*(1), 75–91.

Harnischfeger, A., & Wiley, D.E. (1976). The teaching-learning process in elementary schools: A synoptic view. *Curriculum Inquiry, 6,* 5–43.

Harter, S. (1982). The Perceived Competence Scale for Children. *Child Development, 53*(1), 87–97.

Hedges, L.V., Giaconia, R.M., & Gage, N.L. (1981). *Meta analysis of the effects of open and traditional instruction.* Stanford, CA: Stanford University Program on Teaching Effectiveness.

Hilgard, E.R. (1964). A perspective of the relationship between learning theory and educational practices. In E.R. Hilgard (Ed.), *Theories of learning and instruction: 63rd yearbook of the National Society for the Study of Education* (pp. 402–415). Chicago: University of Chicago Press.

Keogh, B.K., Pullis, M.E., & Cadwell, J. (1982). *A short form of the Teacher Temperment Questionnaire.* Unpublished manuscript, University of California at Los Angeles, Los Angeles.

Levine, J.M. (1983). Social comparison and education. In J.M. Levine & M.C. Wang (Eds.), *Teacher and student perceptions: Implications for learning* (pp. 29–55). Hillsdale, NJ: Lawrence Erlbaum Associates.

Linn, R.L. (Ed.). (1989). *Educational measurements* (3rd ed.). New York: Macmillan.

Marshall, H.H., & Weinstein, R.S. (1984). Classroom factors affecting students' self-evaluations: An interactional model. *Review of Educational Research, 54*(3), 301–325.

Marshall, H.H., Weinstein, R.S., Sharp, L., & Brattesani, K.A. (1982, March). *Students' descriptions of the ecology of the school environment for high and low achievers.* Paper presented at the annual meeting of the American Educational Research Association, New York.

McCombs, B.L. (1991). Motivation and lifelong learning. *Educational Psychologist, 26*(2), 117–127.

McGrail, J., Wilson, B.L., Buttram, J.L., & Rossman, G.B. (1987). *Looking at schools: Instruments and processes for school analysis.* Philadelphia, PA: Research for Better Schools (RBS) Publications.

Mitchell, J.V., Jr. (Ed.). (1985). *The ninth mental measurements yearbook.* Lincoln: Buros Institute of Mental Measurements, University of Nebraska.

Mitchell, J.V., Jr. (Ed.). (1983). *Tests in print III: An index to tests, test reviews, and the literature on specific tests.* Lincoln: Buros Institute of Mental Measurements, University of Nebraska.

Moreno, J.L. (1960). *The sociometry reader.* New York: Free Press.

National Association of Secondary School Principals. (1987). *Comprehensive Assessment of School Environment (CASE model).* Pasadena, CA: McGraw Hill School Publishing.

Newmann, F.M. (1991). Linking restructuring to authentic student achievement. *Phi Delta Kappan, 72*(6), 458–463.

Nitko, A.J. (1983). *Educational tests and measurement: An introduction.* New York: Harcourt Brace Jovanovich.

Pollack, S.D., & Bempechat, J. (1991). *The home and school experience of at-risk youth: An annotated bibliography of research studies.* New York: ERIC Clearinghouse on Urban Education, Teachers College, Columbia University.

Purkey, S.C., & Smith, M.S. (1983). Effective schools: A review. *Elementary School Journal, 83,* 427–452.

Resnick, L.B. (1987). Learning in school and out. *Educational Researcher, 16*(9), 13–20.

Reynolds, M.C. (1989). *ADAPT: Scales for the Assessment of the Accommodation of Differences among Pupils by Teachers.* Philadelphia, PA: Temple University Center for Research in Human Development and Education.

Rutter, M., Maughan, B., Mortimore, P., & Ouston, J. (1979). *Fifteen thousand hours: Secondary schools and their effects on children.* Cambridge, MA: Harvard University Press.

Simon, A., & Boyer, E.G. (Eds.). (1974). *Mirrors for behavior III: An anthology of observational instruments.* Wyncote, PA: Communication Materials.

Stein, M.K., & Wang, M.C. (1988). Teacher development and school improvement: The process of teacher change. *Teaching and Teacher Education*, 4(2), 171–187.

Thurston, P.W., & Lotto, L.S. (Eds.). (1990). *Advances in educational administration: Perspectives on educational reform: Vol. 1. 1990 (Part A)*. Greenwich, CT: JAI Press.

Walberg, H.J., & Wang, M.C. (1987). Effective educational practices and provisions for individual differences. In M.C. Wang, M.C. Reynolds, & H.J. Walberg (Eds.), *Handbook of special education: Research and practice: Vol. 1. Learner characteristics and adaptive education* (pp. 113–128). Oxford: Pergamon.

Walker, H., & McConnell, S.R. (1987). *Walker-McConnell Scale of Social Competence and School Adjustment*: Austin, TX: PRO-ED.

Wang, M.C. (1976). *Student Behavior Observation Schedule*. Pittsburgh, PA: University of Pittsburgh, Learning Research and Development Center.

Wang, M.C. (1982). *Parent Survey*. Pittsburgh, PA: University of Pittsburgh, Learning Research and Development Center.

Wang, M.C. (1989). Accommodating student diversity through adaptive instruction. In S. Stainback, W. Stainback, & M. Forest (Eds.), *Educating all students in the mainstream of regular education* (pp. 183–197). Baltimore: Paul H. Brookes Publishing Co.

Wang, M.C., Haertel, G.D., & Walberg, H.J. (1990). What influences learning? A content analysis of review literature. *Journal of Educational Research*, 84(1), 30–43.

Wang, M.C., & Lindvall, C.M. (1984). Individual differences and school learning environments. In E.W. Gordon (Ed.), *Review of research in education* (pp. 161–225). Washington, DC: American Educational Research Association.

Wang, M.C., & Peverly, S.T. (1986). The self-instructive process in classroom learning contexts. *Contemporary Educational Psychology*, 11, 370–404.

Wang, M.C., & Reynolds, M.C. (1985). Avoiding the "catch 22" in special education reform. *Exceptional Children*, 51(6), 497–502.

Wang, M.C., Reynolds, M.C., & Schwartz, L.L. (1988). Adaptive instruction: An alternative educational approach for students with special needs. In J.L. Graden, J.E. Zins, & M.L. Curtis (Eds.), *Alternative educational delivery systems: Enhancing instructional options for all students* (pp. 199–220). Washington, DC: National Association of School Psychologists.

Wang, M.C., Reynolds, M.C., Walberg, H.J., & Rosenfield, S.A. (1990). *A decision-making framework for description, selection, and evaluation of innovative education programs*. Philadelphia, PA: Temple University Center for Research in Human Development and Education.

Wang, M.C., Vaughan, E.D., & Dytman, J.A. (1985). Staff development: A key ingredient of successful mainstreaming. *Teaching Exceptional Children*, 17(2), 112–121.

Wang, M.C., & Walberg, H.J. (1983). Evaluating educational programs: An integrative, causal-modeling approach. *Educational Evaluation and Policy Analysis*, 5(3), 347–366.

Wang, M.C., & Walberg, H.J. (Eds.). (1985). *Adapting instruction to individual differences*. Berkeley, CA: McCutchan.

Wang, M.C., & Walberg, H.J. (1986). Classroom climate as mediator of educational inputs and outputs. In B.J. Fraser (Ed.), *The study of learning environments 1985* (pp. 47–58). Salem, OR: Assessment Research.

Waxman, H.C., Wang, M.C., Lindvall, C.M., & Anderson, K.A. (1983a). *Classroom Observation Scale*. Pittsburgh, PA: University of Pittsburgh, Learning Research and Development Center.

Waxman, H.C., Wang, M.C., Lindvall, C.M., & Anderson, K.A. (1983b). *Observation Rating Scale for Features of Adaptive Instruction*. Pittsburgh, PA: University of Pittsburgh, Learning Research and Development Center.

Waxman, H.C., Wang, M.C., Lindvall, C.M., & Anderson, K.A. (1983c). *Teacher Attitudes and Assessment Survey*. Pittsburgh, PA: University of Pittsburgh, Learning Research and Development Center.

Waxman, H.C., Wang, M.C., Lindvall, C.M., & Anderson, K.A. (1983d). *Teacher Roles Observation Schedule*. Pittsburgh, PA: University of Pittsburgh, Learning, Research and Development Center.

Webb, N.M. (1982). Group composition, group interaction, and achievement in cooperative small groups. *Journal of Educational Psychology*, 74(4), 475–484.

Weinstein, R.S. (1983). Student perceptions of schooling. *Elementary School Journal, 83,* 287–312.

Wiggins, G. (1989). Teaching to the test. *Educational Leadership, 46*(7), 41–47.

Willson, V.L. (Ed.). (1989). *Academic achievement and aptitude testing: Practical applications and test reviews.* Austin, TX: PRO-ED.

Ysseldyke, J.E., & Christenson, S.L. (1987). Evaluating students' instructional environments. *Remedial and Special Education, 8*(3), 17–24.

Zimmerman, B.J. (Ed.). (1986). [Special issue]. *Contemporary Educational Psychology, 11*(4).

# Afterword: Challenges and Prospects in School Response to Student Diversity

In the United States, as in other parts of the world, children are educated with the ultimate goal of ensuring that individuals learn the essentials for exercising the rights and responsibilities of citizenship and for leading a productive and personally satisfying life. Efforts to build this nation's ability to achieve this educational vision can be traced to 1776 and the American Revolution, or even earlier. As Tyler (1985) noted, the founding fathers of this country

> visualized a society in which everyone would be both a ruler and a worker. They believed that through education all of the citizens of the new nation would learn what was necessary to be intelligent rulers. . . . Leaders of the American Revolution knew the wide range of individual differences in human populations. . . . Nevertheless, they believed that the desire for a democratic community and the dedication of effort to build such a nation would ensure that each citizen acquired the necessary knowledge, skills, and attitudes. (pp. ix–x)

Great progress has been made in ensuring equal opportunity to a free public education for all children in this country by stressing the value of education as a way of achieving social and economic equity. The percentage of the population in school, the diversity of students in regular schools (i.e., students with disabilities, students from diverse ethnocultural and socioeconomic backgrounds, and exceptionally talented and gifted students), and the educational programs offered to respond to this diversity have increased. These accomplishments, however, fall short of visions of schooling success for every child. Significant numbers of students are not achieving well, despite efforts to create "special" programs that provide increased opportunities for a basic education to all children and youth. Many students experience serious problems in schools and have difficulty achieving learning success; they need better help than they are now receiving.

The current call for educational excellence provides an opportunity to harness all the resources and expertise to use the best of "what works" to achieve learning success for every student. School implementation of adaptive education strategies in the 1970s and 1980s has yielded a rich knowledge base on how schools can successfully utilize highly sophisticated instructional and management procedures to effectively respond to the learning needs of their diverse student populations. Furthermore, research and practical wisdom suggest alternative approaches to the delivery of instruction and related services that are substantially superior to traditional practices. The adaptive education strategies discussed in this volume represent a systematic effort to cull from research and practical experience the proven and promising practices that lead to achievement of desired student outcomes.

Nevertheless, widespread implementation of innovative programs requires a major conceptual shift in the way differences among students are regarded, how the purpose of elementary and secondary education is viewed, and the way schools are organized. Instead of attempting to identify a general underlying deficit in students requiring greater than usual instructional support, effective adaptive practices can be implemented to ensure desired student outcomes. Schools seeking to institutionalize adaptive education, which includes innovative practices that require major restructuring and changes in the roles of school staff, face the challenge of overcoming major barriers in the current system. These barriers are described to address the prospects for implementing adaptive education to achieve equity in student outcomes.

## CURRENT SCHOOL RESPONSES TO STUDENT DIVERSITY: A BARRIER TO PROGRESS

For centuries educators have pondered the issues of human diversity and equality and their implications for education. Great teachers and philosophers including Confucius, Plato, and Dewey have all noted that instructional accommodations to differences among students are not only highly desirable but inescapable. The result of such deliberations has been the emergence of a variety of educational policies and practices that address human diversity. The graded school system, for example, is one attempt. Other examples of practices that accommodate individual differences among students include ability grouping, policies on retention and promotion, and the establishment of "special" programs such as Chapter 1, special education, and migrant education programs to accommodate the greater than usual instructional and related service-support needs of individuals.

Despite advances in theories and research on individual differences in learning and effective teaching, this knowledge has had little effect on how schools respond to student diversity. There are serious problems in how individual differences are characterized and the way information is generated and used for educational decision making. In many cases, provisions designed to respond to student differences in learning have been counterproductive to student learning. Students differ as individuals, not as groups. Exceptionally talented students are as heterogeneous across the range of learning characteristics as are those with learning difficulties. In current practice, learning differences are typically addressed by classifications or labels based on perceived differences in macro-level characteristics (i.e., children at risk, low-achieving children from poor families, children with learning disabilities, or socially/emotionally disturbed children). Then the students "identified" or "certified" with these spurious labels are placed "homogeneously" in narrow categorical programs or "special" educational arrangements as a strategy for achieving educational equity.

The practice of grouping students with perceived similar instructional needs has been commonly accepted as a strategy for achieving educational equity, yet it is often instructionally meaningless and counterproductive for students. Placing students with similar classifications in specially designed programs has not worked very well. There is substantial evidence to suggest that students may receive *less* instruction when schools provide programs specially designed for meeting their learning needs. For example, students placed in remedial reading programs (e.g., Chapter 1 or resource room programs in special education) often receive less actual reading instruction than students in regular programs (Allington & Johnson, 1986; Haynes & Jenkins, 1986). Current school classification and tracking practices have not been shown to benefit students. In many instances, these practices have led to further inequity in educational outcomes for students requiring greater than usual educational support (Brandt, 1989; Heller, Holtzman, & Messick, 1982; Jenkins, Pious, & Peterson, 1988; Williams, Richmond, & Mason, 1986). In too many cases, the practice of grouping (or tracking) students for instruction based on certain perceived group differences involves the delivery of radically different and inappropriate content to some students, and there is a tendency to seriously neglect fundamental content (Oakes, 1985).

Schools themselves often compound children's learning problems. There is evidence of the "Matthew Effect" (Stanovich, 1984), in which students who show limited progress in early phases of basic instruction, such as reading, tend to show progressive retardation over succeeding years. It has been estimated that in the middle elementary grades, the lowest achieving students may be reading only one tenth as many words per day in school as the highest achieving students (Reynolds, 1989). Another version of the Matthew Effect occurs when teachers interact differently with students with special learning needs—for example, by giving less feedback on questions to these students than to others, calling on them less often, or waiting less time for them to answer (Cooper, 1983). Children who require different and greater than usual instruction or related services truly have problems, but not because they can't learn. Rather, a flawed service delivery system is in operation.

## PROSPECTS FOR IMPROVEMENT

The adaptive education strategies discussed in this work when viewed collectively represent a movement toward strengthening the correspondence between the learning needs of individual students and standards for the design and delivery of educational and related services to achieve equity in student outcomes. Design and implementation of improved programs based on the adaptive education approach begin by addressing the following questions:

Do differences in learning characteristics contribute to differences in learning and performance? Under what conditions?

In the context of the broad spectrum of schooling tasks required of all students, are certain learning characteristics more critical than others for successful mastery of certain tasks?

Recognizing that there is always a gap between what is known and what is practiced, how is knowledge on learning and effective instruction reflected in current practice? What is the relevance of this knowledge to

designing and managing instruction to achieve intended student outcomes in general and to achieve learning success for students with special needs in particular?

What are some design features of adaptive education programs that effectively incorporate information on individual student learning characteristics and on the nature of learning tasks in planning and program
implementation? Are particular management and organization patterns
associated with the effective implementation of these programs?

Given the effect of current policies and funding guidelines for special programs that respond to student diversity and considering the research
base on learning characteristics and implications for instruction and effective schooling, what policy and implementation reforms are necessary to institutionalize adaptive education in schools?

Experience in school implementation of adaptive education practices indicates that it cannot be assumed that implementation of adaptive education strategies always shows superior results in student outcomes. Programs with well-
implemented features of adaptive education can lead to classroom processes that
have been noted as effective in the literature. A high degree of implementation of
the adaptive education approach can be expected to lead to positive outcomes
for students with diverse learning characteristics and needs. These include student learning success, teaming of educators and related personnel, responsive
accommodation of students at the margins, school coordination with health and
human service agencies, and strengthening the instructional leadership role of
the principal.

## Student Learning Success

Several common features can be found in all adaptive education programs. They
include, for example, instruction based on student needs, materials and procedures that allow students to proceed at their own pace, frequent assessments
of progress, additional learning time for students who need it, and increased
student responsibility for monitoring and guiding their own learning. Effective
implementation of the adaptive education approach can foster continuity in
daily learning experiences and appropriate systematic instruction that meets the
learning needs of each student. Increases in academic and social competence
result in attitudinal and personal growth, help and cooperation among students,
and recognition of individual differences as important instructional and learning resources.

## Teaming Educators and Related Services Personnel

Specialists in adaptive education programs work with regular education
teachers as a team. Special education teachers, school psychologists, and Chapter 1 teachers, for example, provide intensive instruction to students showing the
least progress in the form of small groups or one-on-one in the regular classroom.
They work with the regular education teacher to modify programs for students
who learn rapidly or who require supplementary instruction. These specialists
also work with school administrators in identifying needed resources and expertise and with parents in coordinating and managing special assistance for
students.

## Accommodation of Students at the Margins

Schools using adaptive education programs give particular attention to monitoring the progress of students showing the most and least progress in school learning. Students whose rate of progress in achieving important learning goals is especially low or high are identified, and alternative strategies are implemented that better serve their needs. Rather than classifying, labeling, and referring students to special education programs, students in adaptive education programs are described in ways that reflect their progress toward important school goals and objectives. Procedures for identifying student learning needs in adaptive education programs are similar for high-achieving students, and they too need special adaptations in their learning plans to maximize their progress and learning outcomes.

## School Coordination with Health and Human Services

Coordination and mobilization of all available resources and expertise are central to effective implementation of adaptive education programs. Schools using adaptive education programs seek to establish formal linkages and collaborations with community-based youth programs and health and human services programs, develop agreements with community agencies to exchange information, and engage in developing policy changes to facilitate a coherent pattern of services within the school and in the broader community.

## Strengthening the Leadership Role of the Principal

Principals can be expected to reclaim their role as instructional and administrative leaders in schools using adaptive education programs. Principals are instrumental in reducing the disjointedness of programs implemented as a "second system," instructionally and administratively separate from the mainstream. They provide staff develoment and implementation support that serves all students in a systematic way. In addition, because of the major programmatic changes generally associated with school implementation of adaptive education programs, they assume responsibility for involving parents and the community in decision making and monitoring program implementation and accountability.

### CONCLUDING REMARKS

There is much opportunity for progress. The emerging consensus among educators, policymakers, and educational researchers on improving this nation's capacity to achieve educational equity is explicit about what needs to be done to move the educational improvement agenda forward (President's Education Summit with Governors, 1989; U.S. Department of Education, 1991; William T. Grant Foundation, 1988). The public is demanding better instruction and greater educational accountability for every student, particularly for those who perform below average academically and those considered at risk of failing or dropping out of school. In fact, equality of educational outcomes can be said to be the civil rights challenge of the 1990s. Schools cannot simply provide educational opportunities for students without addressing the issue of quality education and student achievement. National standards of educational outcomes must be upheld for every student, including those with poor prognoses for learning success and those considered difficult to teach.

If widespread implementation of the adaptive education strategies discussed in this book is to occur as a way of achieving educational equity in student outcomes, major restructuring needs to happen on several fronts. Administratively, we need to link school reform efforts with the second-system approach to meet the educational needs of students at the margins. Second system programs have moved beyond the control of school principals, educational administrators, and teachers. Improvement will require establishing responsibility and accountability of teachers and administrators for all programs at their schools. The site-specific decision making and planning initiated in some schools are promising steps toward improvement. School systems and individual schools need to know how to make major changes and to maintain improved programs.

Programmatically, much needs to be done to improve the coordination of instructional and related services to more effectively serve individual student needs. Research and innovative program development efforts during the 1970s and 1980s have provided substantial knowledge of proven and promising practices for improvement. Perhaps more importantly, research and model programs created a standard of accountability for improving practice, resolving well-documented problems, and undertaking serious improvement efforts to ensure the learning success of each student.

Leaders in federal, state, and local education agencies need to support innovative efforts to coordinate programs at all school levels and among schools and health and human service agencies. Although the task of educating children and youth will continue to depend primarily on activities within schools, school capacity for responding to the diverse needs of students can be greatly enhanced by the work of related agencies in the community, state, and at the federal level. Many of the "new morbidities," such as child abuse, drug addiction, poverty, and the erosion of natural support systems as a consequence of broken family structures, have grave effects on children's learning. The school can play a major role in mobilizing and coordinating resources of the community. The major barriers to implementation of coordinated services are surmountable. Although much can be done to repair the current disjointed approach to service delivery with existing resources and laws, sustained improvements will require fundamental changes in the operations of schools and other agencies, and changes in laws and regulations may be necessary. Data on program implementation and effects need to be analyzed and interpreted to consider revisions in policies, legislation, funding regulations, personnel preparation, and other related matters to maintain improvements.

Implementation of the adaptive education strategies discussed in this book can be an important step in gathering knowledge about how research and proven practice can improve education for students with diverse learning characteristics and needs. It is critical to begin accumulating information that distinguishes effective from ineffective practices. Nevertheless, progress in achieving equity in student outcomes will not be made easily. Professional interests and investments are involved, as are the rights of students and parents. Necessary changes in school organization and roles of school personnel present special challenges to implementing adaptive education.

Adaptive education is an evolving process of improving educational effectiveness and incorporating new knowledge and understanding. Graduated increments in educational practices that improve what preceded them is characteristic of the adaptive education approach. As program responses are implemented, and as they succeed in achieving desired educational outcomes for students, including low-achieving as well as academically accelerated students, they become the basis for refined program components, sharpened theories, new knowledge about school implementation, corrections of past errors, and adoption and adaptation of the best strategies.

## REFERENCES

Allington, R.L., & Johnston, P. (1986). The coordination among regular classroom reading programs and targeted support programs. In B.I. Williams, P.A. Richmond, & B.J. Mason (Eds.), *Designs for compensatory education: Conference proceedings and papers* (Vol. VI, pp. 3–40). Washington, DC: Research and Evaluation Associates, Inc.

Brandt, R.S. (Ed.). (1989). Dealing with diversity: Ability, gender, and style differences. [Special issue]. *Educational Leadership, 46*(6).

Cooper, H.M. (1983). Communication of teacher expectations to students. In J.M. Levine & M.C. Wang (Eds.), *Teacher and student perceptions: Implications for learning* (pp. 193–211). Hillsdale, NJ: Lawrence Erlbaum Associates.

Haynes, M.C., & Jenkins, J.R. (1986). Reading instruction in special education resource rooms. *American Educational Research Journal, 23*(23), 161–190.

Heller, K., Holtzman, W., & Messick, S. (Eds.). (1982). *Placing children in special education: A strategy for equity.* Washington, DC: National Academy of Sciences Press.

Jenkins, J.R., Pious, C., & Peterson, D. (1987). *Exploring the validity of a unified learning program for remedial and handicapped students.* Washington, DC: U.S. Government Printing Office.

Oakes, J. (1985). *Keeping track: How schools structure inequality.* New Haven: Yale University Press.

President's Education Summit with Governors. (1989, September). *Joint statement.* Charlottesville : University of Virginia.

Reynolds, M.C. (1989). Children with special needs. In M.C. Reynolds (Ed.), *Knowledge base for the beginning teacher* (pp. 129–142). Oxford: Pergamon.

Stanovich, K.E. (1984). The interactive-compensatory model of reading: A confluence of developmental, experimental, and educational psychology. *Remedial and Special Education, 5*(3), 11–19.

Tyler, R.W. (1985). Foreword. In M.C. Wang & H.J. Walberg (Eds.), *Adapting instruction to individual differences* (pp. ix–xii). Berkeley, CA: McCutchan.

U.S. Department of Education. (1991). *America 2000: An education strategy.* Washington, DC: U.S. Government Printing Office.

Williams, B.I., Richmond, P.A., & Mason, B.J. (1986). *Designs for compensatory education: Conference proceedings and papers.* Washington, DC: Research and Evaluation Associates, Inc.

William T. Grant Foundation Commission on Youth and America's Future. (1988). *The forgotten half: Non-college bound youth in America.* Washington, DC: Author.

# Index